Reading the Bible with Giants

Reading the Bible with Giants

How 2000 Years of Biblical Interpretation
Can Shed New Light on Old Texts

David P. Parris

LONDON ● ATLANTA ● HYDERABAD

First published in 2006 by Paternoster

Paternoster is an imprint of Authentic Media,
9 Holdom Avenue, Bletchley, Milton Keynes, Bucks,
MK1 1QR, UK
285 Lynnwood Avenue, Tyrone, GA 30290, USA
OM Authentic Media, Medchal Road, Jeedimetia Village,
Secunderabad 500 055, A.P., India
www.authenticmedia.co.uk
Authentic Media is a division of Send the Light Ltd., a company limited
by guarantee (registered charity no. 270162)

British Library Cataloguing in Publication Data

A catalogue record for this book is available from the British Library

ISBN-13: 978-1-84227-273-2
ISBN-10: 1-84227-273-X

Design by James Kessell for Scratch the Sky Ltd (www.scratchthesky.com)
Print Management by Adare Carwin
Printed in Great Britain by J.H. Haynes & Co., Sparkford

Contents

Introduction

We are like dwarfs on the shoulders of giants, so that we can see more and farther than they (...), because we are raised up on their giant size.

John of Salisbury, quoting Bernard of Chartres

This book is the result of a long journey. It began about fifteen years ago while I was researching the history of how the concluding verses to Matthew's Gospel have been interpreted. Having a strong interest in missions I was interested in studying the relationship between Jesus' "Great Commission" as recorded in Matthew 28:18–20 and the missionary endeavors of the church. Expecting to find a high level of agreement among the various scholars who have commented on this text I was surprised by the wide range of interpretations that I uncovered for this passage.

The diversity of interpretations offered challenged my preconceptions of what we mean when we speak of the text's meaning. I was educated in a theological tradition which taught that the meaning of a text was determined by attempting to recover the author's original intentions. Most of the interpreters I studied claimed to be doing just this, but arrived at very different conclusions of what they felt the author had originally intended.

Two solutions are usually offered for this dilemma. First, you could regard all those who have gone before you as being partially right, but claim that with all the current research and tools available today, you possess a more accurate understanding of the meaning of the text than those who preceded you. In other words, you can claim the higher ground based on your position in history and view those who came before you as goodhearted but misinformed.

The Dwarf Standing on the Shoulders of a Giant

The metaphor of a dwarf standing on the shoulders of a giant has a rich history and, at the same time, reveals a great deal about how we view our relationship to history. As early as the twelfth century, John of Salisbury quoted his teacher, Bernard of Chartres,

who taught that truth is conveyed to us through tradition:

We are like dwarfs on the shoulders

The second solution is to separate the *meaning* of the text from the *significance* that the various readers attribute to it. While there is some philosophical merit to this argument, it misses the fact that for the past 2,000 years it has been the meaning of the text, not its significance, that scholars and theologians have been wrangling over.

Theories such as Reader Response Criticism give more attention to the role the various interpreters play in how the meaning of a text is constructed. The problem is that all too often too much weight is given to the reader, and, as a result, meaning is reduced to individual preference or taste. But the history of the interpretation of a text like Matthew 28:16–20 demonstrates there are consistent threads and leitmotifs that crisscross one another and give a degree of continuity and coherence to a tradition of interpretation. The consistency that is present in the history of the interpretation of this passage seems to indicate that both the text itself and other factors limit the possibilities of what is considered an appropriate reading.

> *Neither author-oriented approaches nor reader response theories can account for what I encountered in the history of the interpretation of the Bible.*

Neither the author-oriented approach nor the reader response theories could account for what I encountered in the history of the interpretation of the text. As a result, my attention shifted from the practice of biblical exegesis to questions about *how* we read or interpret a text: from biblical studies to hermeneutics (a discipline which I have found to be not only intellectually challenging but also immensely practical). In particular, I was trying to find a hermeneutical model which could account for and explain the twists and turns that occur in a text's interpretive history, a model that recognizes the importance of what the author was trying to communicate to his audience and at the same time reflects appreciation for how different readers have understood a biblical text in the history of the church. And perhaps most importantly, it had to be a model that not only enables us as contemporary readers to learn from the gifted commentators of the past, but also allows the biblical texts to speak to us in new and even provocative ways today.

Why Reception Theory?

I was originally exposed to Reception Theory while working on my doctorate at the University of Nottingham. Reception Theory is a literary theory that was formulated in Germany during the late 1960s. While Reception Theory is well known in Germany and continental Europe, its acceptance has been relatively slow in the English-speaking world and it is just now being recognized as a viable approach in biblical studies. One of the original proponents of the theory, Hans Robert Jauss, once joked that "to the foreign ear, questions of 'reception' may seem more appropriate to hotel management than to literature."[1]

Reception Theory was conceived at the University of Constance, Germany, when a group of literary scholars sought to overcome what they thought were two major weaknesses in contemporary literary theory. Their first complaint was that contemporary theories of literary history were organized around the poles of great authors or masterpieces. While

of giants, so that we can see more and farther than they, not by virtue of any sharpness of sight on our part, or any physical distinction, but because we are raised up on their giant size. Our age enjoys the gifts of preceding ages, and we know more, not because we excel in talent, but because we use the products of others who have gone before.

This image was used up to the Enlightenment to indicate that just as the dwarf owes his keen vision to the giant, so also we are indebted to our tradition; and not only that – the dwarf's vantage point actually allowed it to see a bit farther than the giant could.

This simple metaphor was used to show the progress of knowledge and the dependence of contemporary thinkers on the past.

The metaphor of the giant and the dwarf allows a certain interpretational freedom. It gives credence to both tradition and contemporary thinking and allows some latitude regarding where we place the emphasis, depending on how we perceive the relationship between the ancient and the modern.

this approach provided some skeletal structure to literary history, it was a very bare one. In particular, too much attention was devoted to the great authors and many of the lesser known authors and their works were overlooked. At the same time, the inter-relationships between various texts, the development of genres, and the ability to assess the value of a particular text was not possible, or only very minimally. Finally, there needed to be some means to evaluate the influence and impact of a particular author's works on subsequent writers. This final aspect is often neglected, but is one of the most significant features of a text's history.

The second question Jauss and his colleagues sought to address was how to bring a text from the distant past back to life for present-day readers. Jauss's work focused on medieval tales and poems written about the royal court. Traditional methodologies of literary history allowed one to understand the meaning of these tales but did so in a way that made these stories dry and dusty, historical relics from a distant time and place. The question for Jauss was how to bring these stories back to life so that we as modern readers not only understood what they meant but could also appreciate and enjoy them once again.

> *How can we read the Bible so that it speaks in fresh and even provocative ways?*

The second question also applies to the Bible: How can we read and interpret the Bible so that it speaks in fresh and even provocative ways? This may seem like a moot point to many in the church today, especially given the abundance of contemporary translations and other books written on the Bible.

With the Enlightenment this metaphor was interpreted

However, two things must be kept in mind. First, the Bible is not a modern book but an ancient one (or more accurately, a collection of ancient books). The most recent portion of the New Testament was written almost 1,900 years ago, by authors who spoke Aramaic or Greek and were subjects of the Roman Empire. Their language, daily experience, and understanding of the world were profoundly different from ours. To devalue or ignore the historical, cultural, and linguistic distance between the biblical authors and ourselves is not only naïve but can easily lead to unexpected (mis)understandings of the text.

Second, the old adage that "familiarity breeds contempt" also operates against us. The Western European and North American cultures are saturated with words, images, ideas and stories from the Bible. When a housing developer advertises new homes for sale as "your sanctuary" we see an appropriation of a biblical concept for a place set apart for the worship of God being applied to single-family, detached houses on a quarter acre of land, with a two-car garage This saturation is even more profound for those who have been raised within a believing community. We have heard the same Bible stories and passages told and taught over and over since we were small children. As a result, a certain reading lethargy sets in. When we sit down to read the Bible it is yesterday's news to us. Our mind races ahead of our eyes for something to catch our interest. Soon we are no longer reading the Bible, but pondering the weather or our plans for the day. When our attention finally snaps back to the page we ask, "Now just where was I? Did I make it to the end of this line, paragraph or page?" So we back up a few sentences, or start at the top page all over again.

in a different manner. Sir Isaac Newton and others claimed that while we have benefited from the past we are independent of and above the giant. The emphasis now fell on the dwarf's superior vision and understanding, and ability to know better than those who came before. Since it was not possible for those in the past to possess the same level of truth that Renaissance thinkers progressed to, the authority of tradition was reduced, if not denied.

Gerald Holton (Professor Emeritus of the History of Science at Harvard) is a contemporary embodiment of this spirit: "In the sciences, we are now uniquely

> *The question, "How do we approach the biblical text so that it speaks in new and fresh ways?" is critical for the contemporary church.*

It is for these reasons that the question of "How do we approach the biblical text so that it speaks in new and fresh ways?" is critical for the contemporary church.

privileged to sit side by side with the giants on whose shoulders we stand." We are tempted to think that since we know more than those who came before us, there is neither a great deal we can learn from them nor much value in studying their works.

The metaphorical image of the dwarf on the giant's

Three-way Dialogue

While I personally enjoy diving into the deep and technical discussions surrounding the philosophical principles of interpretation, that is not the aim or focus of this book. Instead, the emphasis of this book will be on introducing the reader to the basic concepts of Reception Theory and the role these concepts can play in our personal reading of the Bible and how we teach it to others. At times this will mean that the reader may be required to wrestle with a few of the hermeneutical issues in order to understand Reception Theory. But I will attempt to keep these discussions to a minimum. The essence of this book will be on practice rather than theory.

> *The reader must move from a two-way dialogue with the Bible to a three-way dialogue.*

What I hope to accomplish with this book is to help the reader move from a two-way dialogue with the Bible to a three-way dialogue. By "a two-way dialogue" I am referring to the normal interaction we think of between a reader and the Bible. We come to the scriptures with particular questions or needs as readers. As we engage the text we may find the answers we seek or come away with even more questions. This two-way dialogue between us and the text is

shoulders raises questions about, and illustrates the significance, authority and proper interpretation of, classical an almost universal aspect of every interpretive approach. The third active participant I would like to introduce into the picture, so that it becomes a three-way dialogue, is the tradition of biblical interpretation. The problem is not that we are members of a tradition that has commented on and applied the biblical texts in various ways and means. Rather, it is the question of how we engage our tradition in a receptive and critical manner – to bring it to the table, so to speak, as an active dialogue partner when we read the Bible.

When I teach on the idea of a three-way dialogue the example I like to use is a chess game. Imagine walking into a room where a game of chess has been played for a very long time (we have to stretch our concept of a chess game at this point, since most games do not last very long, and I am speaking about years, decades, and even centuries in this illustration). This game has been going on for so long that the original players are no longer present and their spots at the board have been filled by others. At some point in time you may be asked to take a turn at the table.

Now in terms of the analogy, a two-way dialogue would be like jumping right in and beginning to play the game. We may even make our moves based on lectures we have heard about how to play chess, or on a book we once read, *Great Chess Moves for Dummies*. But would we know what moves to make in this particular game? Would our moves be legal? Would they be wise or foolish moves in light of the opponent we were playing?

On the other hand, a three-way dialogue would mean, in terms of the chess analogy, changing the way we approach the game. We would want to learn from others in the room,

texts such as the Bible. How indebted are we to those who preceded us, and is there anything we can learn from them? The image of the dwarf standing on the shoulders of the giant is an appropriate image. We stand on the shoulders of giants and need to learn to read the text with them.

especially if they had been there a while and were known to have made some good moves in the past. We may want to ask if there were any special rules for this particular game, learn something about the history of the game and its players. When did the game start? Have the rules changed over time? What type of player is the opponent? What have been some of the best moves made in the past? Based on all this information, what would be the wisest move to make in a situation similar to this one?

Let me apply this analogy to biblical interpretation. The normal approach to reading the Bible is that of a two-way dialogue. Now I don't want to be misunderstood as claiming that this is an invalid approach. However, since most of the book will be presenting an approach based on a three-way dialogue, it may be possible to read my work as an argument against the two-way approach. What I hope to demonstrate are the benefits that we can derive from engaging our tradition as we study the biblical text. Just as we would want to learn from the experiences and wisdom of other chess players, it would be wise to learn from those who have wrestled with the biblical message before us. What have been some of the best interpretations and applications of this particular story? What mistakes have others made when interpreting this passage? Have the rules for what counts as a valid interpretation changed over time? Have believers always read the text in the same manner as we do today?

For us as believers this three-way dialogue is very important. After all, we claim that God speaks to us through this book we call the Bible and that our personal faith and Christian community rest on it. We believe that through the illumination of the Holy Spirit, God uses this book to inspire, console, correct and guide us. If I claim that God speaks to me through the Bible I should be open to what others claim God has revealed to them through the same text. Especially if I consider that in the 2,000 years since Christ inaugurated the church there have been countless individuals who were more sensitive readers, had sharper minds, were more gifted Greek and Hebrew scholars and were more devout than I am, I should be grateful to sit at their feet!

Threefold Structure of this Book

Time for a quick disclaimer. This book examines and attempts to demonstrate how Reception Theory enables the reader to engage the Bible and the tradition of biblical interpretation in a three-way dialogue. Such an exclusive focus could give the impression that I think this is the only method to study the Bible. This is not the case. On the contrary, I believe that there is a wide variety of valuable methods available. The different approaches (historical studies, lexical and grammatical studies, narrative analysis, etc.) can be likened to the various tools a handyman possesses. A good do-it-yourselfer doesn't have only a hammer in his or her toolbox, but a collection of tools. (I use this line regularly to justify my spending when I visit a home improvement center!)

I decided once to attempt to replace a faulty water pump on my car. In order to do this I first had to remove the serpentine belt (obviously named for its relation to a certain biblical character) which connected the water pump to about ten other pulleys on the engine. The instructions called for the use of a "tension adjusting wrench" to relieve the pressure which held this belt in place. A quick call to the local automotive supply store revealed that the tool cost about twenty-five dollars. So I improvised using a crescent wrench, then a larger, adjustable wrench, and finally a pipe wrench with a rusty old piece of pipe slipped over the end for extra leverage. After several hours of frustration, a bruised forehead and losing a fair amount of skin from my knuckles I resigned myself to paying the twenty-five dollars for the tension-adjusting wrench. In less than ten seconds the serpentine belt was off. The right tool can make all the difference.

The same is true in biblical interpretation – the right approach can make all the difference. A word study on the name *Corinth* will not yield the same results as a historical background study on what life was like in ancient Corinth. Reception Theory is an excellent tool for engaging the history of biblical interpretation along with the Bible, but it is only one tool among many that the reader should have at his or her disposal.

Unfortunately this analogy fails at a certain point. Applying the appropriate interpretive tool will not produce results in ten seconds most of the time, but may involve long hours, days or even years of diligent study. However, I believe the results are well worth the sacrifice.

The Reception Theory model presented in this book will be summarized under three historical contexts and three levels of reading.

Three historical contexts

First, the biblical text is a product of history itself. The New Testament is the result of the early church's understanding of God's revelation in the life, death, and resurrection of Jesus Christ. The authors of the New Testament take a very particular perspective on the person and message of Jesus and seek to persuade the reader to adopt that same view. At the same time, when these same authors read various passages in the Hebrew scriptures (which was the entire Bible to them) they read them through the lens of Jesus' resurrection.

The clearest illustration of this is the experience of the two disciples on the road to Emmaus. Prior to the resurrection Jesus' followers did not understand the relationship between various scriptural passages and Jesus' life and teachings. So Jesus gave these gentlemen a crash course on how to read the scriptures from a new perspective: "Beginning with Moses and all the prophets, he explained to them all the things in the scriptures concerning him" (Luke 24:27). This allowed them to read passages in their scriptures in an entirely new light. It was like putting on a pair of glasses for the first time and seeing things in an entirely new way. Similarly, in order to understand the New Testament the reader must understand how the authors of these texts perceived the life, death, and resurrection of Jesus, and how this became the lens through which they read and interpreted the message of the Old Testament.

So the first historical context we need to understand is that of the situation in which the text was originally written and how the original audience would have understood the text. Why didn't the disciples recognize the references to Jesus in the Hebrew scriptures before he explained it to them? How would the original readers of Paul's letters have understood his writings given their religious, cultural, and social background? Determining how a text would have been received in its original historical context is very similar to the traditional hermeneutical method that seeks to determine what the author intended when he penned the text.

The second historical context Reception Theory considers is the history of the reception of the biblical texts as recorded in the various commentaries, sermons, creeds and confessions of the church. Art

> *A text's reception history exposes the reader to the great repository of understanding and significance that other Christians have found in the Bible.*

and music can play an important role, since how a biblical text or story is perceived by a generation may be more clearly communicated through a work of art than a sermon. One of the primary tenets of Reception Theory is that a text possesses a potential for meaning which is realized only in the history of its interpretation. As such, both the New Testament and the history of its interpretation are witnesses to the creative power of the transmission of the gospel message to new generations of believers in new historical and cultural situations.

The biblical text is like the trunk of a tree. It is the document that we appeal to and which forms the center of our theological reflection and thought. The branches correspond to the history

> *A text's reception history exposes us to the great repository of understanding and significance that other Christians have found in the Bible.*

of how these biblical texts have been understood. They emerge from the same tree but can be very different in quality and character from one another. Some branches are incredibly productive. They have a long history of providing valuable insight and guidance for the church. Some of these trajectories of interpretation have been forgotten and may need to be retrieved from a neglected recess of history. At the same time, there are other branches which have proven themselves through history to be theological dead ends or, worse yet, whose fruit have been found to be unhealthy for the church.

> *Unfortunately, the history of a text's effects and interpretations is often treated as ancillary material that gets tucked away in a commentary's appendix.*

The analogy of a tree and its branches helps us to see the organic relationship between the Bible and its interpretations. Reception Theory does not take the perspective that a text is hermetically sealed off from how it is interpreted but perceives an organic relationship between the text and the interpretations that grow off it. Understanding springs from the interaction between readers and the text. These interpretations, in turn, influence later readers and how they will then understand the message of the Bible.

Unfortunately, the history of a text's effects and interpretations is often treated as ancillary material that gets tucked away in a commentary's appendix or called upon as an occasional illustration to make the commentary more readable or interesting. But a text's reception history exposes the reader to the great repository of understanding and significance that other Christians have found in the Bible. It allows us to learn from previous interpretations and may also reveal to us why we read a particular passage the way we do. History reveals to us what we owe to those who preceded us. To cite a famous metaphor, we are like dwarves standing on the shoulders of giants.

This brings us to the third historical context. We need to understand to a certain extent how and why we read a particular story or epistle the way we do.

In order to do this, we must be students of our own culture, historical context and religious tradition. However, this is often the most difficult step to perform, because

> *We know more, not because we excel in talent, but because we use the products of others who have gone before.*

the network of assumptions, preconceptions and beliefs that shape the way we understand something the way we do is often invisible to us. For example, when we read the word *whale* in the story of Jonah we don't think of it as an evil creature on a par with the devil, as earlier interpreters did. Rather, we instinctively envisage a giant whale as we have been conditioned by our educational system and our modern biological view of the world to see it: as a gentle, graceful creature of the sea.

Three levels of reading

Parallel to the three historical contexts, I want to position three levels of reading.

The first level of reading is what I would term pleasure or devotional reading. At the devotional level of reading we are not asking technical questions of the text. Rather, we want to enter into the world of the text. If we are reading Psalm 23 we are not asking questions about the meaning of the word *shepherd* or *sheep*. Instead, we want to enter devotionally into the text, to allow our spiritual imagination and the words of the text to affect us. Seeing our relationship to God in terms of sheep and shepherd creates new ways to understand that relationship.

The second level of reading focuses on literary features. At this level of reading we are interested in the macro-structure of the text. If we are reading a narrative we will be concerned with the plot structure of the story. For an epistle we would be more concerned with the outline of the letter's argument. In order to understand the conclusion to Matthew's Gospel we need to understand the rest of the gospel. I doubt whether many of us would accept someone's conclusions to a detective novel if that person had not read anything except the last chapter. Yet we do this all the time in Bible studies, Sunday school lessons and sermons. We fragment and atomize the text and examine small portions of it and then claim to understand the whole. At the literary reading level we want to reverse this trend and keep the whole of the book in mind, keep the big picture before us.

The third level of reading examines the nuts and bolts found in the text. The intention at this level is to try and determine the answer to two questions. The first is, "What does the text say?" This may involve questions about the meaning of a word, what the background to this particular idea may be, what the literary structure or genre of the text is, and so on. This is the level with which most readers will be familiar. It is at this level that other methods and approaches to biblical interpretation are incorporated. The second question asks, "What does the text say *to me*?"

These two questions unite the hermeneutical concepts of interpretation and application. Meaning and application are not separate concepts but are directly related to each other. And in some instances it is impossible to discuss one without reference to the other. For example, any discussion of the meaning of Psalm 23 without reference to its effect on the reader misses the thrust of the psalm – it was originally written and structured in a particular manner to produce an effect in the reader.

To a greater or lesser extent all texts have the same relationship between "what it says" and "what it says to me". What distinguishes the third level of reading from the first two is that the interpreter is focused on particular questions or aspects of the biblical text and its post-history, such as a word, phrase, idea, or grammar of a verse. This contrasts with the first two levels of reading, which focus on the big picture, or the whole into which all the parts fit.

There is a constant ebb and flow between these three levels of reading. Our understanding of the whole gives us a context in which to understand how the parts operate and relate to one another. And as we study the parts, we form a better grasp of the inner workings and intricacies of the whole.

These three historical contexts and three levels of reading form the backbone or outline for this book. The first four chapters will focus on the three historical contexts and the history of interpretation. The fifth chapter will try to pull all the parts of this book together with practical advice on the three levels of reading and some guidelines for engaging in a study on a text's history of reception. While the fifth chapter could be read on its own, it is built on the preceding chapters and should be read in that light. Finally, in the sixth chapter I will explore how the material presented in this book can be applied to teaching or preaching situations.

A Word About Sources

Before someone starts to complain about the types of resources and texts I cite in this book (for example, "He does not use the original Hebrew or Greek manuscripts ...") I need to clarify the type of resources I have used.

Since the ideal reader I am trying to write for is someone who has been actively involved in his/her Christian community for several years (and is, therefore, presumably familiar with his/her tradition's history), is conversant with both the Old and New Testaments, and has a fair amount of intellectual curiosity (or else why pick this book up in the first place?), I will attempt to use sources with which they would be familiar or to which they should have access. What this means is that texts like lexicons and dictionaries that require a strong grasp of Greek or Hebrew will only make the occasional appearance. Instead, all attempts have been made to use reference materials that are accessible in English. The corollary to this is that exegetical resources that are written for the informed lay person have been chosen over the more technical reference works that require a specialized theological education. Books that are widely available have been preferred over those which, while they may be more accurate and reflect the most recent research, might be found only in a large library.

This brings me to the final criterion I had in choosing texts, namely, are they available on the internet? While there are definite drawbacks to the internet, one of its strengths is its democratizing power. A person sitting in his or her stone farmhouse on the Scottish Isle of Butte has the same access to internet texts as the condo dweller in Los Angeles. Since one of the goals of this book is not merely to explain how to engage in a three-way dialogue with the Bible, but to enable the reader actually to go and do so, it is only appropriate that I should have I selected texts that would make that possible.

One

The Original Horizon of Author and Audience

I lift up my eyes to the mountains –
from where will my help come?
My help comes from the LORD,
who made heaven and earth.
            Psalm 121:1–2 (NAS)

Many if not all of us have sung the words of this psalm in a worship service at some time. The words of the psalmist call us to consider creation and the greatness of the creator who stands behind it. As I write this book, the door to my office opens onto a view of Pikes Peak, a majestic Colorado mountain that

In the process of transmission from the first readers to the present, elements of distortion or domination have crept into how the Bible is read and taught, and even into the text itself, elements which need to be raised to consciousness and examined if we are interpret and apply the text in an appropriate manner.

rises from a base elevation of six thousand feet to over fourteen thousand feet at its peak. It is the mountain that inspired Katharine Lee Bates to write the line "from purple mountain's majesty" in her poem "America the Beautiful" in 1893. Almost every time I look upon this mountain my heart is lifted up to the Lord in praise and the words of this psalm echo in my mind. The wonders of creation point us to the creator.

However, is that what the psalmist had in mind as he composed this psalm? Are these the associations that

1

would have sprung to mind in the Jewish pilgrims as they sang this song either going to Jerusalem for one of the religious festivals or returning from there afterwards?

The actual words of the psalm are fairly easy to understand. However, reading a psalm involves more than just understanding the words printed on the page. It evokes our thoughts and calls for a response.

Psalm 121 appears to have been written originally to elicit or affirm the ancient pilgrims' trust in the Lord, YHWH, as they made their way to or from Jerusalem. But if this psalm calls for the reader to trust the Lord for protection, then this meaning of the psalm is found in more than just the dictionary definitions of the words on the page. The first stanza, "I lift up my eyes to the mountains", forms a natural association with how we view nature and the environment from our contemporary perspective. For example, the grandeur of the Rocky Mountains or the Alps inspires our imagination and has inspired the work of countless artists. We see God's handiwork in nature and this leads us to associate it with God's creativity. In my office I even have a panoramic picture of Pikes Peak with the words of Psalm 121:1–2 in calligraphy below it.

But we need to consider whether this is how the Jewish pilgrim would have been moved by this psalm. First, we need to understand that this is labeled a psalm of ascent or procession. It is part of a larger collection of psalms (120–134), entitled "Songs of Ascent" or "Pilgrimage Psalms", that were written for use during pilgrimages to Jerusalem for one of the prescribed feasts. Jerusalem is located on the top of a mountain, surrounded by other hills, especially to the north and east. Pilgrims would have approached Jerusalem by roads that either followed the valleys between these hills or led up one of the long ascents from the coastal plain or the Jordan River valley. Reciting the psalm in this context, they would have naturally formed associations with the mountainous terrain they were traversing. How would they have looked upon these hills? Would the first thoughts that crossed their minds have been about the beauty of God's creation? Or would they have been worrying about their personal safety from thieves hiding among the hills (see Jesus' parable of the Good Samaritan for an example of this)? If the second association was the one which came to their minds when they recited this psalm, then the message is quite different from the one we perceive. For them the first stanza would have called for them to recognize the possibility of their suffering misfortune on the pilgrimage, and as a result the second line, "from where will my help come?" asks the faithful to consider who they trust in for protection.

Another option is perhaps equally valid. As the pilgrims made their way to Jerusalem the psalmist called for them to look at the hilltops they were passing. As they gazed upon these hilltops they may have caught glimpses of the small temples, sanctuaries or altars dedicated to other gods – the "high places" that are frequently denounced in the Old Testament. This idea fits nicely with the overall thrust of Psalm 121 as well. As the travelers made their way to worship in the temple, line one calls them to look upon the high places and temples to foreign gods on the hills. This leads to the question in the second line, "where does my help come from?" In this case the pilgrim looks upon the sanctuaries of the foreign deities and asks, does my help come from them? The expected response is, "No, my help surely does not come from those gods. My help comes from the Lord, the Maker of the heavens and the earth!" It turns their eyes from these pagan shrines and reaffirms Israel's monotheistic dedication to YHWH.

In both of these cases the association which is formed by the reference to looking to the mountains is negative. These associations stand in stark contrast to the positive connotations contemporary readers form when looking upon or thinking about mountains.

> *The Jewish pilgrims' associations with mountains stand in stark contrast to the positive connotations modern readers form when looking upon or thinking about mountains.*

What is interesting about this particular psalm is

that while the way in which the psalmist and the earliest audiences would have understood the reference to the mountains and the way we perceive the same reference today are almost diametrically opposed, the basic affirmation of the psalm remains the same: both the Jewish pilgrims of old and the contemporary worshippers are called to place their confidence in God as their protector. As creator, God keeps watches over us all at all times and places.

The Original Horizon of Understanding

Psalm 121:1–2 illustrates the value of understanding how the way a text was perceived in its original context can play a part in our interpretation of the text today. It raises to our awareness just how different our reading of a text may be from how it was read by those for whom it was originally written. At the same time it exposes us to alternative

Three Reasons Why we Need to Understand the Original Horizon

Investing the time and energy into understanding how a particular text in the Bible was originally understood can be time-consuming. However, there are three reasons why I believe it is time well spent, and why it is important for us to go digging around in the historical, cultural and religious background of a passage.

Firstly, as we study the historical and cultural differences between us and the writers and original readers of the text we realize that we may be reading the text in an inappropriate manner. When we read Psalm 121 with some knowledge of these differences we will not come to the text with a blank slate upon which the message will be inscribed. Rather, we will approach the text with a number of expectations and pre-understandings. Some of these are very helpful. Knowing something about Israel's history and religion gives us a basic theological pre-understanding with which to enter into the psalms. In some cases the pre-understanding we bring to a text plays a significant role. For example, being familiar with the story of King David and Bathsheba is almost essential to understand Psalm 51. Knowing the basic contours of the history of Israel in the Old Testament allows us to place the various books in an appropriate context so that we can pick up on the various historical and intertextual references made in these texts.

At other times our pre-understanding can cloud our understanding or even lead us down the wrong avenue. Many of us have listened to countless sermons, attended Bible studies and read various books on the Bible. All of these experiences shape our pre-understanding of what the Bible means. It is like the Sunday school teacher who asks her young charges, "What is grey, has a bushy tail, eats nuts, and lives in a tree?" After a moment all of the five- and six-year-olds look at her eagerly and raise their hands. One particularly sharp child jumps to her feet and volunteers, "Jesus!" Why? Because they have learned that the correct answer to just about *any* question in Sunday school is "Jesus"! Their previous experiences have created a pre-understanding of what the answer to any question in this class should be.

Every time we approach a text we bring with us certain presuppositions and expectations. This is true not only for us today, but was also true for the original audiences of the various biblical texts. If we do not attempt to understand something about their pre-understanding and expectations we may continue to think, naïvely, that the way we read the Bible is the way it has always been read.

In order for the text to be intelligible to a reader today, the little black marks on the white

> *Our pre-understanding of a text can cloud our understanding or even lead us down the wrong avenue.*

readings of the text that may not naturally occur to us. **In this** way our understanding of the text is corrected and expanded. However, in this particular instance, it also helps us to see that while we read Psalm 121 very differently from the way the original readers would have, the basic substance of our understanding of this psalm is affirmed.

page which constitute the words and sentences must be linked to the reader's background knowledge. The background knowledge you as a reader bring to this book includes the mastery of the English language and the associated reading skills to understand what I have written. But even this is not enough. Even if I approach a text like Psalm 121 with the skills and knowledge that all my contemporaries possess in order to read or communicate effectively I still may not be able to read a biblical text appropriately. The reason is that I will associate *what I consider to be the literal meaning* of the passage with my contemporary presuppositions. I will be reading the Bible in a naïve manner. A more adequate reading requires more than knowing what the words on the page mean. It also requires knowing something about the network of ideas and beliefs that the author and the original audience associated with those words and concepts.

Denotation and Connotation

The way we use words to signify, indicate, or refer to a person, thing, or idea is what is labeled *denotation*. Denotation is the aspect of meaning that probably first comes to mind when we inquire about

Studying the author's or the intended audience's network of ideas and beliefs, or what is often called the original horizon of understanding, is not a static event but a journey. As we study the historical, cultural and religious contexts in which a text was written we begin to realize some of the differences between how a passage may have been received by the people it was originally written for and how we read it today. In the case of Psalm 121, we noticed that there is a gap between what we think the text means and how it would have been received by the Hebrew pilgrims on their way to Jerusalem. A distance opens between us and the text. Psalm 121 becomes unfamiliar and a little strange. Until we invest the time and energy into this type of study we are naïve in thinking that we read the psalm in the same manner as the author or early pilgrims did. In reality we are only repeating, in an unexamined manner, what we assume the text means. Studies like this call into question how we read the psalm.

The second reason why it is important to try to understand how the text would have been received by its original audience is that as we begin to perceive just how great the historical, cultural, linguistic and religious differences are between us and the people to whom the text was originally addressed, new possibilities for understanding the text and its relevance for us are opened. We are familiar and comfortable with this psalm because we subconsciously assume that the psalmist saw the splendor of creation the same way we do. We tend to read Psalm 121 as if it had been written by someone alive today, who thinks, believes, and evaluates the world the same way we do – that is, until we raise questions like this. When we begin to realize that the early Jewish pilgrims probably did not look at the mountains the same way that we do, the message of the psalm becomes foreign. In order to overcome this alienation between us and the psalm, we must wrestle with its message in ways that we have not had to do before as we try to incorporate this new information into how we understand the psalm. In the process, a perceptual opening is created, a transitional space between how we previously understood Psalm 121 and how we will come to understand it. This transitional space opens the possibility not only for us to gain a new understanding of the psalm, but also for the text to address us in ways we had not considered before. Our thoughts are provoked, our interest is raised, and we think about what this poem may mean to our lives in fresh ways. We not only come away from our study with a deeper

a word's meaning. Oftentimes, *denotation* is spoken of as the literal or objective meaning of a word. *Connotation,* on the other hand, is often defined as the subjective feelings, associations or ideas that are added to or associated with a word's denotation. The Latin root for this term, *connotare,* which means "to make along with," probably contributes to this view.

If, however, we limit the "real" meaning of a word to its denotation, and consider connotation as mere window-dressing that is tacked on, a number of problems arise. Anyone who has traveled internationally has most likely experienced the following first hand: using phrases from a guidebook you may be able to order food

or better understanding of the text, but we may also realize new possibilities for how we orient ourselves within the world. In the case of Psalm 121, I now no longer read it in terms of how the majesty of the mountains inspire my thoughts to praise God, but in terms of how it comforts me with a message of God's protection in dangerous situations and calls me to guard my mind from the enticements of false religions.

> *Transitional space opens the possibility not only for us to gain a new understanding of the psalm, but also for the text to address us in ways we had not considered before.*

Finally, this type of research is crucial because the communication processes through which the Bible has been passed down, interpreted, taught and applied from when the text was originally

in a restaurant or secure a hotel room, but this is a far cry from being able to express an idea that requires a familiarity with the connotations associated with the words you are using.

What makes exploring the reception history of a biblical passage so interesting is that both denotations and connotations shift across time and

written until we read it today may have been broken somewhere along the line, perhaps due to changes in cultures and languages that have taken place over time. Psalm 121 was originally written in Hebrew. The early church read it in Greek, then Latin. And finally, we read it in English. Because the transmission of any message from one language to another is never perfect, there is the possibility that *distortions* may occur in the process of transmitting the Bible from the original authors to later readers.

At the same time there is also the possibility that elements of *domination* may have entered into the transmission of the biblical text. How someone interpreted or translated the Bible may have been intentionally or unintentionally used either to support or to suppress a particular teaching, practice, institution, or group of people. Perhaps one of the best known examples of domination is how Americans in the Confederate states interpreted the New Testament in a manner that supported slavery.

As I write, there is an energetic debate taking place over a recent Bible translation, *Today's New International Version* (TNIV). For the sake of our discussion I will consider only one issue and only a few of the points in regard to how questions of distortion or domination have been raised in this debate. One of the hottest topics concerning this translation is the decision the translators made to eliminate "most instances of the generic use of the masculine nouns and pronouns" found in the Greek text.[1] As an example, in the TNIV Luke 17:3 is translated as, "If any *brother or sister* sins against you, rebuke the offender; and if they repent, forgive them." If we were to follow a word by word, literal translation from the Greek, then we should not include "or sister", since that word or its equivalent is not in the Greek text. Those who claim that the translators of the TNIV have fallen prey to the spirit of political correctness argue that the word *brother* is a generic term and can refer to both men and women, and that since it is not an offensive term it should be maintained in the translation, since that is the way it was originally penned. They fear that translation practices such as this lead down a slippery slope where theologically significant gender references, such as those to the various members of the Trinity, will also be removed. On the other hand, those who defend the validity of the TNIV translation claim that while the Greek word *adelphos* which is used in Luke 17:3 can mean "brother", in other instances it is used to refer to a fellow believer (which could be male or female, cf. 1 John 2:9–11); thus the translators tried to bring across this idea when they translated the Greek word *adelphos* as *brother or sister*.

cultures. George Caird used the statement, "I am mad about my flat!" to illustrate the profound effect that different denotations can have on understanding. In England the speaker would be expressing how excited they are about their new living accommodation, while in the U.S. someone hearing the same words would understand them as referring to someone venting their frustrations over the condition of their bicycle tire. The same statement denotes different things in different cultural contexts and only a knowledge of the two cultures can make one aware of just how disparate these denotations are.

[1] Committee on Bible Translation, "A Word to the Reader", in TNIV, *New Testament* (Grand Rapids: Zondervan, 2001).

The meaning of some terms, such as *Luke* or *Timothy*, are grasped primarily through denotative function – they identify particular people. But other terms, such as *cleanliness*, *justified*, *sinner*, or even *the cross*, need to be understood in light of their connotations as well. In many cases, the connotative aspect of a word's meaning can play a more significant role when we interpret a passage, as we saw with the use of *mountains* in psalm 121.

They claim that the use of inclusive language, when appropriate, by the TNIV's translation committee is a welcome improvement on the NIV translation, and that a failure to make these changes would reflect a capitulation to a male-dominated mindset that has influenced the church and biblical translation for too long.

From the committee's perspective, to continuing the practice of translating the pronouns as exclusively masculine in English Bibles represents an instance of *domination* in the communication process that should be rectified. Those who criticize the TNIV claim the same thing from the opposing position, namely that our current climate of political correctness has become the norm by which the Bible is interpreted and thereby introduces a *distortion in the translation*.

Which side is correct? They both have valid points. If we are attempting to produce a literal, word by word translation, then the use of masculine pronouns in the English translation should be preferred. However, the idea of a literal translation is fraught with problems, because no two languages line up with words that correspond to each other on a one to one basis (with the possible exception of indexicals such as a person's proper name or numbers). If the goal is to produce a dynamic equivalence (which aims for understandability, not a word for word translation), then we need to ask, "Did Luke intend for only men to be included in the reference to *adelphos* in 17:3, or would women have been included also? Would the female members of Luke's audience have perceived that they were included in his use of this term when they read his gospel?" I think the answer to both of these questions is yes. As a result, the use of the phrase *brother and sister* is an appropriate translation that communicates clearly to contemporary readers how it would have been understood by Luke's original audience. This example demonstrates that questions about distortion or domination are not just part of an academic debate, but are as relevant to us as the question of which version of the Bible we choose to read or teach from.

The point of this discussion is not to resolve the disagreement over the TNIV. Rather, I hoped to illustrate the third reason why we need to study how a text would have been received by its original audience. In the process of transmission from the first readers to the present, elements of distortion or domination have crept into how the Bible is read and taught, and even into the text itself, elements which need to be raised to consciousness and examined if we are interpret and apply the text in an appropriate manner.

In the next chapter this question will be revisited when we consider how words shift meaning over the course of time. In particular, we will look at William Tyndale's translation for a case in point of how powerful this type of study can be.

Two Primary Questions

Two questions should jump to the forefront when we are studying the original horizon of understanding.

The first question is: What did the author and the original audience believe? Or to put it differently: What were the presuppositions that they brought to the text? Sometimes this type of study is spoken of as looking "behind" the text. This is an apt metaphor, since it illustrates that the goal is to look "behind" the written page to see where the author's ideas came from, how these terms were used by other writers, what the average person believed about these concepts. The answers to this type of investigation are often found in word studies, the examination of historical evidence, and comparing this text with others (especially within the biblical canon).

The second question is: How did the author employ these expectations and beliefs in the text? Did the author affirm, negate, correct or expand those beliefs and ideas? In contrast to looking "behind" the text, the second question is often referred to as looking "inside" the text. How did the author use these particular terms or concepts in this particular passage? What clues are embedded in the text which would enable us to make these types of determinations?

> *We might compare some of the questions we should be asking to the work that detectives do in a blackmail case.*

We might compare these two questions to the work that detectives would do in a blackmail case. To answer the first question, the detectives would interview friends of the intended victim, potential suspects, their background and history, and gather any other relevant information that might help them solve the case. But in relation to the second question, the detectives would focus their attention on the actual blackmail letter itself: What is said in the letter? How is it said? What other clues can be gleaned from the manner in which it was written that may help them to crack the case?

The Original Horizon of Understanding: Behind the Text

One of the strengths of the traditional approach to the study of the Bible, often referred to as the historical-grammatical approach, is its concentration on the meaning of words, the grammatical relationship between those words, the literary structure and style of that particular text, and the historical elements of the text in order to determine what the author was trying to communicate.

Since there is an abundance of excellent books which already cover most of this material there is no need to duplicate their work here. Instead, I will simply refer the reader to three of them. *Understanding and Applying the Bible* by J. Robert McQuilken is the most accessible of the three. Written with the lay reader in mind it includes reproductions of the actual pages from the various sources, such as lexicons, to help the reader actually see what he is discussing. A workbook with exercises that follow the material of this book is also available. The second, *Introduction to Biblical Interpretation*, is by three professors at Denver Seminary, William Klein, Craig Blomberg and Robert Hubbard. While this text was written as a seminary level textbook and includes a certain amount of Greek and Hebrew, it is not overly technical and gives an overview of almost every aspect of the conventional approaches to biblical interpretation. Finally, for those who prefer a bit of a challenge, *The Hermeneutical Spiral: A Comprehensive Introduction to Biblical Interpretation* by Grant Osborne goes into greater depth, especially with regard to some of the philosophical issues behind the various principles of interpretation. Like the second book mentioned, *The Hermeneutical Spiral* was also written with the university or seminary student in mind.

Unearthing the presuppositions, events and beliefs which form the network of ideas that stood behind the text requires sifting through every possible piece of evidence that we can find. This will most likely involve lexical studies of the words used in the text, background studies into the culture of that time and place, comparative studies with literature outside of the Bible, historical studies, and so on. Alongside historical and lexical background studies there are several issues that are especially relevant in regard to the author. In particular, we need to consider how this particular text was a response to a particular question or problem. Why did the author write this text? What was his or her purpose in doing so?

Sometimes the text will answer some of these questions for us. For example, 1 Corinthians appears to be Paul's response to questions which the Corinthian believers had written to him about, for example 8:1 Cor. 7:1 (marriage); 7:25 (virgins or engagement); 8:1 (food offered to idols); 12:1 (spiritual gifts), and to oral reports from others about problems in the church at Corinth, for example 1:11 (factions in the church) and 5:1 (sexual immorality). For other texts, such as Psalm 121, we need to look at clues in the text itself to ascertain why the author composed that particular text, as we have already seen.

As I've mentioned above, how I answer the question, "Why did the author write this?" can have a profound impact on how I interpret and apply a particular passage. In 1 Timothy 2, Paul writes that women are not to "teach or exercise authority over a man". If Paul's purpose in writing this letter to Timothy was to communicate universal principles that were to be applied in all situations at all times, then it would appear that churches that promote women to positions of leadership and teaching are diverging from the pattern Paul envisioned for the church. However, if Paul was writing to address specific problems that were confronting Timothy as a leader, then the question becomes much more complex. In particular, if Timothy was faced with the threat of false teachers who were entering into the church and gaining a platform for propagating their teaching by deceiving the women in the congregation (who would not have had the same level of education as the men in that culture), then we need to ask how universally applicable this injunction was intended to be. Thus, how I answer the question, "Why did Paul write this text?" or "What was his purpose in doing so?" will, to a large degree, shape how I interpret the relevance of 1 Timothy 2 in relation to women's ministry in the church today.

There are numerous other issues and questions which could be raised in regard to how the text would have been understood by the original audience. These include such questions as the relationship of the text to other texts (especially when a New Testament author quotes the Old Testament), what the literary structure of the text is, or whether the author was employing some form of classical rhetoric or argumentation to make his or her point. The discussion of any of these questions would more than exceed the limits of this book. However, for the purposes of our study, questions like the ones we have posed about the how the original audience would have understood the concepts in the text and why the author wrote the text will more than satisfy our needs at this time.

The original horizon of understanding: Inside the text

The difference between studying the network of beliefs, ideas, values and word meanings "behind" the text and what we can learn from "inside" the text can be compared to learning a sport. When we moved to England I knew very little about cricket, having seen it played only a few times. Talking to others about the game helped me learn something about the concepts "behind" the game. But this was a far cry from actually watching a cricket match. Theoretically, I understood the rules of the game. However, that knowledge did little to help me follow what was taking place on the field, let alone figure out the strategy either team was using. This required the patient help of a British friend who labored to explain the finer points of the game as it unfolded. Having said that, I am still confused as to whether it was the fact that I am an American, he was a poor teacher, or the complexities of the game itself which explains why I am still unclear about cricket!

A similar principle pertains to biblical interpretation. We may have done the most comprehensive background study on a particular term, but that does not mean we are equipped to determine correctly how it was used in a passage. As readers we need to be attentive to the various literary devices and elements the author employs in the text, and the various moves he makes.

The story of Nathan and David in 2 Samuel 12 is an example of this. Nathan was sent by God to rebuke the king. Once he had been granted a royal audience Nathan seemed to beat around the bush by telling David a story about a rich man who steals a precious ewe from a poor man (we are told this sheep was like a daughter to the poor man, 12:3). As he listened, David became indignant and declared not only that the rich man must repay the poor man fourfold, but that he was deserving of death as well. David correctly perceived the injustice done – however, that was not the point of the story. Rather, Nathan had carefully crafted his story so that David saw the injustice committed (because the man did not have pity, 12:6) and was led to pronounce a judgment. Like a skillful cricket bowler Nathan's first pitch was set up only for the second more crucial move: "You are that man!" (12:7). By using this story Nathan was able to skirt David's defenses and self-justification concerning his adultery with Bathsheba and the murder of her husband. Before David had a chance to raise his defenses he realized that he had exercised judgment upon himself ("I have sinned against the Lord", 12:13).

Nathan's story was not about sheep-stealing but was a clever rhetorical move by which he is able to bring God's message of judgment to the most powerful man in the nation. This is a nice, clear example, because in a single chapter we have Nathan's story, its explanation and its impact.

The issues are a bit more complicated when an explanation is not included in the text. Jesus' parables often follow this pattern. When Jesus answered the lawyer's question about "Who is my neighbor?" with the parable of the Good Samaritan (Luke 10) he was not giving a lesson on showing charity to those in need. Rather, Jesus was undermining the lawyer's preconceptions and beliefs about who was a member of his community and therefore to whom he had a social obligation. There was a subversion of the lawyer's values not only at the level of the story as a whole, but also at the level of the characters. As a person associated with the religious class, the lawyer most likely had positive connotations of and expectations about priests and Levites and just the opposite with regard to Samaritans – preconceptions Jesus would have been familiar with and which he used to undercut the lawyer's belief system. Because we approach this parable with contemporary preconceptions of what the story means and with Christian preconceptions about the characters, we prejudge the Levite and priest. But if we did our background study we would have discovered that these men were usually respected individuals within their communities in Israel. At the same time, the phrase *good Samaritan* would have been an oxymoron to Jesus' audience. By doing a background study and paying careful attention to how the text is written we can experience something of the same shocking and surprising turns this parable would have taken for the original audience.

At the sentence level careful attention must be given to the various figures of speech which the author used. For example, it is hard to miss the sarcasm in Michal's voice when she greets her husband, King David, after he had danced naked before the ark as it entered Jerusalem: "How the king of Israel distinguished himself today!" (2 Sam. 6:20 NIV). Or the sarcasm in Paul's words to the Corinthians: "Already you have all you want! Already you have become rich! Without us you have become kings!" (1 Cor. 4:8). Paul even teased the thought along a little farther in the next sentence when he wrote, in effect, "I wish that this were true, because I would like to get in on this" (4:9). In contrast to the Corinthians' inflated and distorted view of the spiritual blessings they had in Christ, Paul wanted them to see, instead, the fallacy of their theology when he continued to describe how God has put the apostles on display as "men sentenced to death ... the very scum of the earth."

Trying to determine *how* the author communicated his or her message is often more difficult than researching *what* is in the text. Often I find that students who have studied the sciences, math, engineering or medicine have difficulty when examining the literary features of a text. Their educational background has trained them to look for facts, which is helpful when examining background or historical material. But when we start considering the literary features of a text I get the impression that the students think I am speaking a foreign language. Becoming a careful reader is not something that can be learned by applying a set of rules. Rather, it is a skill that is learned by practice, especially when done in the presence of a gifted reader (either their personal presence or their presence vicariously through their work).

Considerations of what is behind and what is inside a text are significant because a text does not just appear out of a vacuum. Every text evokes in its readers the literary conventions that they are familiar with from their interaction with other texts and their social and religious traditions. By examining both what is behind and what is inside a text we can gain a better understanding of how the text was understood by its original readers and the impact it would have had on them. The original impact a text had on its readers is all too easily overshadowed or erased by the impact it has on successive generations of readers. In the case of the parable of the Good Samaritan the subversive effect this parable had on the lawyer, and on Luke's original audiences, is almost totally lost on contemporary readers who see it as a moral lesson, namely that we should follow the example of the "good" Samaritan, not the "bad" priest and Levite. We miss how this parable negated the original audiences' presuppositions about who was a member of their community and for whom God held them responsible.

Putting it all together

How does all this fit together, especially if all the historical information does not agree, or may even appear to be contradictory?

Let's return to the example from Psalm 121 and consider where to find some of the background information and how to deliberate the exegetical decisions about the preconceptions or beliefs that stand behind the text.

> The first point we should note relates to the preconceptions we bring to the text, or how we would naturally read it, namely that we naturally assume the words of the psalmist, "I lift up my eyes to the mountains," to be a reference to the splendor of God's creation as seen in the mountains.

Commentaries are often an excellent source for information on how the early Jewish pilgrims would have understood the words in Psalm 121:1. In the Word Biblical Commentary series, Leslie Allen offers three possibilities as to how this reference may originally have been heard – one positive and two negative. Firstly, in a positive sense, the phrase *the mountains* could have been referring to the heavenly heights where God dwells. In a negative sense, this phrase may be intimating either the danger of traveling through the mountains around Jerusalem or the presence of the pagan sanctuaries dotting the hilltops. William Van Gemeren, in his commentary on the psalms (*Expositor's Bible Commentary*), reiterates the idea of the pilgrims' anxiety about the potential danger from bandits that may await them. The result is that we have three exegetical possibilities from these two commentaries alone that help us grasp the possible range of options of how the original audience might have perceived the opening lines of this psalm. If we consider the wider intertextual context of the Old Testament as a whole, then all three of these possible readings can all be fairly well substantiated from other passages. This information provides us with some answers, provisionally at least, regarding what may be *behind* the text.

There are several indicators *inside* the text of Psalm 121 that help narrow the choice between these three options. First, the Hebrew adverbial particle translated as *whence* ("from where") which starts the second stanza introduces not only a question but a contrast as well. When the pilgrim looked on the mountains and asked, "Where does my help come from?" the implied reasoning was that his or her help did not come from the surroundings but from the Lord who made heaven and earth. Second, as the reader moves through Psalm 121, God is portrayed in contrast not only to the mountains (looking to the hills in the first stanza of verse one as opposed to God being the creator of them in the second stanza), but also to the dangers that may come from the sun, moon or evil (vv. 6–7). God is depicted as the one who provides for and who protects the pilgrims from the dangers they may face on their journey. Based on the immediate context of psalm 121, the positive connotation that the psalmist is speaking about the heavenly heights in which God dwells should be eliminated as a potential reading. Rather, the negative readings which suggest danger from robbers or the sight of pagan temples on the high places fit the context not only of the Old Testament generally but specifically of the immediate context *inside* this psalm better. By alluding to dangers on the road or to pagan shrines, the psalmist is attempting to move his readers' hearts so that they affirm their trust and faith in the Lord.

Summary

The late historian R.G. Collingwood compared the task of the interpreter or historian to the relationship between a hiker and his or her wilderness guide.

[T]he historian may very well be related to the non-historian as the trained woodsman is to the ignorant traveler. "Nothing here but trees and grass", thinks the traveler, and marches on. "Look", says the woodsman, "there is a tiger in the grass." The historian's business is to reveal the less obvious features hidden from a careless eye in the present situation.[2]

When the woodsman directed the hiker's attention to the tiger crouching in the grass his perceptions of the forest were transformed. His previous assumptions about his surrounding were negated and that situation will never appear the same way to him again because where he once saw only grass he now sees the tiger. In the same manner, one of the tasks of an interpreter is to raise to consciousness aspects or features of a text that may be hidden from the view of a contemporary reader, to point out what is hidden from the untrained eye. The purpose of this type of study is not the accumulation of lifeless historical facts. We need to keep our eyes not only on the question, "What did the text mean to the original readers?" but also trained on, "What does the text mean to us?" Just as the hiker will alter his or her route once the tiger is pointed out, we also need to be open to change based on what we now see in the text. As we begin to grasp the original questions or issues that the text was addressing, we begin to see how it was an answer to a question or addressed a situation which is very different from the questions we bring to the text today.

This opens up the historical distance between us and the Bible and creates the possibility for new avenues of understanding that challenge our theological preunderstanding. We are forced to ask how this new understanding of Psalm 121 addresses us today. Thus, the question "What did the text originally mean?" is intimately connected to the question of "What does the text mean to us?"

---

[2] R.G. Collingwood, *An Autobiography* (London: Oxford University Press, 1939), 100.

The Hermeneutical Spiral

Most contemporary books on biblical interpretation view the goal of interpretation as recovering the original meaning of the text by means of the historical method and stop at that point. The problem is that this approach is not historical enough. It does a great job at providing a method and structure for studying the original historical horizon in which the text was written, but provides little room for including the various interpretations that have resulted from all those who have read and applied the Bible over the centuries. This brings us to the topic of the hermeneutical spiral.

Theologians like to throw around impressive terms (it's is one of the perks of the job!), and one such popular term is the term *hermeneutical circle* or *hermeneutical spiral*. It's hermeneutical because it concerns the philosophy of how we understand, interpret, explain and/or apply just about anything: from texts to artworks, form the conventional symbols and signs we communicate with to our perception of the natural environment. It's a spiral or circle because every act of understanding is circular by nature. As we've already examined in this chapter, we approach every text with a certain set of presuppositions. As we read and interpret that text our presuppositions are either confirmed or corrected. The result is that we come away from our encounter with a different set of presuppositions. These revised preconceptions then form part of the pre-understanding we will bring to that text the next time we read it. They also carry over to other books we read. We move from one understanding of a text to the next, constantly shifting, expanding, and revising our understanding. Thus many authors prefer to speak of this relationship as a hermeneutical spiral (which conveys an image of progress or development) rather than the more static idea of a hermeneutical circle.

This chapter has examined how the reconstruction of the original readers' horizon of expectations helps us to grasp how they would have understood or experienced the text. However, our reconstruction of their understanding will never be identical to their pre-understanding or experience of the text. While our goal is to get as close as possible to how the original readers would have understood or experienced the text, we need to keep in mind that our results will always be provisional. We will never reach an exhaustive or definitive understanding of the network of beliefs and values that they brought to the text. Therefore, we must keep ourselves open not only to learning more about the text, but also to the fact that someone else may have a better grasp of the text than we do. Our reconstruction will always take place within the sphere of our contemporary horizon of understanding. We will always approach the Bible with specific questions that we have been either taught to ask or that are raised by contemporary situations. Each generation of readers has brought and will bring different questions to the Bible. The answers that are found then shape the pre-understanding and questions the following generations of readers bring to the text. As a result, each generation of readers will understand the Bible differently.

> *Each and every generation of the church is called upon to interpret the Bible and apply it to their situation.*

This hermeneutical spiral has been going on since the day the biblical authors laid down their pens. It will continue until we are ushered into the next age. For some, this can be a rather discouraging thought. "You mean to tell me that we will never arrive at a definitive understanding of the Bible? What point is there to studying it then?" I prefer to see this as a point of encouragement and challenge. It means that we are pilgrims on a road to understanding. Each and every generation of the church is called upon to interpret the text and apply it to their situation. We do not have a definitive interpretation of the text. Rather, we are called upon to be faithful stewards of

God's word, to study it, to allow it to address us in our life situations, and to help others to listen to its message more closely. In the next chapter we will turn to this historical aspect of the hermeneutical spiral.

Original Horizon of Expectations

Art museums are one of my favorite places to visit, even though I would not presume to call myself an art critic or historian. I feel privileged by the fact that from time to time I have had the chance to see some of the great masterpieces, which I would not be able to see if they were not part of the museum's collection. At the same time, I am often frustrated by the fact that once a work of art becomes part of a collection it has been removed from the culture, location and community in which it was created. I love Vincent van Gogh's impressionist paintings of southern France, but I have never been there and do not fully appreciate what he was trying to represent in his paintings. The explanatory plaques placed beside the paintings, audio guides and museum attendants help supply useful information that helps me appreciate and understand what van Gogh was trying to portray, the techniques he used, the innovative features in his work, and how the public received his work. They provide some of the original context that van Gogh's work was originally part of but which has been erased by both the passing of time and the dislocation it suffers when it is incorporated into a museum collection. The museum's curators realize that if the public is going to appreciate the invaluable items in their collection they must educate their patrons. This is what we are trying to achieve at this level of biblical research. We are trying to locate the resources so that we can better understand the original context in which the biblical texts were written.

Two

Words

*Because we are so at home with our
preconceptions and pre-understandings
we are usually unaware of how powerfully
they shape how we read.*

What better place to start than with the basic unit of language
– words. But we need to guard against thinking that by
starting with words rather than entire passages we are merely
doing the obvious by learning to crawl before walking. The
situation is not that simple, however. The decision to use
words as our entry point is an entirely pragmatic one: it is
easier to illustrate the twists and turns through history for
the meaning of a word than similar shifts of interpretation
for an entire passage. So, in a sense, the choice of starting
with the basic building block of sentences, a word, may
give the appearance of starting at the most fundamental
level, but this is really not the case. If anything, because
a word always needs to be understood within the larger
context in which it is used, special care needs to be exercised
whenever studying the history of an individual word. Having
said that, though, the history of how a word has been
understood offers a rather simplified, if not slightly artificial,
access to the history of how a text has been received and
read.

We tend to assume that the meanings and use of words
remain stable over time, especially those that carry little
connotative meaning, such as a name. After all, doesn't the
word *Paul* designate the same person today as it did almost
2,000 years ago? That is true, but the meanings of other words
are quite flexible, and can therefore change or drop out of

use completely. One hundred years ago, *consumption* referred to a complex of illnesses that often resulted in death; today it conveys an entirely different set of ideas, such as is found in a sentence like *Our economy is built upon a culture of consumer consumption.*

In *The Structure of Scientific Revolutions*, Thomas Kuhn documented how our understanding of a term like *the world* has changed in relation to scientific theories. Under the

> *For Copernicus's contemporaries to shift from the Ptolemaic to the Copernican model entailed something more fundamental than just exchanging one theory of the cosmos for another.*

Medieval Ptolemaic theory of the heavens, the world stood at the center of the universe. The sun, moon, stars and planets revolved around the earth. Copernicus challenged this view when he proposed a radically different model of the universe: the sun occupied the center of the universe and the earth orbited around it along with the other planets. For his peers to shift from the Ptolemaic to the Copernican system entailed something more fundamental than just exchanging one theory of the cosmos for another. Copernicus's theory required the redefinition of a whole constellation of terms such as *earth* and *planet* before someone could understand, let alone accept, his system. The vocabulary of the Ptolemaic worldview defined the earth or the world as the center of the universe. The world was not moving, it was stable, and not spinning through space. This is one reason why Copernicus was initially ridiculed when he presented his theory. The idea that the earth not only orbited the sun but revolved on its axis daily was not part of the network of beliefs and presuppositions by which they understood and viewed the world.

This shift in the scientific worldview also required the redefinition of related terms such as *planets*, since the earth which formerly was not one, now was. If we had access to a time machine and could go back and conduct "before and after" interviews with people who adopted Copernicus's cosmology, the difference this shift made in how they saw the world would be striking. Thomas Kuhn described it this way: "The scientist who embraces a new paradigm is like a man wearing inverting lenses. Confronting the same constellation of objects as before and knowing that he does so, he nevertheless finds them transformed through and through in many of their details."[3]

Figure 1

We might compare these changes in understanding to how someone views the line drawing in figure 1. If you were asked what this was a picture of, you would answer, "It is a duck" or "It is a rabbit", depending on which aspects of the sketch caught your eye. In a similar manner, if a Medieval scientist was asked what "the world" was, prior to Copernicus, he would have described it in terms of being the steadfast center of the universe and not a planet, since planets "wandered" across the heavens (the word *planet* is derived from the Greek verb *planáô*, "to wander"). After the Copernican revolution, the same person would have replied that the world was a planet hurtling through space at incomprehensible speeds. This is like a person looking at this drawing – they might notice only those features that resemble those of a rabbit (round nose and ears), but then, once other features (the duck's bill and the rounded shape of its head) are pointed out, they would see how the drawing can also represent a duck. The drawing has

---

[3] Kuhn, *Scientific Revolutions*, 121.

not changed, but the viewer has "read" and understood the picture differently.

In a similar manner, the person before and after Copernicus would have seen the term *world* as denoting the same thing (this terrestrial sphere on which we live) but how they defined the denotative meaning of *world* would have been radically transformed. Unlike the duck/rabbit drawing, however, in which both perspectives seem to present adequate characterizations of the sketch, the reason why someone would switch to Copernicus's theory was that it explained their observations in a more consistent manner, solved problems the old view could not, or was a more elegant theory.

Our perception of the world affects the definition of words and vice versa. The revolution which Copernicus introduced is only one of a myriad of semantic transformations that have occurred over the past 2,000 years. The scientific revolution transformed our understanding of the natural world from viewing it as the realm in which God's creativity and providence are displayed to that of a clock-like mechanism governed by natural laws.

> *Our perception of the world affects our definition of words and vice versa.*

These and other cultural shifts transformed not only a word's denotation but also its connotations. Often the connotations of a word are more difficult to define as they involve beliefs, value judgments, and/or emotional associations. The shifts from the classical Greco-Roman culture to the Medieval period, the Reformation, Renaissance, Enlightenment, the Industrial and Scientific Revolutions, and – some would argue – from modernity to post-modernity, all reflect profound cultural transformations, each of which introduced a multitude of semantic transformations. As if this were not complicated enough, we also need to layer on top of this all the shifts in meaning that

occur as we translate a text like the Bible from one
language to another.

The goal of this chapter is to explore how these
semantic shifts affect biblical interpretation. Along the
way we shall examine the historical journey of the
whale that swallowed Jonah. In this context I hope
to show why the work of biblical translators and
commentators is so significant. And, finally, I hope
that I can remain faithful to one of the goals of this
book, and that is to illustrate how to do one of these
studies in the process.

The Best Fish Story Ever Told

One of the most interesting facts about the book of
Jonah is that its immensely provocative and challenging
message is best known for the part about the "whale"
that swallowed Jonah. The reliability of this story is
questioned and/or rejected by liberal critics, and some
conservative scholars speculate about what species of
whale could best support the claims of the narrative.
Instead of entering into
our contemporary debate
about what this text could
be referring to I would like
to take a historical tour of
the words that have been
used to translate Jonah
1:17, 2:1 and Matthew
12:40. Along the way
we will gain a glimpse of the various ways the fish
that swallowed Jonah has been understood and
interpreted and in the process hopefully gain a richer
understanding of the book of Jonah as well.

> *Liberal critics question or reject
> the story of Jonah's whale,
> while conservatives speculate
> about what species of whale
> could best support the claims of
> the narrative.*

In the Hebrew text of Jonah, all we are told is that
God appointed a "big fish" to swallow Jonah. Aside
from the adjective describing to the size of this "fish",
the text does not provide us with any more details

about its nature or the species. The generic word used for *fish* in the Old Testament is the Hebrew *dâg*. Outside of Jonah, the most significant uses of this term are in passages that prohibit the eating of fish without fins or scales, which were considered unclean. Based on the fact that elsewhere in the Old Testament *dâg* is a rather generic word for *fish* it is probably prudent to restrict our interpretation of Jonah's "fish" in the same way, albeit a very big "fish".

This generic understanding of the Hebrew word is also evidenced outside the scriptures in the rabbinic writings (see the sidebar on the Mishnah, Talmud and midrash). The Babylonian Talmud preserved a debate between Rabbi Simeon ben Eleazar and Rabbi Papa about whether the Mishnah prohibited the eating of small or large fish. Part of their discussion revolved around how the Hebrew word for *fish* was understood. The masculine form of the word *dâg* appears to have been understood by the rabbis as referring to a large fish, while the feminine form, *dâgâh,* denoted a small fish. This raised a question for the rabbis, since in Jonah 1:17 the masculine form of the noun was used but then switched to the feminine form in 2:1. By way of a solution Rabbi Papa cited Jonah 1:17, where the masculine form of the word is used, and 2:1, where the feminine form is used. "How do we know that *'dâg'* implies large ones only? Because it is written, 'Now the Lord had prepared a great fish *dâg* to swallow up Jonah'. But is it not written, 'Then Jonah prayed unto the Lord his God out of the fish's [*dâgâh*] belly'? ... Hence *dâgâh* implies both large and small."[4] The masculine

Mishnah, Talmud and Midrash

Any research into the interpretation of a passage in the Hebrew scriptures should take into consideration Jewish readings of a text. Three of the most significant of the Jewish sources are the Mishnah, Talmud, and the midrashim.

The Mishnah is one of the earliest rabbinic documents and dates from around 200 AD It is a collection of Halachic (from the Hebrew word *hâlak*,

---

4 Quoted from *Nedarim* 51b in the *Soncino Talmud,*

"to walk")
teachings
focused on
how to live
in accordance
with the Torah
and is divided
into six topical
sections (for
example,
the division
entitled
"Seeds"
discusses
agricultural
laws).
Traditionally
it is held that
the Mishnah
represents the
oral Law that

form connoted the idea of a larger fish, while the feminine form could be used to indicate any size of fish.

In regard to the meaning of the word *fish* in Jonah, this discussion illustrates that the rabbis understood the Hebrew word as denoting a fairly broad concept of a fish. When the text says, "Jonah was swallowed by a great fish", we are supplied with about the same amount of information as when someone says, "He was bitten by a dog." Well, what type of dog? We are not told. But the type of dog makes a significant difference to how we understand the nature of the attack. It is one thing if someone was bitten by a pit bull terrier that was roaming free, and something completely different if their neighbors' dachshund nipped at the person's ankles.

Some passages in the Talmud recount a fish of such size that the modern reader has difficulty swallowing their stories.

There is another very interesting trajectory in the rabbinic writings that offers a completely different perspective on how the rabbis may have read Jonah. In this trajectory of

was given to
Moses and was
passed down
from teacher
to disciple.
After the
unsuccessful
Jewish
rebellions from
Rome in 68
and 135 AD the
various leaders
of the Jewish
community
saw the need
to compile and
systematize

rabbinic interpretation the size of the "great fish" that swallowed the prophet is explored. Several passages in the Talmud recount a fish of such size that the modern reader has difficulty swallowing their stories. Two consecutive stories from Rabbi ben Bar Hana epitomize this trajectory:

> Once we were travelling on board a ship and saw a fish in whose nostrils a parasite had entered. Thereupon, the water cast up the fish and threw it upon the shore. Sixty towns were destroyed thereby, sixty towns ate there from, and sixty towns salted [the remnants] thereof, and from one of its eyeballs three hundred kegs

of oil were filled. On returning after twelve calendar months we saw that they were cutting rafters from its skeleton and proceeding to rebuild those towns.

Rabbah ben Bar Hana further stated: Once we were travelling on board a ship and saw a fish whose back was covered with sand out of which grew grass. Thinking it was dry land we went up and baked, and cooked, upon its back. When, however, its back was heated it turned, and had not the ship been nearby we should have been drowned. (*Baba Bathra* 74a, in the *Soncino Talmud)*[1]

These stories appear to be the product of a fertile imagination from a modern viewpoint. However, for the ancient seafarer (or perhaps even more importantly, the non-traveler) such stories reflected some of their beliefs about the world. We may be tempted to think that their views were based on ignorance and that we know better today. I have a copy of an etching by Rembrandt on the temptation of Adam and Eve in the Garden of Eden. Adam is hesitantly accepting the apple which Eve is proffering to him. Coiled in the tree is the serpent, which is depicted more like a small dragon than a snake. But the feature I find most interesting is an elephant loping through the garden in the background. It is not like any elephant you would see in an encyclopedia. It is fat and round with short, stumpy legs. In many ways it looks as though

this oral Law into a codified text, the Mishnah.

The Mishnah in turn forms the organizational core of the Talmud. There are two versions of the Talmud: the Babylonian (450–500 AD) and the Jerusalem (325 AD) Talmud. The Babylonian version is the more extensive of the two. The Talmud contains not only the Mishnah but also the Gemara – the interpretations and teachings of various rabbis on the Mishnah. In the printed version of the Talmud you can see its organizational structure clearly. A passage from the Mishnah is usually printed in the middle of the page in a slightly bolder text. Around

---

[1] Edited by David Kantrowitz (Brooklyn, NY: Institute for Computers in Jewish Life, Davka Corp & Judaica Press, 1975) – with some grammatical simplifications made to the text in order to conform with contemporary conventions of English usage.

it was lifted from the pages of *Winnie the Pooh*.

Rembrandt's elephant catches the eye not only because it seems out of place, but also because of its comical appearance. It is this incongruity between the elephant and the other characters that captured my attention. I don't think Rembrandt was trying to interject a humorous note into this work, but rather was actually depicting an elephant according to the conventions of his day, when news of African wildlife was just returning to Europe from various colonial exploits.

Returning to the rabbinic views on the "great fish" in Jonah, then, their chimerical view of the great fish reflects, in part, their lack of familiarity with creatures that inhabit the depths of the sea, just as Rembrandt portrayed the elephant in the manner he did. Perhaps if we contemplate some of our contemporary conceptions about aliens from outer space (in particular, images from science fiction/horror films), the Bermuda Triangle, crop circles or the Loch Ness monster we can empathize a bit more with the rabbinic descriptions of the incredible fish that swallowed Jonah.

By way of summary: We have covered two rabbinic trajectories of thought on the "great fish" in Jonah. The first was that it was a generic fish – a rather large one, but still just a fish nonetheless. The second concerned the fantastic size that they thought a fish could grow to. The proportions of the fish may have been deliberately overstated by the rabbinic interpreters in order to spark their readers' imagination about the size of this fish that God commands.

To these two lines of thought we need to add a third. When the Hebrew text of Jonah

---

this is arranged the Gemara. The Gemara makes for some very interesting reading as it is comprised of commentary, parables, legends and various illustrations (Haggadah) on various topics in the Torah and the Mishnah. These comments and stories range from wonderfully insightful, to contradictory and theologically outrageous if you were to read them literally. Rabbi ben Bar Hana's big fish story cited in this chapter is one example.

The term *midrash* (the plural form is *midrashim*) is derived from the Hebrew verb *dâras*, "to study, search or investigate" and can refer to a type of commentary as was translated into the Greek text of the Septuagint some very interesting semantic transformations occurred. The translator(s) could have employed at least three different Greek terms for the Hebrew word *dâg*. The first is the generic term *ichthus*, which is perhaps the closest equivalent to the generic Hebrew word for fish, *dâg*. The second is *enalion*. This is a bit more inclusive and refers to any creature that lives in the sea, fish being one of them. The third is *kêtos*, which denotes a huge fish, whale or sea monster. It is from the third word that we get the English word *cetacean*, the biological term for the family of whales. The connotations for *kêtos* in ancient Greek are much darker than for the first two terms, and this is the word that the Septuagint's translators chose to use.

There are several reasons why they may have thought this was a more appropriate word. First, the fact that it must have been an extraordinarily large creature that swallowed Jonah would have made *kêtos* a logical choice. Second, the more foreboding and monstrous connotations associated with *kêtos* agree with the metaphorical comparison between Jonah's time in the stomach of the fish and a descent into hell (Jonah 2). At the same time, these connotations associated with the Greek term *kêtos* were not part of the semantic range of the Hebrew word *dâg*. As a result there is a transformation in the denotations and connotations from the Hebrew *dâg* to the Greek *kêtos* once the translators made this choice. This semantic transformation allowed for and created a different field of possible meanings that the reader could construct when reading the story of Jonah in the Septuagint.

Before moving on to consider how this word was interpreted within the Christian tradition, well a method of interpretation practiced by the rabbis from the time of Jesus through the first millennium. As an interpretive practice, midrash explored various types of intertextual relationships between different biblical passages. It utilized allegorical or typological forms of interpretation which allowed the rabbis to see multiple levels of meaning within the biblical text. Some of the interpretive goals of midrash included explaining apparent contradictions between certain passages, demonstrating the unity of the scriptures, and illuminating the teachings of the Law and its application to daily life. Midrash may appear to go beyond the text from our perspective, but the task of midrash was productive – to produce new readings, thereby preserving the relevance of God's word in new cultural and historical situations. The various midrashim are scholastic commentaries on the Hebrew Bible by some of the most influential rabbis and were often drawn upon by of some of the church fathers, such as Jerome and Augustine, in their work.

we need to briefly appraise the Greco-Roman background associated with it.

While the semantic range for the Greek word *kêtos* includes both the idea of a huge fish and that of a sea monster it is the later concept and its connotations that would most likely have come to mind first for most Greek readers. Two well-known and similar stories from classical Greek mythology illustrate this. In the first, Perseus discovered the beautiful Andromeda chained to the cliffs along the Aegean coast. She was in this predicament because her mother, Queen Cassiopea, had boasted about Andromeda's beauty exceeding even that of Poseidon's daughters. Infuriating one of the Titans was never a wise move and this was no exception. Once Poseidon's anger was kindled he dispatched a sea monster, or *kêtos*, to destroy the coastal cities of their kingdom as retribution for the queen's hubris. In order to avert the total destruction of their realm and placate Poseidon, Andromeda's parents had her chained to the cliffs as a sacrifice for the sea monster. As it rose from the depths of the ocean to claim its prize Perseus killed the creature. As a reward for saving both their daughter and their kingdom he was given Andromeda's hand in marriage.

In an another adventure story, Herakles rescued Hesione from a similar fate. Only this time Herakles was swallowed by the *kêtos* in his attempt to defend Hesione. Three days later he emerged from the side of the monster, having hewed it to death from the inside. The stories of Perseus, Andromeda, Herakles and Hesione illustrate not only the malevolent nature of whales, *kêtoi*, but also their incredible size, and would have been part of the network of beliefs that informed how readers from a

Greco-Roman background would have conceived of the *kêtos* that swallowed Jonah.

Tales of "great fish" or "whales" were widespread in the Ancient Near East, around the Mediterranean Sea, and in most of Europe. There are stories of Alexander the Great's men encountering a school of whales in the Indian Ocean. The men were so frightened by the sight of them that they dropped the oars from their hands.However, the quick thinking of their captain, who ordered them to splash their oars in the water and sound the battle trumpet, saved the day as they scared the monsters away. Pliny described the size of the *kêtos* that swam in the Arabian Sea as 300 staffs long and 360 wide in his *Natural History* (XXXII §10). His description of the *kêtos* parallels Rabbi Hana's account of the great fish in the Talmud.

> *Tales of "great fish" or "whales" were widespread in the Ancient Near East, around the Mediterranean Sea, and in most of Europe.*

Lucian took the ancient fish story one step further when he narrated his adventures of sailing past the Pillars of Hercules (the Straits of Gibraltar). Once in the Atlantic Ocean, he and his comrades spotted whales (*kêtoi*) and other sea monsters which were over 150 miles long according to his description. Being a masterful teller of tall tales, Lucian was not content just to embellish the size of the creatures but also included a dramatic encounter with the monsters. As they attempted to navigate between the monsters one whale turned upon the ship,

> ... open-mouthed, raising the waves on all sides, and beating the sea before him into a foam, and shewing teeth much larger than our colossal phalli, sharp pointed as needles, and white as ivory. We therefore took our last leave of one another, and while we were thus in mutual embraces expecting him every moment, he came on, and swallowed us up, ship and all, at one gulp; for he found it unnecessary to crush us first with his teeth,

but the vessel at one squeeze slipped between the interstices, and went down into his maw. (Lucian, *True History* I.30 ff)

Inside, the sailors found not only the remains of other ships but also an island with mountains and forests that was composed of what it had swallowed. After exploring the vast interior of the beast and surviving several adventures the crew began to plot their escape. Their first attempt to cut their way out through its side, as Herakles did, proved futile. So they decided to set fire to the forests growing on the island. The fire raged for seven days before the smoke began to affect the beast. By the eleventh day it was near death. On the twelfth day they propped open its lifeless jaws and sailed their vessel out between the gaps in its teeth (Lucian, *True History*, II.2).

Tales of the *kêtos*, or "whale", were not unique to Greco-Roman literature. The seventh-century British theologian and historian Bede chronicled St. Brendan's encounter with a sea monster so large it appeared to be an island upon which the other monks in the ship disembarked. However, their shore leave was abruptly canceled when their cooking fire, on what they thought was a beach, scorched the giant's flesh. The monks barely made it safely back to the ship, where St. Brendan in his wisdom had waited, before the beast began to stir violently from its rest and return to the depths of the ocean.

Around 1500 AD Olaus Magnus, the archbishop of Upsal (Norway) listed, in his *Carta Marina*, the various types of "whales" that were known to live in the ocean. Some grew to over 1,000 feet long and 150 feet across. Their eyes were so massive that twenty men could sit on one, and each eye was protected by 200 horns six feet long. Some whales were like a giant lamprey that could discharge huge waves from its mouth that capsized ships so that it could suck the helpless victims into its mouth. A leitmotif we are familiar with is also found in Magnus's work: "The backs of whales are pebbled like gravel, so that mariners fix their anchors to them, disembark and light fires to have a picnic, whereupon the whale wakes and drags sailors and ship under."

This guided litany of the "Greatest Fish Stories of All Time" could easily be extended, since these stories are found in the literature and in folk tales across the Middle East, around the Mediterranean, and to the North Atlantic regions of Europe. Not only were these fish stories geographically dispersed but they persisted through history from the time of Jonah until the sixteenth century.

Across all these times and locations there are three motifs that occur in the various stories. The first is the incredible proportions of the fish – far larger than most of us, skeptics that we are, could ever accept. The second is the *kêtos* appearing as an island that lured the sailors to go ashore but had them beating quick retreats to their ships when their activities roused the beast. And finally, there is the theme of being swallowed by the sea monster, whether individually, in groups or by the ship load, ship and all.

From Kosher Fish to Gentile Monsters

Why give all this attention to these fish stories? Because we need to start from the premise that no act of interpretation occurs in a vacuum, that we always bring our cultural and traditional baggage with us. These fish stories provide us with a window to understand how the network of beliefs, preconceptions and connotations came into play as the various church fathers and others interpreted the "fish" in Jonah. If we can grasp just the smallest portion of their worldview we can read their comments on these passages in a manner that is much more sympathetic. Not just to learn intellectually, but to come under their

> *Other ancient fish stories provide us with a window to understand the network of beliefs, preconceptions and connotations that came into play as the various church fathers and others interpreted the "fish" in Jonah.*

teachings in a manner that allows us to learn from them about the meaning and relevance of the Scriptures.

The Sign of Jonah

The first port of call in the post-history of how Jonah's fish was interpreted is the Christian Scriptures. The only reference to the fish is found in Matthew 12:39–40, where Jesus drew a typological correspondence between Jonah's being in the belly of the whale, and his (Jesus') death and burial. In response to a request for a sign Jesus answered, "No sign will be given to it [this generation] except the sign of the prophet Jonah. For just as Jonah was three days and three nights in the belly of the sea monster (*kêtos*), so for three days and three nights the Son of Man will be in the heart of the earth" (NRSV). A rather cryptic reply at best. Does this "sign" refer to the person of Jonah, his being swallowed by the sea monster, his being in the earth for three days, the fact that he descends to the bowels of the earth and returns to preach to the Ninevites, his prophetic mission, or the fact that Jonah's mission was to the Gentiles? Matthew does not help us answer this question, and the enigmatic nature of Jesus' answer has sparked a great deal of exegetical discussion down through the ages.

Nevertheless, two conclusions can be made about Matthew 12:40. The first is that Matthew followed the Greek version (the Septuagint) of Jonah with the word *kêtos*. This, as we noticed above, carried connotations of a huge, evil, sea monster – connotations which were not associated with *dâg*, the Hebrew generic term for fish. The second is that the typological correspondence that Jesus drew between himself and the story of Jonah launched a trajectory of interpretation that many commentators in the church would follow, not only for understanding what type of creature it was, but also for how they would read the rest of the book of Jonah. These two trajectories of interpretation will be tackled in reverse order.

The typological reference in Matthew 12:40 became one of the primary lenses through which many Christian interpreters, from the early church up to and including the present, have understood the reference to the Jonah's fish story: Jonah's experience foreshadowed what Christ would undergo in his death, burial and resurrection. The *kêtos*, or whale, became synonymous with hell in the early church. Jonah's prayer to God from the depths of the earth, and the reference to the bars of Sheol encircling him (Jonah 2) were recognized as clear support for this line of interpretation by many of the church fathers, especially since the Greek translation of Jonah used the same word to refer both to the belly of the great fish and to Sheol in Jonah 2.

The authoritative role which Matthew's Gospel played in the church set a furrow in which many would exegetically plow. St. Cyril of Jerusalem (315–387 AD) clearly followed this lead in his fourteenth Catechetical letter:

> If we seek for Scripture testimony in proof of such facts, the Lord Jesus Christ Himself supplies it in the Gospels, saying, For as Jonas was three days and three nights in the whale's belly; so shall the Son of man be three days and three nights in the heart of the earth. *And when we examine the story of Jonas, great is the force of the resemblance. Jesus was sent to preach repentance; Jonas also was sent ... The one was cast into a whale's belly: but the other of His own accord went down thither, where the invisible whale of death is.* And He went down of His own accord, that death might cast up those whom he had devoured, according to that which is written, I will ransom them from the power of the grave; and from the hand of death I will redeem them (italics mine).

For Cyril, Jonah illustrated or articulated the mystery of Jesus' life and sacrifice in a number of ways. As we noted above, the use of the same Greek word for the belly of the fish and for the belly of hell (Jonah 1:17 and 2:2), and Jonah's descent into the heart of the earth (Jonah 2:6) provided Cyril with the textual clues by which he read the text. Most importantly, when Cyril read Jonah, it was through the lens that Matthew supplied and it would be hard to see how Cyril could have come to this particular understanding of Jonah if he had not read Matthew 12:40.

Augustine continued this trajectory when he addressed the question, "What was prefigured by the sea monster restoring alive on the third day the prophet whom it swallowed?" In his response, he pushed the correspondences between Matthew's and Jonah's texts further. Not only did Jonah and Jesus both suffer a similar descent, but in both instances there was also a redemptive purpose to their experiences.

> As, therefore, Jonah passed from the ship to the belly of the whale, so Christ passed from the cross to the sepulchre, or into the abyss of death. And as Jonah suffered this for the sake of those who were endangered by the storm, so Christ suffered for the sake of those who are tossed on the waves of this world. And as the command was given at first that the word of God should be preached to the Ninevites by Jonah, but the preaching of Jonah did not come to them until after the whale had vomited him forth, so prophetic teaching was addressed early to the Gentiles, but did not actually come to the Gentiles until after the resurrection of Christ from the grave. (Augustine, *Epistle* 52 §34)

This trajectory of interpretation continued unbroken for nearly 1,600 years. The primary point of disagreement (if you can call it a disagreement) between the various writers was a minor one: What, specifically, was the "sign of Jonah" that Jesus was referring to? At the most basic level, most perceived a parallel between the whale's belly and hell. At the same time, most commentators noticed more correspondences than a descent to the netherworld and return. Augustine and Cyril are examples of interpreters that recognized a redemptive purpose in the "sign of Jonah." Almost a millennium later Calvin summarized the different points of correspondence between Jonah's fish story and Jesus' crucifixion identified by various readers before him in his commentary on the gospels. In the end, Calvin's conclusions are very close to Augustine's reading.

> I am aware, display greater ingenuity in expounding this passage; but as the resemblance between Christ and Jonah does

not hold at every point, we must inquire in what respect Christ compares himself to Jonah. For my own part, leaving the speculations of other men, *I think that Christ intends to mark out that single point of resemblance* which I have already hinted, *that he will be their prophet after that he is risen from the dead.* "You despise," he says, "the Son of God, who has come down to you from heaven: but I am yet to die, and to rise from the grave, and to speak to you after my resurrection, as Jonah came from the bottom of the sea to Nineveh" (Calvin, *Commentary on the Harmony of the Evangelists:* Matthew 12:39, italics mine).

Pull any commentary from a library shelf on Matthew's Gospel (or almost any commentary written on Jonah from a Christian perspective) and you will likely find a discussion on the "sign of Jonah."

There are three aspects I wish to focus our attention on here. The first is how a text which is recognized as authoritative can set an entire line of interpretation for 2,000 years. Now I admit, Matthew's Gospel serves as an example par excellence because of its inclusion in the New Testament canon. But other texts can serve this same type of normative function for setting an interpretive trajectory, albeit to a lesser degree. The second aspect is how the various interpreters recognized the "belly of the whale" as symbolic of the grave, death, or hell. The fact that the same Greek word is used for the stomach of the *kêtos* and for the belly of hell in Jonah 2 in the Septuagint adds weight to this line of interpretation. But more significantly, this trajectory of reading is the result of Jesus' enigmatic expression that has dramatically shaped how the church read Jonah. Finally, these connotations, especially those of hell, have influenced how readers have conceived of Jonah's fish.

Do Christians Tell Fish Stories?

We return now to our original question: What swallowed Jonah? Being acquainted with rabbinic and Greco-Roman stories about sea monsters places us in a better position to read alongside many of the early commentators on Jonah.

Tertullian (160–220 AD) reflected the accepted beliefs of his day when he wrote, "Jonah was swallowed by the monster of the deep, in whose belly whole ships were devoured, and after three days was vomited out again safe and sound" (*On the Resurrection of the Flesh*, ch. 58). This train of thought is reflected in a third-century ode about Jonah (traditionally ascribed to Tertullian; see side-bar). It is almost as if the author of this poem wrote with both the book of Jonah and Lucian's work in his hand. The whale not only devoured

---

A Strain of Jonah the Prophet
(lines 124–150)

And from the eddy's depth a whale
Outrising on the spot, *scaly with shells,*
Unravelling his body's train, 'gan urge
More near the waves, shocking the gleaming brine,
Seizing – at God's command – the prey; which, rolled
From the poop's summit prone, *with slimy jaws*
He sucked; and into his long belly sped
The living feast; and swallowed, with the man,
The rage of sky and main. The billowy waste
Grows level, and the ether's gloom dissolves;
The waves on this side, and the blasts on that,
Are to their friendly mood restored; and, where
The placid keel marks out a path secure,
White traces in the emerald furrow bloom.
The sailor then does to the reverend Lord
Of death make grateful offering of his fear;
Then enters friendly ports. Jonah the seer
The while is voyaging, in other craft
Embarked, and cleaving 'neath the lowest waves
A wave: *his sails the intestines of the fish,*
Inspired with breath ferine; himself, shut in;
By waters, yet untouched; in the sea's heart
And yet beyond its reach; *'mid wrecks of fleets*
Half-eaten, and men's carcasses dissolved
In putrid disintegrity: in life
Learning the process of his death; but still –
To be a sign hereafter of the Lord –
A witness was he (in his very self).

Jonah, but within its bowels are flotsam and jetsam of entire fleets. Notice the size of the whale and how its appearance is described. Its body is like that of an eel, it is covered with scales, has slimy jaws and sucked its prey in like a lamprey. His description of the whale certainly conjures up an image unlike any I have seen or would have imagined, but is in complete harmony with how others in those days catalogued their appearance.

Augustine, by contrast, is restrained. Once again we return to his 102nd letter, where he tried to refute the pagan critics who derided the thought of Jonah surviving his gastronomical misadventure. It is interesting to note (from what we can glean from Augustine's letter) that Augustine's interlocutors do not question the whale or Jonah's being swallowed, but the idea that Jonah survived the ordeal.

"In the next place, what are we to believe concerning Jonah, who is said to have been three days in a whale's belly? The thing is utterly improbable and incredible, that a man swallowed with his clothes on should have existed in the inside of a fish ..." Questions such as these I have seen discussed by Pagans amidst loud: laughter, and with great scorn ... Since, however, our friend did not on this ground ask whether it is to be believed that Lazarus was raised on the fourth day, or that Christ rose on the third day, I am much surprised that he reckoned what was done with Jonah to be incredible; unless, perchance, he thinks it easier for a dead man to be raised in life from his sepulchre, than *for a living man to be kept in life in the spacious belly of a sea monster. For without mentioning the great size of sea monsters which is reported to us by those who have knowledge of them, let me ask how many men could be contained in the belly which was fenced round with those huge ribs which are fixed in a public place in Carthage, and are well known to all men there? Who can be at a loss to conjecture how wide an entrance must have been given by the opening of the mouth which was the gateway of that vast cavern?* unless, perchance, as our friend stated it, the clothing of Jonah stood in the way of his being swallowed without injury, as if he had required to squeeze himself through a narrow passage, instead of being, as: was the case, *thrown headlong through the air, and so caught by the sea monster as to be received into its belly before he was wounded by its teeth* (Augustine, *Epistle* CII §30-31, italics mine).

Augustine's replies may not contain the same amount of detail as those found in "A Strain of Jonah", but he too envisioned a sea monster of disproportionate size. It had a cavernous stomach (a theme repeated by many later interpreters) capable of holding not just our prophet but a multitude of victims. For support he appealed to two facts: that the ribs of a sea creature were supposedly on public display in Carthage and that there were reliable reports of sea monsters from knowledgeable sources (sailors, travelers, or perhaps Lucian?). These are interesting interjections on Augustine's part, because by appealing to these sources he consciously raised to the surface the expectations and network of beliefs that his readers brought with them when they read Jonah. We owe him a debt of gratitude since these preconceptions often remain deep in the uncharted waters of pre-understanding that ancient readers brought to the act of reading.

Monstrous Pictures

During the Medieval and Reformation periods artistic depictions of Jonah's whale display, from our perspective, a profound ignorance of and unfamiliarity with their subject. But if we judge these artworks according to the texts we have just considered, then we need to reassess our judgments about how faithful these depictions are. In some of the earliest Christian art depicting the story of Jonah the whale is often portrayed as a giant fish, often resembling what we would recognize as a dolphin. What is interesting is that if we compare these representations of Jonah's encounter with the whale with the Greco-Roman depictions of Perseus and Andromeda the whale is often portrayed in a very similar manner. With the passage of time, the whale often takes on the appearance of a scaly sea monster or an immense sea serpent. Some artists accentuated the whale's connotations with hell in their work. In many of these works the monster's mouth is wide open, allowing the viewer an unobstructed glimpse of the multitudes suffering in the blackness of its stomach. As a whole, the history of artistic representations mirrors the textual interpretation of Jonah's fish story.

From Bestiary to Zoology

One of the forces which we have not discussed so far that propels a reader to link a word in a text to a certain denotation or connotation is other sources which are considered authoritative. These authoritative sources may be institutions (such as schools or the teachings of the church), oral literature, or other texts. Since we have been asking questions about Jonah's great fish the natural place to look would be texts that discuss marine life.

> *From the second century* AD *to the Enlightenment any good exegete would have relied upon the Physiologus or a bestiary.*

From the second century AD up to the Enlightenment one of the primary texts any good exegete would have relied upon would have been the *Physiologus* (from the Greek *physis*, "the nature of something", and *logos*, "study") or a bestiary (Latin "book of beasts" based on the *Physiologus*). The *Physiologus* was actually a family of closely related texts (while technically there was supposed to be one *Physiologus* several different versions attributed to different authors have been preserved) that described the various types of known (real or fantastic from our perspective) animals. They were incredibly popular and influential texts that not only catalogued a particular creature's appearance and how it lived but also provided moral and/or allegorical significances that this animal represented. The *Physiologus* is quite different from a modern zoological guidebook. The goal was not to provide detailed biological information about the various creatures (although this was included); the goal of the *Physiologus* was to furnish a study of nature so that the readers could learn about God and their place within the created order. Nature was viewed as a mirror through which readers could discern the deeper truths of God's creation and their role within it. For example, the pelican was accurately depicted as a large fish-eating bird. But then the text continued, describing how this bird would shed its own blood (by cutting its chest with its beak) so that it could sprinkle this on its young that had died in order to revive them. As such, the pelican represented a type of Christ who shed his blood on the cross so that we may live. The qualities or traits of various animals epitomized virtues that readers were either to imitate or shun.

Some creatures, like the whale, personified the cunning and deceitful nature of the devil. The whale was the largest of all fish that appeared to the human eye as an island when it floated on the surface. In this manner it deceived unsuspecting mariners into disembarking upon it only to descend to the depths without warning and take its victims down with it. It enticed fish to swim into its gaping mouth by means of a sweet aroma in its breath. Some versions of bestiaries also included stories of whales devouring men and entire ships on the high seas. These traits mirrored the schemes of the devil, who seduced men through their sinful desires and human weaknesses, only to draw them in and drag them down to perdition. Many included a reference to the whale swallowing Jonah at this point as well, solidifying the connection between the whale, the devil and hell which we have seen in other sources. If someone had questioned Thomas Aquinas about why he read the reference to Jonah's fish in terms of a sea monster he could easily have pointed his critic to a copy of the *Physiologus* in the monastic library to settle the debate, just as we would point someone to, say, the *Encyclopedia Britannica* to settle a similar question today.

Luther, Calvin and the Books They Read

In the rabbinic stories, Greco-Roman literature, the writings of the church fathers, the *Physiologus* and bestiaries the *kêtos* or whale was often portrayed as a colossal sea creature. Its malevolent nature was portrayed either as devouring men and ships whole or how it deceived mariners into thinking it was an island. One of the strongest connotations associated with the whale was how it illustrated the deceptive wiles of the devil. While we may look upon such views as backward we must remember that these beliefs reflected the best and most authoritative knowledge of the day. With this in mind I would like to summon one last spokesperson for this view – Martin Luther.

Jonah's encounter with the whale surpassed the other miracle stories in the Old Testament, according to Luther. The fact that Jonah spent three days in the belly of the whale when most would have been digested in less than three hours into the "flesh and blood of that monster" is more incredible than Israel's crossing the Red Sea (*Table Talk* §DXLVII). But it is in his *Lectures on Jonah* that Luther really displayed his hand. Luther attempted to put the reader in Jonah's position as the prophet was cast overboard and left to drown as the ship sailed off. However, God was not content with a drowned prophet, but greatly increased the horror of Jonah's predicament by appointing a sea monster to ingest him.

> It must been a horrifying sight to poor, lost, and dying Jonah when the whale opened its mouth wide and he beheld sharp teeth that stood upright all around like pointed pillars or beams and he peered down the wide cellar entrance to the belly. Is that being comforted in the hour of death?

The reformer painted a picture that surely would have terrified his readers – a picture that included razor sharp teeth the size of pillars and a throat like a dark stairwell descending into the depths of hell. Feeling his way among the ribs and intestines in the dark the prophet contemplated his life and God's hand sustaining him in the midst of death. There is a vividness and power in Luther's interpretation that is absent from recent commentaries when they speculate about what species of whale could swallow a man or if such a thing is even biologically possible. They do not confront us with the monster death and hell as Luther did to his readers. It is the monstrosity and horror of the whale that assaulted Jonah and it is precisely in the midst of this that Luther wants us to re-experience the miracle that occurred. God was present with Jonah in the midst of these horrors. Luther wanted his readers to learn vicariously from this story to trust God in the midst of their trials, which pale in comparison with Jonah's dreadful experience.

With the rise of the Renaissance and the Enlightenment texts like the bestiaries and the *Physiologus* fell from their prestigious positions. Nature was no longer perceived as reflecting the attributes of the creator but was now perceived in terms of a giant, well-oiled clock. Its operation was studied not to learn about the clockmaker but rather to learn how the individual parts of the mechanism operated. The goal of inquiry was now nature itself. Galileo, Sir Isaac Newton and Darwin typify this line of inquiry that continues down to our day. One of the most significant individuals for our study at this point is Guillaume Rondelet (1507–1566).

Rondelet was the sixteenth century's equivalent of Jacques-Yves Cousteau. He lived on the Mediterranean coast of France and practiced a naturalistic approach in his study of marine biology. In 1554 he published *The Book of Marine Fish* (*Libri de Piscibus Marinis*), in which he described over 250 different kinds of marine life in great detail based on either his own observations and dissections or on the most reliable information he could collect. A Lamia (there is a debate over whether he was describing what we would call a Whale Shark or a Great White Shark), according to Rondelet, was a huge fish with an incredible appetite that ate primarily tuna but was known to snack on the occasional human. His personal observation of specimens seems to have been limited to one that was beached on the coast and another that was caught by fishermen and required two ox carts to carry it from the docks. In his description of the Lamia, Rondelet noted that there were reliable reports that Lamia have swallowed men whole and in one specimen an entire man in armor was discovered in its stomach. In particular, Rondelet claimed that it was a Lamia, not a whale, that was responsible for swallowing Jonah. Rondelet's book represents a major turning point and watershed when it comes to how Jonah is now read.

If we laid Luther's commentary on Jonah 1:17 alongside Calvin's, one of the most notable differences we would see is the tone they employ when commenting on the Jonah's whale. For Luther the whale that ingested the prophet was more than a sea creature; it was a living personification of hell. When we turn our attention to Calvin we are greeted with a whole new vocabulary and tone. All the monstrous terms and references to hell are evacuated from his text. The most frequent type of phrase Calvin employed to describe the same referent in Jonah was "a fish prepared by the Lord". When Calvin considered the specific question about the nature of the great fish that swallowed Jonah he wrote:

> I therefore refer what is said here, that a *fish was prepared*, to the preservation of Jonah: for it is certain that there are some fishes which can swallow men whole and entire. And William Rondelet, who has written a book on the fishes of the sea, concludes that in all probability it must have been the *Lamia*. He himself saw that fish, and he says that it has a belly so capacious and, mouth so wide, that it can easily swallow up a man; and he says that a man in armor has sometimes been found in the inside of the Lamia. Therefore, as I have said, either a whale, or a *Lamia*, or a fish unknown to us, may be able to swallow up a man whole and entire; but he who is thus devoured cannot live in the inside of a fish. (John Calvin, *Jonah, Micah, Nahum*, vol. 3 in *Commentaries on the Twelve Minor Prophets*, lecture 86)

Aside from the dramatic change in tenor in Calvin's commentary, the reference to Rondelet (the translation above uses his English name, William) should immediately strike us. A new authority had emerged on the scene, and as a result Calvin's conceptualization of the whale had been transfigured. Rondelet's *Book of Marine Fish* functioned like a new pair of glasses through which Calvin read Jonah. As a result, he read Jonah in a manner that was markedly different from those of his contemporaries, such as Luther.

Calvin's interpretation is extraordinary for several reasons. First, his commentary signals a new direction in the interpretation of the great fish in Jonah. Second, his citing from *The Book of Marine Fish* testifies to the impact of Rondelet's

> *Rondelet's Book of Marine Fish functioned like a new pair of glasses and transformed how the book of Jonah was read.*

work. Calvin's use of Rondelet bears witness to a whole new trajectory of thought and inquiry. He adopted Rondelet's identification of the Lamia as being the guilty party based on Rondelet's observations, measurements and anecdote about the man in armor. The *Physiologus* and bestiaries were knocked off their pedestals, to be replaced by books that took a more "scientific" approach to marine life. And finally, the stamp Rondelet's book placed on Calvin's reading of Jonah raises an important concept for the history of reception. It is not just what someone writes, but the impact of their work on subsequent readers that should be carefully noted – in this case, how Rondelet informed Calvin's interpretation of Jonah and how Calvin influenced his readers. The impact of Calvin's writings on the Christian tradition cannot be overstated. He is the 800 pound gorilla that cannot be ignored when biblical interpretation is being discussed. Calvin set an agenda for how many who followed him perceive what the "great fish" in Jonah denoted and connoted. Calvin's appropriation of Rondelet's research reveals how one person's work can impact how generations after him or her read the Bible.

Whale-eating Sharks

Calvin and Luther, while contemporaries, represent two very different trajectories for reading the book of Jonah. Luther represents the older view; Calvin ushers in the new. Luther's reading followed the approach taken in the *Physiologus* and bestiaries: that nature mirrors spiritual realities. The fantastic and monstrous denotations and connotations associated with Jonah's fish are to a large degree abandoned after Luther.

Calvin followed the lead of Rondelet who studied nature from a rationalistic, biological perspective. As we turn to those that come after the two reformers the number of commentaries greatly increases, in large part due to the invention of the printing press. Since there is no possibility of tracing all the various trajectories of interpretation from the Reformation to the present in what remains of this chapter, we will concentrate on a select number of commentaries that discuss the nature of the fish/whale.

Perhaps the most widely read English commentary is Matthew Henry's. First-year seminary students often pepper their papers with footnotes to his commentaries. This is most likely due to the fact that a copy of his work is included in almost every

> *The fact that Matthew Henry's commentary is 300 years old (written between 1706 and 1721) does not mean it is unsuitable for exegesis, but only that we need to remember he was a child of his age.*

package of Bible software, that his commentary is available on the internet, in many libraries, and that book distributors often place his work on sale. What surprises many of my students is to learn is that Matthew Henry's commentary is 300 years old (written between 1706 and 1721). This is not to say that Matthew Henry's commentaries are unsuitable for exegesis, but only that we need to remember that he was a child of his age, as we are of ours, and when we use his commentary we need to read it within that historical context. For example, Henry arrived at an interesting reading of Jonah's fish. He seems to attempt to steer a middle course between Calvin and Luther. In favor of Luther he referred to Jonah's fish as a "whale" in places and associated it with the Leviathan of the Old Testament. In Calvin's favor he referred to it as a "fish" and also related that in its belly "has sometimes been found the dead body of a man in armor". Henry did not appear to have read

Rondelet directly, but was apparently indirectly influenced by him through Calvin's work. By carefully comparing Henry's work with Calvin's we can observe Rondelet's impact on how people read Jonah 150 years after him.

Rondelet's influence did not die with Matthew Henry. On the contrary, Rondelet's work has a rather impressive list of followers. For example, in his *Exposition of the Bible* (1746–66) John Gill noted that the fish in question was most likely a Lamia, in which whole men in coats of mail had been found. Other well-known commentaries in this company include Keil and Delitzsch's *Biblical Commentary* (1866), Gray and Adams' *Bible Commentary* (originally published under the title of *Bible Museum*, 1871–81), E.B. Pusey's *Commentary on the Minor Prophets* (1885; more on this book in a moment), and Frank Boyer's *Jonah in Fact and Fiction* (1899). Three hundred and fifty years after its original publication, Rondelet's book *The Book of Marine Fish* was still being quoted as the authoritative reference in regard to the identification of the creature that swallowed Jonah. There are two exegetical themes that evidence this influence. The first is how the various commentators identify the "great fish" as a Lamia. The second is seen in the way that the story of the man in armor was passed down from commentator to commentator.

Rondelet's influence on subsequent generations of commentators was not static. Modifications to Rondelet's view can be found in Keil and Delitzsch's comments on Jonah. They added two new anecdotal accounts to Rondelet's man in armor, which only serves to thicken our plot. First, they added an account of an entire horse being found in the stomach of a sea-dog (Lamia?). And second, they recounted a story of a sailor who fell overboard in stormy seas and was swallowed by a sea-dog before he could be rescued. The captain quickly ordered the carnivore to be shot with the deck cannon. As the predator thrashed about in its death spasms it disgorged the sailor. About ten years later Gray and Adams extended these anecdotes. Instead of a sea-dog, the predator was now a Great White Shark which the captain gave to the sailor after his rescue. Gray and Adams appealed to the widespread story (or what they thought was a commonly known account) that the former would-be meal had the shark preserved and took it on the European speaking circuit. This story was repeated in *Jonah: Fact and Fiction* (1899) and continued to be cited as late as the 1950s in the *Pulpit Commentary* (which also mentioned men and horses being swallowed whole).

Another incident that came to be associated with these anecdotes was that of a sailor who was swallowed by a whale off the Falkland Islands. This particular story first appeared in English commentaries around 1900. A certain James Bartley was reported to have fallen overboard and swallowed alive by the whale he was hunting. Several days later his shipmates harpooned a whale and began the process of harvesting their catch, only to discover Bartley bleached white but still alive in its stomach.

This story received attention in various commentaries (including the *Beacon Bible Commentary*, 1966), *Expository Times* and the *Princeton Theological Review*. While the veracity of this tale was refuted (the thrust of the *Expository Times* article) both this story and the previous anecdote about the sailor swallowed by the shark reintroduced a mythical, or tall-tale, aspect to the interpretation of Jonah similar to that found in ancient and Medieval literature. At a popular level these stories satisfied the human curiosity for the unknown that has made publications such as *Ripley's Believe or Not* successful. Their inclusion in the commentaries highlights two ideas. First, these stories were cited because they were found in authoritative (e.g. Rondelet and Calvin) that the commentators consulted in their research. And secondly, these stories were grafted into a trajectory of interpretation by the way they were cited by various interpreters to support a particular reading of a text.

It was not until around 1880, with the publication of E.B. Pusey's *Commentary on the Minor Prophets*, that Rondelet's work began to fall from its authoritative position. Pusey's work was quickly recognized as the new authority. The influence of his thoughts on Jonah is felt down to and including Frank Gaebelein in his commentary *Four Minor Prophets* (1970). His examination of what swallowed Jonah is one of the most thorough and detailed discussions of the great fish in Jonah. It stretches over nine pages and covers not only zoological considerations but also many of the Greco-Roman stories we looked at earlier. As opposed to Luther, Pusey favored a scientific approach. He meticulously quotes numerous biology texts to identify Jonah's mystery fish. The size of jaw bones and teeth of various specimens is used to calculate the possibility of either a Lamia or a White Shark swallowing someone. Whereas Calvin cited Rondelet, Pusey turned to a fellow professor at Oxford, Dr. Rolleston, who personally informed Pusey that:

> In all modern works on Zoology, we find 30 feet given as a common length for a shark's body. Now a shark's body is usually only about eleven times the length of the half of its lower jaw. Consequently a shark of thirty feet would have a lower jaw nearly six feet in semicircular extent. Even if such a jaw as this was of hard bony consistence ... it would qualify its possessor for engulfing one of our own species most easily. (E.B. Pusey, *Minor Prophets*, 386)

Once again, notice how different this discussion is from Luther's. All supernatural language is absent from the discussion and in its place is the precise, calculated language of the scientific revolution. The dialogue Calvin initiated when he cited early marine zoologist Rondelet was continued with Pusey's quoting Rolleston. The revolutionary changes introduced by the sciences not only transformed how we understood the world but also introduced a new type of authority and a new list of authorities that were consulted in research. Both of these cultural transformations also profoundly impacted how the Scriptures were read.

Conclusion

One of the main goals of this chapter was to explore how the unspoken network of beliefs and pre-understanding every reader brings with them shapes their act of reading. Because we are so at home with our preconceptions and pre-understandings we are usually unaware of how powerfully they shape how we read.

Gleason Archer's *A Survey of the Old Testament* (1974) is representative of how our contemporary presuppositions delineate what we count as a valid interpretation for Jonah's whale. Working from the Hebrew text of Jonah, Archer commented that in the original language the term used was *great fish* and the popular word *whale* was not a very accurate translation. However, since a whale is the only sea creature known with a stomach large enough to accommodate a human he revises his argument and states that this popular understanding is valid after all. To support this reading Archer writes how the author of Jonah could not have used the alternative Hebrew word *tannîn* because it was too vague and "could also mean shark, sea-serpent, or even dragon". It is precisely because of what he considers the unacceptable monstrous connotations communicated by *tannîn* that Archer argues that the author used the Hebrew *dâg* instead. His comments illustrate how the network of beliefs (in this case our modern, scientific presuppositions) we bring to every act of reading shapes and constrains how we read a text, even down to the level of the meaning of individual words.

In order to appreciate how Jonah's fish has been transformed through time imagine, if you will, that you are a passenger on two ships. The first is a Medieval sailing ship with St. Brendan, the second a nineteenth-century clipper. On both a cry goes forth, "Whale port bow!" Along with Brendan and his crew you would most likely have dropped to your knees to petition the Almighty to protect you from this personification of the devil. Pusey's and Rolleston's contemporaries, by contrast, would most likely have rushed to that side in order to gain a better glimpse of the whale, gauge its size, or possibly harpoon it for study.

It is at this point that I need to interject an autobiographical confession. When we lived in Southern California my wife and I took our children on a one-day whale-watching excursion. Yes, we deliberately boarded a ship with the intention of spotting Grey Whales as they migrated north along the coast. It is difficult to convey how impressive the sight of these creatures was, even though we saw only a small portion of their entire body when they surfaced. Once or twice we caught sight of their flukes as they raised them out of the sea for one slow, majestic thrust. Excitedly we pointed for our kids, "Look, look, there's another one!" I certainly live in a world foreign to that of the rabbis, Lucian, the authors of the Latin bestiaries, Rondelet, and even Pusey.

> *Words are not stable, but transform over time.*

Words are not stable, but transform over time. Not only are a word's *connotations* (e.g. as the devil and hell were associated with *whale*) transfigured, but so too are their *denotations* (e.g. "sea monster", "Lamia", "shark", or "whale" for what swallowed Jonah). Some of these lexical shifts occur when a text is translated into another language (from Hebrew, to Greek, Latin, and finally English). Each time the text is translated some of a word's range of meaning is lost in terms of the subtleties of the text and the play on words.

At the same time something is gained. New perspectives and possibilities for understanding a text are opened up. The meaning of a word is also sculpted by how we understand the world. Do we perceive nature as a mirror that reflects God and his purposes or do we study nature to learn about nature itself (the *Physiologus* as opposed to Rondelet's *The Book of Marine Fish*)? As a result, whenever we read someone's comments on a biblical passage we need to be attentive to what presuppositions they brought to the text, their place in history, and the resources and references they used for their research. The more distant we are from an author's historical situation the more attention we may need to give to these considerations.

One of the prejudices shared by many modern commentators concerns their approach to how the biblical text has been received and read historically. The history of a text's interpretation is often seen as something that must be eschewed. They attempt to jump from our historical horizon over 2,000 years of interpretation and application back to the original Greek or Hebrew text. Instead of seeing it as a rich, living heritage and connection from the text, down through the centuries to us, this heritage of interpretation is perceived as a hindrance to reading the Bible. I hope this chapter has demonstrated how the way a text is received and read down through history not only allows us to understand what the biblical text may mean, but allows us to do so in a fuller and more historically embodied sort of way than the historical-grammatical method makes possible. We learn how we got where we are today and why we translate certain words the way we do. It opens other avenues of interpretation and perspectives on the text that we may have never considered. As such, the writings of the doctors of the past may be as profitable as the Bible dictionaries and Greek or Hebrew lexicons we rely so heavily on today.

> *We need to come to the giants of the past with the attitude of a student rather than treating their readings as outdated or ignorant.*

If we are going to learn from the giants of the past then we must learn to read them sympathetically. We need to come to them with the attitude of a student ("What can I learn from you about this passage?") rather than treating their readings as outdated or ignorant. For example, Luther's comments on Jonah expose me to unimagined visions of judgment, horror, repentance and God's presence. He also provokes my modern biological presuppositions (e.g. "Save the Whales") when he speaks of the monster's teeth being razor sharp pillars and says that its throat was a dark stairwell plunging into hell. By contrast, many modern commentaries are limp and lukewarm with their biological discussions of what type of marine animal may be physically able to swallow a human. I would also argue that Luther's view of the whale and the miraculous in the book of Jonah are closer to the original author's view than are our contemporary beliefs. In this sense his reading of Jonah represents a more appropriate reading of the text than many of the commentaries written during the last half century. Luther provokes my thought and imagination and, as a result, my engagement with the book of Jonah. His exposition of Jonah's fish story is a prime example of the three-way dialogue between us as readers, the Bible and tradition.

> *Luther's comments on Jonah provoke my thoughts and expose me to unimagined visions of judgment, horror, repentance and God's presence.*

Three

The Second Historical Context: A Living Tradition

Tradition is not something to be jumped over in an attempt to gain access to the pristine texts of the New Testament. Tradition is what we dwell within. And we need to cultivate our mindset of dwelling within a tradition.

It was springtime in Paris and I was staring into the eyes of one of the most famous women in the world. A number of thoughts kept running through my mind. Was she smiling? Or was there just a transparent hint of a smile on her lips? What was she thinking of? What was there about her that had caused her to become one of the most celebrated and speculated upon faces in the world? Ah, *Mona Lisa*, why are you the most famous artwork depicting the smile when you really are not smiling all that much, if at all?

Angus Trumble considers these questions, and documents how we "read" the *Mona Lisa*, in his enlightening book, *A Brief History of the Smile*. He argues that our perception of Mona Lisa's mouth is not a neutral reading of the portrait. Rather, our artistic heritage has handed down to us very specific ways in which to view this artwork.

When Leonardo da Vinci first unveiled his masterpiece it was not the smile that captured the attention of his patrons. During that age it was common for wealthy husbands to commission portraits of their wives or fiancées. These portraits were a means for the man to exhibit the status of his household. In most of the portraits the subjects appear inert, almost as if they were a still life. By contrast, Da Vinci represented Mona Lisa as relaxed and poised. "The *Mona Lisa* is very different from this earlier genre, and the striking manner in which Leonardo realized his subject in space and light seems to reflect not only an entirely different working method, but also radically different ideas about how a woman might inhabit a painting," says Trumble (p. 28).

Until the middle of the nineteenth century these were the aspects of the painting that occupied the art critics. Then, beginning around 1850, a series of French art critics began to comment on the seductive, treacherous or hypnotizing power of Mona Lisa's smile. Even Sigmund Freud contributed a psychological analysis of this portrait and the artist: *Mona Lisa* depicted Leonardo da Vinci's fleeting memory of the smile of his mother, whom he was tragically separated from at an early age, said Freud. Since then the number of contemporary articles about this work of art has "obscured the fact that the smile of the *Mona Lisa* was essentially the creation of nineteenth-century French critics who were determined to see the work as a miraculous achievement in the history of art ... and the smile as the seat of the painting's mesmeric power" (Trumble, p. 22).

Trumble's book embodies much of what has been covered in the previous chapters and is a fascinating study to read. By considering the original historical context in which the *Mona Lisa* was painted he helps us to understand the context in which it was commissioned and how it was originally intended to function, and to appreciate a bit of da Vinci's creative genius. The history of the *Mona Lisa*'s reception and analysis discloses how the way an artwork is perceived and appreciated is not as neutral as we tend to think. Every generation of viewers has been shaped and trained to look at an artwork like the *Mona Lisa* in a certain manner and to ask certain questions about it – questions that shift and change with the passing of time. The goal of this chapter is to consider how our tradition shapes us as readers of the Bible and how to actively engage that tradition as we read the scriptures.

A Non-traditional Tradition

One of the most difficult hurdles to clear when I am teaching the concept of the three-way dialogue (the Bible, tradition and the reader) is the Western tradition of thought since the Enlightenment. The Enlightenment and the scientific revolution ushered in profound changes on many fronts. In regard to theology, the most dramatic change introduced was the adoption of the historical-critical method in biblical interpretation. One of the basic presuppositions undergirding this approach is that through the proper application of method we are able to determine objectively the reality or truths about the world in which live.

The impact of modern scientific or historical methodology in the field of biblical studies has been a double-edged sword. On the one hand, the work of sunburnt archeologists carefully excavating sites in the Middle East, or linguistic scholars poring over papyri in a library's special collections, has produced an incredible explosion of knowledge. Most of the commentaries, historical studies, lexicons, and most recent biblical software testify to the value and role that historical-critical methods have played. This is something we should cherish and use as wise stewards, and it is not my goal to reject or undermine the value of these types of studies or their results. Rather, what I want to offer is a complementary model for reading and studying the scriptures.

Inherent within many contemporary methods of interpretation are problematic presuppositions and prejudices – prejudices which, while often unspoken, lead us to make judgments about what is a valid interpretation in ways that we may not be aware. One the one hand, I do not want to be accused of undermining 200 years of biblical research. On the other hand, by way of criticism, I hope to raise several of the presuppositions that accompany our methodological approaches to conscious reflection so that we may productively engage in a three-way dialogue with the Bible.

Inherited Presuppositions

1. The first presupposition we need to examine concerns the epistemological regard in which individual judgment is held. One of the apologetic strategies of the scientific revolution is

that a lone individual, sequestered in a lab or library, rethinking accepted knowledge on a subject, is able to overturn conventional understanding with a dramatic new breakthrough through the use of a methodology or procedure. René Descartes (1596–1650) is perhaps the person from whom we inherited this prejudice. In his *Discourses on Method and the Meditations*, Descartes says that he rejected all that he had learned from his parents, religion and teachers in order to arrive at some absolute, bedrock certain truth he could base his life and knowledge on. After clearing away all the clutter of conflicting opinions he had been taught he arrived at the final, irrefutable, bedrock truth that he could build his philosophical system on: "I think, therefore I am."

> *As Descartes's children we have inherited a philosophical presupposition that places a high value on the individual who questions everything, with the result that we have become intellectual orphans, cut off from culture, community and tradition.*

As Descartes children we have inherited a philosophical presupposition that places a high value on the individual who questions everything. The result is that we are no longer the dwarfs standing on the shoulders of the giants who came before us, but have climbed down from their shoulders and claim to know better than they did.

However, this disconnection from our tradition is one that our intellectual tradition has fabricated. As a result we deceive ourselves into thinking that we are able to escape our position in tradition and history and impartially study the Bible. The significance of our Cartesian legacy is that we have been trained to become intellectual orphans, cut off from culture, community and tradition as we pursue the ideal of a neutral, detached, objective researcher.

Yet from a *diachronic* (from the Greek *dia*, meaning "through", and *chronos*, "time or history") point of view, we need to recognize the formative role that tradition and community have had in our lives. For example, I never chose to be born in the country I was born in, my mother tongue, my parents or siblings, the culture in which I was raised, or even the color of my hair. Any lofty ideas I may have about my individuality are like a spider that walks on the surface tension of water. In fact, the very conceptions I have about my individuality are part the deep waters of tradition upon which my individuality floats ever so delicately. From a *synchronic* (from the Greek *syn*, meaning "with" or "at", and *chronos*, "at one point or period in history") point of view we need to recognize just how embedded we are within a particular community. Long before I realize that tradition is something that belongs to me, I belonged to a tradition. I am an individual, but my individuality must be seen in terms of the relationships and roles I have within a larger community: as a teacher, cyclist, believer, husband, father, etc. The attempt to enter into (only) a two-way dialogue between the reader and the Bible is based on the over-estimated role of individuality (that can be understood and exist apart for their tradition) which is part of our Western tradition. In order to engage in a three-way dialogue with the Bible we need to realize how embedded we are in our community and tradition. Otherwise the idea of engaging in a dialogue with our tradition, along with the Bible, is just a lofty ideal.

2. The second unspoken presupposition in many modern hermeneutical models is that of method itself, the belief being that the proper use of method insures the correct result. There are several corollaries that attend this premise. The first is that the Bible can be studied like any other object. Like a specimen under the microscope, the Bible is reduced to something that can be objectively mastered.

The second corollary is that there is one correct interpretation that the proper use of method will yield. Often this objective meaning is referred to in terms of recovering the author's intentions when he or she wrote the text, and various methods are proposed for doing this. For example, I have seen flow charts that are two pages long on how to interpret a Greek verb correctly. You drop the verb in question in the top of this chart. It tumbles down various chutes, its direction decided at different points along the route by its tense or other grammatical information, and finally drops out the bottom of the chart in a slot that indicates exactly how we should interpret it.

One of the simplest illustrations of this occurs in Ephesians 5:18 where Paul wrote, "Do not get drunk with wine, for that is debauchery; but be filled with the Spirit" (NRSV). The imperative (command, instruction) *be filled* is in the present tense in Greek. Any first-year Greek student should be able to tell you that one of the grammatical aspects of the present tense is that it conveys continuous or ongoing action. This leads some to read Paul's command in this verse as conveying the idea of "keep being filled with the Spirit." The problem is that this verse contains another present tense imperative which is often translated as "do not get drunk." If we are consistent in how we interpret these commands then the verse should read, "Do not keep getting drunk (on a regular basis) for that is debauchery; but keep being filled (on a regular basis) with the Spirit." But this raises the problem that the Ephesians were living a rather inebriated lifestyle while being filled with the Spirit of God! It is better to read these two imperatives as simple commands without any emphasis in regard to duration: "Don't get drunk" and "Be filled." This might seem to be a rather common sense line of interpretation, but I have heard this verse taught with emphasis to the continuative aspect of the present tense in some very respectable contexts. This may be an overly simplified example (so that the reader is not bogged down in a technical discussion of Greek grammar), but it gives an idea of how the rise of methodology, and our trust in it for accurate results, has shaped the way we exegete the scriptures.

> *If we approach the Bible as an object that we master by means of methodology, we are coming at it from the wrong direction. Rather than our mastering the Bible, the Bible should master us.*

Let me quickly raise a few of the objections to this second presupposition. First, if we approach the Bible as an object that we master by means of methodology, we are coming at it from the wrong direction. Over and over we are told in the Bible that its purpose is to transform our lives (Psalm 119, 2 Timothy 3:16–17). Rather than our mastering the Bible, the Bible should master us. This requires that we approach the Bible in a manner that is open and receptive to its claims, a stance that is difficult to maintain if we are trying to study it objectively.

The second problem with the idea that the proper use of method insures the correct result is that a method determines in advance what you will find. Using a method is similar to casting a net: it determines in advance what we will catch. If I fish in a lake with a net that has two-inch spacing between its lines I will only catch fish that are too big to pass through that net. I may be able to draw some conclusions about the fish that cannot pass through the net, but I may not be able to draw any conclusions about smaller ones, or about the fish that live in parts of the lake where a net cannot be used. In the same manner, each method of studying a text has its strengths and weaknesses. Just because someone has correctly applied all the procedures and principles of a method, that does not guarantee that he or she will accurately interpret a verse.

The idea that a text possesses only one correct interpretation or meaning is related to this modern, objective, methodological approach. Now to a certain extent it is proper to speak of a "correct" interpretation within the context of a particular methodological approach. For example, if the meaning of a sentence appears to hinge on the tense of its main verb then we can present evidence from various Greek grammars to support how that sentence should be understood. However, once we move beyond the level of a clause or sentence so many factors come into play that the idea of one "correct" interpretation or meaning becomes problematic. Later in this chapter we will discuss an alternative way of conceiving of meaning, but for now I have just wanted to focus on a few of the problems this view raises.

Taken as a whole, these two presuppositions present some major obstacles to a three-way dialogue. If I as an individual, through the correct use of a particular method, determine that the church has misread the closing passage in Matthew's gospel, then I am elevating myself as an authority over all that have gone before me. There are instances where a criticism of tradition is perfectly valid and justifiable, but I would argue that this is not as common as is assumed and that in most instances the consequences of taking a critical approach are counter-productive, for various reasons.

First, it leads to a hardened position. Both fundamentalists and liberals (for they really are flipsides of the same coin in this respect) proclaim that if you read the Bible the way they did (used their methods to arrive at their conclusions) then you would arrive at the proper position or reject opposing views. Second, the proliferation of sects and cults is another reflection of these unspoken presuppositions. The fact that they are often based on a particular person's interpretation of the scriptures should be a clear indication of this. And third, our modern consumerist approach to churches is an outgrowth of this mentality at the individual level. "I think I will fellowship at this church because I like the music or fellowship, but I will pick and choose which of its doctrines and teachings I will agree with." The removal of statements of faith or the credal formulations from the public life and teaching of many churches may be an attempt to cater to these narcissistic tendencies.

> *Removing statements of faith or the credal formulations from the public life and teaching of many churches may be an attempt to cater to narcissistic tendencies.*

In regard to the actual practice of biblical interpretation we end up with a double chronological prejudice. (I know it sounds really academic, but float a term like this in a Sunday School class and see how much *gravitas* it carries!) On the one hand, the oldest archeological artifacts, manuscripts, lexical information or other forms of evidence are preferred. The evidence that comes closest to the actual timeframe within which the text was written is given priority. While this preference is useful for historical or background studies it has borne unfortunate consequences for the type of studies we want to engage in. In particular, the post-history of the text, such as how the church fathers read and taught the Bible, is devalued, since it comes chronologically later and is often separated from discussions concerning the meaning of the text. This is demonstrated by the way most universities or seminaries separate the biblical studies departments from the departments of church history and the history of biblical interpretation (if they offer anything in this area at all).

On the other hand, more weight is given to the most recently published commentaries, lexicons, reference works or journal articles. Because they bear a more recent copyright date the unspoken presupposition is that they are more valuable. Older commentaries, especially if they are over 50 or 100 years old, are seen as dated (in both senses of the word).

The aftermath of this double chronological prejudice is that we clear away the vast middle ground between the earliest artifacts and the most recent publications. We push 2,000 years of biblical interpretation off to the side. The illusion is created that we can jump over the entire span of the history of the church when we interpret the Bible, from the twenty-first century directly back to the first. When modern commentators consider this vast middle ground of history they are often ambivalent about the value of their interpretations, or reject how they read the text, because it does not agree with our views and methodological conclusions ("Did you read what Luther said about the whale?"). Markus Bochmuehl, for example, complains about the lack of attention given to the Christian tradition's rich history of biblical interpretation:

> Road engineers know that when you are trying to build a new road from A to B, quite often the best route is more or

less to follow the course of the old road from A to B. Thus one can make all the necessary road safety improvements while gaining from one's predecessors collective understanding of the local terrain. To this day, the main westbound motorway from Cambridge follows the straight course of an ancient Roman road through the Fens. Nineteen centuries of biblical interpretation generally followed an analogous procedure. For the last century and a half, however, we have not been building and improving a road on which to travel back and forth, but have attempted to slash a wide swath through the woods with picks and machetes and, one suspects, often without much sense of direction or sensitivity to the terrain.[5]

The history of biblical interpretation and reception presents both a challenge and a compliment to biblical scholarship which has been dominated by questions concerning the origin of the text for the past century. Once again, this is not to deny the value of such research, but asks why such a disproportionate amount of research in biblical studies is devoted to the historical reconstruction of the text's origin while so little is devoted to the history of the interpretation of the Scriptures and the effects of those interpretations. Reading with the giants requires a different set of reading glasses from those used by many of our contemporary methodological approaches. The rest of this chapter is devoted to considering some of the basic values and attitudes behind this different approach to reading.

> *Why has such a disproportionate amount of research in biblical studies been devoted to the historical reconstruction of the text's origin and so little to the history of the interpretation of the Scriptures and the effects of those interpretations?*

---

[5] Markus Bochmuehl, "A Commentator's Approach to the 'Effective History' of Philippians", *Journal for the Study of the New Testament*, 60 (1995), 58.

Resurrecting the Role of Tradition

Tradition in the New Testament: Oral teachings and Paul's traditions

The Christian faith has been shaped by tradition from its very inception. We often read the New Testament without consciously realizing that the traditional and oral teachings that stood behind the text are preserved within the text in numerous locations.

For example, the authors of the New Testament texts appeal to, or quote directly from, what appears to be an oral body of teaching that was handed down from teacher to disciple within the primitive church. Indirect references to these teachings can be found in texts such as: Acts 2:42 (the believers being devoted to the apostles' teachings); Philippians 2:16 (Paul's admonition to "hold fast to the word of life"); Colossians 3:18–4:1, Ephesians 5:22–33, 1 Timothy 2:1–15, 5:1–2 and 1 Peter 2:13–3:7 and other passages where appeals are made for the believers to follow a household code. Then there are what appear to be word for word citations from creeds or hymns widely known among the believers. These include, but are not limited to, the following: 1 Corinthians 8:6, Ephesians 5:14, 2 Timothy 2:11–13.

The two direct quotations from this oral body of teaching that I wish to consider are 1 Corinthians 11:23–26 and 15:3–8. Both of these passages begin with almost identical expressions: *What I received ... I handed on to you.* The two verbs *received* and *handed on* are recognized by many New Testament scholars to be formal rabbinic terms used in the transmission of traditional material from teacher to student. In essence, Paul is reminding his readers that these teachings concerning the Eucharist and the resurrection did not originate with him. He had been taught these statements and had passed them on exactly as he had received them, probably implying a word for word memorization on both his part and his readers'. The fact that he not only reminds them that he had handed the teachings down to them, but also quotes these teachings in 1 Corinthians, implies that the teachings carried authoritative weight within the early church.

In both cases we see a living tradition functioning in Paul's life and ministry. First, this brilliant theologian learned from those who had gone before him and accepted their teachings as binding. Paul's theology is not just the result of personal reflection and thought on the life and death of Jesus, but he is operating within an authoritative theological framework that is already highly developed in certain respects. Second, Paul is an active participant in this tradition. Not only does he pass this tradition along, but he actively uses it in his ministry and teachings. And third, having the Lord's Supper and the creed of the resurrection preserved in the text of 1 Corinthians gives us a glimpse into the oral teachings of the apostolic church ten or more years prior to the inscription of the New Testament epistles.

The middle ground of tradition: The canon and the illumination of the spirit

What about the intervening period between the composition of the text and today? There are a number of different illustrations that could be used to demonstrate how different ministers, theologians and commentators have engaged in a three–way dialogue. One of the most noteworthy concerns the formation of the New Testament itself. A common phrase used to describe how the canon came about is that "the church did not decide on the canon but discovered it," the idea being that the church did not sit down at any one point in time, lay out all the various candidate texts on a table and then decide by committee which texts should be included in the New Testament. In fact, none of the ecumenical councils during the first three or four centuries ever issued a definitive decision on the New Testament canon. While there are earlier lists of which books and letters were recognized by the church it was not until 367 AD, when the bishop of Alexandria, Athanasius, composed his Easter encyclical letter, that we have the earliest preserved list of texts that matches the table of contents of the New Testament today. Rather, the church discovered the canon through the reception and impact of the various letters to and writings on the church. The authoritative status of an epistle such as Hebrews grew as different believers and congregations experienced the relevance of that letter's message for Christian life and practice, for its theological contributions on the person and nature of Jesus, salvation, or the church, and for its literary features and style.

At a secondary level, the authoritative status of a text was also buttressed as various authors quoted it in their works. I Clement (90 AD) cited extensively from the Epistle to the Hebrews, as did Justin Martyr (100–165 AD) and Hippolytus (170–236 AD). The manner in which the church fathers and councils quoted from Hebrews helped establish its authority within the church, both geographically and chronologically, as their letters and decisions were copied and dispersed.

The main point I want to bring out in this discussion is that the New Testament canon was formed through a three-way dialogue between the various New Testament texts, the reading community of the early church, and the impact these texts had on other readers, primarily preserved in the writings of the church fathers.

> *The New Testament cannon was formed through a three-way dialogue.*

John 8 – The woman caught in adultery

The inclusion of the story of the woman caught in adultery in the Gospel of John demonstrates the role of tradition in the formation of the New Testament text. Based on the earliest manuscripts we are fairly certain that this story was originally not part of the text of the Gospel of John. At the same time many biblical scholars believe it is an account of an actual event from the life of Jesus that was circulated independently, most likely orally transmitted within the early church, that managed to wrestle itself a place within the canonical Gospel of John around 400 AD.

Before its final location in John 8, various scribes who copied the New Testament tried to insert it in several different settings, including Luke 21 and 24, John 7 and 21. The persistence of this episode in continually popping up in different textual locations attests to the reception of this story within the teaching and tradition of the early church.

The early historian Eusebius of Caesarea (260–340 AD) partially documented the oral transmission of this story: "Papias, an ancient man who was a hearer of John ... relates another story of a woman, who was accused of many sins before the Lord, which is contained in the Gospel according to the Hebrews" (*Ecclesiastical History*, 3:39.1 and 16). Eusebius seemed to know of two different sources for this story: one from Papias and the second in the Gospel of the Hebrews. Augustine thought the text was originally removed from the Gospel of John by the church fathers (and was reinserted at a later date) because the early church fathers feared it might be read by women as permission to engage in adultery. Thus the story would have been provocative at best and challenging to the church's teachings. This is especially true if we consider that the early church held to some very strong and rigid views in regard to sexual immorality and in this particular story Jesus not only forgave the woman's sins but took a very light hand in disciplining her. However, if the lesson of this story had lined up exactly with the church's morality then it may not have been passed on either, as its message would have been considered obvious and as making little contribution to the formation of the church's teachings. As a result, this story walks a thin but highly illuminating line. The fact that it challenged the accepted norms of the church gave it a provocative power and this is perhaps one of the main features of the story that made the church wrestle with it.

The popularity of this story in the church fathers' writings testifies to its authoritative status throughout the earliest Christian communities. At the same time, each time they cited this story they reinforced its authoritative status. For example, Augustine included an entire exposition of it in his *Tractates on the Gospel of John*. While he did not discuss the actual sin of the woman, or whether she was set up, he saw the primary point of the story as a demonstration of the gentleness and grace of the Lord. Jerome was aware that not all the manuscripts of John included this story; however, his decision to include it at its present location in John in the Vulgate (between 386 and 404 AD) virtually guaranteed its presence in the Gospel of John for the next 1,000 years. The presence of this story in John 8 in our contemporary Bibles testifies to the influence of the decision Jerome made almost 1,600 years ago.

The historical path this story took before arriving at its final resting place in John 8 is similar to the way epistles like Jude or James achieved their canonical status. The primary difference concerns the nature of the text itself. Unlike the letters of Jude or James this passage was not a self-contained whole, but was a single narrative episode that required a larger context within the life of Jesus. Instead of being including it in the New Testament as an individual narrative fragment the early church found it necessary to situate this account within one of the gospels. This provided the story with a context in which to make sense of its purpose and meaning and also gave it an authoritative position as part of the New Testament canon.

Our present preoccupation with questions of historical accuracy and the restoration of the original manuscripts means we either deny this story its place in the Gospel of John or treat it with marginal notes that state the earliest manuscripts did not include it. As a result, we have lost contact with the teaching of this story, which the early church found authoritative, wrestled with and finally recognized. As such, the story of the woman caught in adultery illuminates how our methodological concerns may conflict with the teachings of the early church and the tradition that has been handed down to us.

When we turn to consider the writings of the church fathers and medieval theologians we discover that their interpretations of the Bible are often considered imaginative or uncritical by many today. While I do not want this to be taken as a blanket statement that covers all the commentators on the Bible during this period, this negative attitude toward their work is not justified in most instances. As we saw in the previous chapter, in most cases they interpreted the Bible in light of the best resources and information available at that time. They just had a very different set of reference works and understanding of the world from what we have today. They also employed a very different approach to the scriptures and asked a different set of questions of the text.

Perhaps one of the best ways to illuminate the differences between the exegetical practices of the early and medieval church and contemporary practices is by means of a brief consideration of the allegorical method. While it is not quite accurate to label this as a single method, since it varied quite a bit over time and from interpreter to interpreter and there were often alternative methods of interpretation being put forward, we can roughly group these variations over a millennium of biblical interpretation under this one method for the purposes of our discussion.

One of the basic presuppositions that undergirds the allegorical method is that words possess multiple levels of meaning. At the most fundamental level a text has a literal meaning that can be found by considering the grammar and vocabulary. It also possesses a secondary, deeper, or allegorical level of meaning that could be very different from the literal meaning. Origen claimed that when the author of the Bible employed an anthropomorphism to describe God we should read this allegorically. For example, Job's petition, "Have pity on me, my friends, for the hand of God has touched/struck me" (19:21) should not be understood literally as that God reached out his arm and physically touched Job. Rather, the allegorists argue (rightly), we should understand this at a secondary level signifying that God has allowed a number of afflictions to befall poor Job.

In other instances we are struck by the secondary levels of signification that an allegorical intepreter perceived in the text. Augustine's interpretation of Noah's ark in terms of the nature of the church and Christ's work of salvation is a case in point:

> *Any modern student who turns in a paper that includes an Augustinian explanation of some texts will probably not have a promising academic future.*

Moreover, inasmuch as God commanded Noah, a just man, and, as the truthful Scripture says, a man perfect in his generation, – not indeed with the perfection of the citizens of the city of God in that immortal condition in which they equal the angels, but in so far as they can be perfect in their sojourn in this world – inasmuch as God commanded him, I say, to make an ark, in which he might be rescued from the destruction of the flood, along with his family, i.e. his wife, sons, and daughters-in-law, and along with the animals who, in obedience to God's command, came to him into the ark: this is certainly a figure of the city of God sojourning in this world; that is to say, of the church, which is rescued by the wood on which hung the Mediator of God and men, the man Christ Jesus. For even its very dimensions, in length, breadth, and height, represent the human body in which He came, as it had been foretold. For the length of the human body, from the crown of the head to the sole of the foot, is six times its breadth from side to side, and ten times its depth or thickness, measuring from back to front: that is to say, if you measure a man as he lies on his back or on his face, he is six times as long from head to foot as he is broad from side to side, and ten times as long as he is high from the ground. And therefore the ark was made 300 cubits in length, 50 in breadth, and 30 in height. And its having a door made in the side of it certainly signified the wound which was made when the side of the Crucified was pierced with the spear; for by this those who come to Him enter; for thence flowed the sacraments by which those who believe are initiated. And the fact that it was ordered to be made of squared timbers, signifies the immoveable steadiness of the life of the saints; for however you turn a cube, it still stands. And the other peculiarities of the ark's construction are signs of features of the church. (Augustine, *City of God*, 15.26)

Any seminary or university student who turns in a paper to their Old Testament professor that includes an explanation of the text along the lines of Augustine's will most likely not have a promising academic future.

But is it fair to judge Augustine's work in this manner? What appears to be rather creative exegesis on his part is actually restrained by the rules he was working under. First, he believed that the text possessed four levels of meaning: a literal meaning, an allegorical meaning that signified the faith the church was to possess and teach, a moral level that taught the responsibility of individual believers, and finally the so-called anagogical meaning of the text pointed to the church's future or hope. At each of these four levels the meaning that was perceived by the reader should be in agreement with the "rule of faith." No interpretation should be contrary to the teachings of the church that have been handed down.

The most quoted summation of the multiple levels of signification found in the allegorical method is from Nicholas of Lyra (1270–1340):

The literal sense teaches what happened,	*Littera gesta docet,*
allegory what you are to believe,	*quid credas allegoria,*
the moral sense what you are to do,	*moralis quid agas,*
anagogy where you are going.	*quo tendas anagogia.*

What is most striking about how we perceive the differences between this earlier hermeneutic and ours is the distrust that many feel today or voice about the early and medieval church's practices. Andrew Louth expresses our contemporary cynicism of the allegorical method:

It is Patristic allegorization that sticks in the gullet of modern theology ... at all levels this allegorization is something deplored ... Why is this? Basically, I think because we feel

> *It is Patristic allegorization that sticks in the gullet of modern theology ... at all levels this allegorization is something deplored. – Louth*

that there is something dishonest about allegory. If you interpret a text by allegorizing it, you seem to be saying that it means something which it patently does not. It is irrelevant, arbitrary: by allegory, it is said, you can make the text mean anything you like.[6]

This brings us back to the problem of method that we discussed earlier. Because we have been taught that a text possesses one correct, or objective, meaning that we can arrive at through the proper use of a method, we think the medieval interpreters were playing fast and free with the text. So when the allegorists speaks about the spiritual, moral, anagogical, or Christological meaning of the text they are blatantly violating our presuppositions of what counts as a valid reading of the text. How can anyone arrive at the same conclusion as Augustine, that the door to the ark signified the wound in Christ's side, by means of any of the methods we are taught in Sunday school, Bible studies, university or seminary?

But are we not guilty of the same type of criticism? The allegorists were seeking to answer certain questions about the text and to fill in certain gaps (e.g. "How does the story of Noah's ark relate to the believer?"). In a similar manner, we also seek to fill in gaps that we perceive in the text. However, the gaps we notice, the way we try to fill those gaps and the

---

6 Andrew Louth, *Discerning the Mystery: An essay on the Nature of Theology* (Oxford: Clarendon Press, 1983), 96–7.

methods we use are different from theirs. In both instances (the allegorical approach and our methods) we ask questions about the meaning of the text. In the process of answering those questions we find new answers and something is brought to light that was not noticed before (otherwise why feel the need to explain it if it was obvious?). This new insight into the text adds to our understanding and contributes to the formation of the tradition as a whole.

We may well ask why, if the allegorists' approach was so different from ours, we should listen to them then? Do they have anything to teach us?

In his book *Listening to the Past: The Place of Tradition in Theology* (2002), Stephen Holmes presents a similar argument to this book's for the value of engaging the giants of our tradition (the primary difference being that his work focuses on theological issues while this book addresses questions of biblical interpretation). He contends that the idea of a "saint" to help us grasp how the interpretations passed down from the great theologians of the past can function in our studies and lives. A saint, he says, is someone whose life has been recognized by the wider church as an appropriate imitation of Christ in their unique situation. By studying their life we can learn more about what it means to imitate Christ. Their life is not a photocopy of Christ's. Rather, it is comparable to that of a small child who dresses up and imitates their mother of father. We observe some of the parent's traits, qualities or mannerisms in the child's imitation of their parent that we may not have noticed before.

> *How a doctor expounded the scriptures has been recognized by the church as especially lucid and beneficial when it comes to the message of salvation, an insight into a specific passage, or its relevance to the body of Christ.*

Holmes points out that the teachings of a certain doctor (Latin *doctores ecclesiae*, "the teachers or great writers of the church") or theologian may have been recognized by the church, in a manner similar to what has happened in the case of a "saint", as being lucid and beneficial when it comes to expounding the scriptures, the message of salvation, or perhaps insight into a specific passage and its relevance to the body of Christ. This does not mean that they explained the passage perfectly, but rather that the way they unpacked the text has been recognized over time as extremely valuable. The recognition and reception of their work can extend beyond just their statement of what the passage means.

Sometimes the impact of a particular interpretation may have little to do with what someone said the text means. Rather, it might be the way they worded it, the context in which they presented their explanation, or any number of factors that contributed to the influence of their reading of a passage.

> *The impact of a particular interpretation may sometimes have very little to do with what someone said the text means.*

For example, when William Carey asked if the Great Commission in Matthew 28:18–20 was still binding on the church of his day he did not present a new perspective on the passage. Rather, it was the way he combined the exposition of Matthew 28 with the knowledge England was gaining about the four corners of the world and England's access to them that made his work so compelling. (We will cover this in more depth later.)

If we just consider what an interpreter claims the text "means" we may miss the real significance and nature of their contributions to our tradition. For example, the fact that someone like Calvin has been widely recognized for 500 years for the perspicuity of his commentaries should give a great deal of weight to the argument that he has something to say to us as well. The same logic can be applied to the writings of Origen, Augustine and others, even though their modes of thought may appear more foreign to us than those since the Reformation.

> *If we accept that the Holy Spirit is active and guiding the church today in its interpretation of the Bible then we must also grant that the Spirit worked in the same manner with every previous generation.*

One last idea needs to be covered in regard to the vast host of commentators that inhabit this middle ground called tradition. That is the doctrine of the illumination of the Holy Spirit. One of the roles the Holy Spirit fulfils in the church is that of guiding the church into the truths of Jesus' teachings and, by extension, of the rest of the scriptures. If we accept that the Holy Spirit is living and active, leading and guiding the church today in its interpretation and teaching of the Bible then we must also grant that the Spirit worked in the same manner with every previous generation. Therefore, if we value the illuminating work of the Holy Spirit today it would seem heretical if we did not place the same value on how the Spirit worked in the hearts and minds of the doctors of the church. The legacy they have left us is a treasury of insight into the Bible from various perspectives and applied in multifarious situations. To use an analogy, instead of having just a hammer (my default tool) or a screwdriver we have an entire tool chest full of tools at our disposal – and it would be a shame not to take advantage them.

Tradition today: Biblical competency and the body of Christ

How does all of this relate to us today, on this side of the second millennium? As in the previous two sections I want to demonstrate how the past functions in our lives when we read the Bible. On the practical side, we will reflect on how tradition enables us to engage in the actual practice of reading. Then we will turn to the theological question, raised in the preceding section of this chapter, of what it means to be part of the communion of saints, or the body of Christ.

Our ability to communicate via language rather than resorting to grunts and physical gestures is an incredibly complex skill, and one that we often overlook because we use it all the time. The ability to control our breath, vocal cords and mouth in order to vocalize a word is a truly amazing ability, especially if you consider that most of us master these skills by the age of two or three. Aside from the phonetic skills, there is also a wide body of conscious and unconscious knowledge we need to learn in order to communicate effectively. How dependent communication is on culture and tradition struck me when I, an American, was studying in England. The old joke of two nations separated by a common language was an almost daily experience. The same words often yield different meanings in England from those they do in the States. One particularly embarrassing episode involved my inquiring at church where a friend had purchased his pants, as I needed some new ones. The comedy – or at least *they* thought it was funny – revolved around the fact that what I should have asked about were "trousers," since "pants" are what you wear *under* you "trousers" in England, while hardly anyone uses the word *trousers* in America.

The broader framework of background knowledge that is required if we are going to communicate effectively with others is, to a large extent, passed down to us from our parents and elders and gained from our interaction with others in our social environment. In other words, both the linguistic and extra-linguistic competencies involved in language are handed down to us. They are part and parcel of what we call tradition.

Reading is no exception to this; if anything, the argument is even stronger. The idea of approaching a text objectively or with a blank slate is in all reality a

> *The idea of approaching the Bible with a blank slate is in all reality a myth.*

myth; we must bring all the skills and knowledge we have learned from other forms of communication to bear on every act of reading.

But even that is not sufficient. In order for us to convert the little black marks on a page into either oral vocalizations or internal thoughts we need to be trained in the art of reading. This involves much more than the intellectual act of being able to recognize the letters and words on the page. In order to read with any degree of comprehension the reader must possess a certain degree of literary competency. Literary competency involves training in rules, conventions and forms of literature. The need for this training can easily be seen in the widespread practice of literature courses in schools and universities.

The level of literary competency required of the reader will depend on the genre and complexity of the text. A general experience of the language, the world and society is not sufficient to make a reader competent to understand literary works. Reading requires interaction with others who either train us in our reading skills or with whom we can confirm or correct how we have understood a text. It involves learning from our mistakes, being shown where and how we made a mistake and learning to recognize it as a mistake – a process of training by which the reader slowly gains a fuller understanding of the nature of texts and how to read them. The reader's training in literature instills in him or her a pre-understanding of literary conventions which enables an understanding of the work. This knowledge is not something that is personal, but is highly interpersonal by nature. In this sense, reading is built upon and requires a community. And communities are, in a sense, the present instantiation of a tradition.

Reading also requires a connection with the past through other texts. Any book we read is always read in relation to other texts we have read which provide a grid of pre-understanding and expectations that enable us to perceive the style, structure, plot and other salient features of the book.

For example, as a literary genre or family, mystery novels have certain features in common. If I knew nothing at all about mystery novels I would be rather confused by the first one I read. However, once I had a few under my belt, and had perhaps taken a class on them or discussed them with my friends, I would have gained a level of literary competency in regard to this genre of literature, as the reading of one mystery facilitates the reading of the next. I would now know to expect clues as the plot unfolded, to try and solve the case before the end of the novel, and to watch for certain types of characters or twists in the plot. I would not only have gained an awareness of what to look for and of how this particular novel differs from others, but would also have developed a repertory of questions to ask as I read; and (most importantly) I would also have gained a sense of how to read mystery novels in general. In a sense I would, in future, be extrapolating from one mystery novel to read the next. The experienced or competent reader has acquired a sense of how to proceed with certain literary works by reading others of that genre.

As the reader progresses to more complex forms of literature the level of literary competency demanded increases correspondingly.

> *The specific act of reading the Bible requires a remarkably high level of literary competency.*

If we turn to the specific act of reading the Bible, the level of literary competency that is required is remarkably high. In fact, I would argue that it is one of the most demanding books to read in this regard. Many of us who have been members of a church for years may be incognizant of just how daunting the Bible is to read, because of our familiarity with it.

The idea that the Bible is fairly clear and straightforward to understand is a presupposition that we have inherited from the Reformers. One of William Tyndale's goals (1495–1536) when he translated the Bible into English was that a plough-boy should be able to read and understand it. This same goal is reflected in may modern translations that try to produce a text that is readable by the average thirteen or fourteen year old.

But even if the translators and editors manage to fashion an accurate translation with the appropriate words and grammar for that level of reader there are still other aspects of biblical competency that will be demanded of those readers. For example, they will need to be able to recognize the differences between letters (epistles), gospels, historical narratives, wisdom literature, poetry, prophecy and apocalyptic literature and the rules that apply to that genre.

Readers gain their biblical competency from three primary sources. The most significant is that of the biblical canon. Because Paul's letters are grouped together in the New Testament the reader should acquire an exposure to one of his letters by reading it in light of the others. The same point applies to the gospels, psalms, or prophetic writings. The canons of both the Hebrew and Christian scriptures provide another level of intertextual connections that create a reading context in which readers should be able to develop their biblical competency.

A second source is the religious tradition the reader belongs to. If you attend a church that holds to a dispensational form of theology you will have been trained in a very different approach to reading a text like Revelation than if you were attending an Anglican church, say.

Part of our competency as biblical readers is inherited. The larger context of the culture that we are raised in shapes our reading skills and competency. On the whole there is a marked difference in the level or form of biblical competency between someone raised in an Eastern European country under communism, someone raised in a Muslim nation, and someone raised in Western Europe or North America. Books like Herman Melville's *Moby Dick* or movies such as Cecil B. DeMille's *The Ten Commandments* inform our pre-understanding of the Bible and how we read it. Texts, movies, dramatic arts and artwork are all part of our tradition and contribute to the expectations we bring to the activity of reading the Bible.

Revelation: A complex case study

To complicate matters even more, some of the books of the Bible contain more than one genre. The book of Revelation is such a book.

Revelation opens with, "The apocalypse of Jesus ... to his servant John." While the Greek word for apocalypse, *apokalupsis*, could also have been translated as *revelation* (hence the title of the book), the use of the word *apocalypse* in the first verse gives the reader useful information about what type of literature they are about to read: it is an apocalyptic text. This type of "signalling" in a text to alert the reader as to what to expect is a common feature in literature. For example, when we read a story that opens with the words *Once upon a time*, we are immediately able to recognize (if we are familiar with fairy tales) what type of story it is going to be, what type of relation it will have to reality, what main themes and characters

> *When we read a story that opens with Once upon a time, we immediately know what type of story it is going to be ...*

we may expect (princesses, fairies, evil godmothers, etc.), and whether we should look for a moral in the narrative.

Apocalyptic literature was a literary genre used in the Ancient Near East. It was revelatory in nature, most commonly in the form of a dream or vision that was interpreted by an angel. In many instances apocalyptic literature was a theological response to a nation's experience of foreign invaders overthrowing what they saw as their divinely ordained kingship. (Daniel in the Hebrew Bible is an example.) Often this was accompanied by the suppression of their culture and religion and being excluded from economic and social privileges. As a genre, apocalyptic literature was a means to provide an oppressed people with hope by projecting a future in which order would be restored to their nation by divine intervention. One of the primary purposes of apocalyptic literature was to reveal how God has all things under his control, despite how things appeared on the earth.

However, John's composition is more complex than most apocalyptic texts, as it is not only apocalyptic, but also *prophetic* in character (see 1:3; 22:7, 10, 18–19). While prophetic literature and apocalyptic literature share certain features (e.g. a concern with God's plans for the future) there are significant differences between the two genres. Prophetic literature tends to portray God accomplishing his divine plans in human history through human agents. An apocalypse, in contrast, tends to present God accomplishing his plans by divine intervention in history, usually in very dramatic ways.

Besides being prophetic in addition to apocalyptic, Revelation also contains certain stylistic features of an *epistle*. It opens with a typical greeting of a letter (1:4–5) and closes with a standard benediction (22:21). It also contains the seven letters to the seven churches. But while the book is addressed primarily to those churches (1:11), it also includes an exhortation that other congregations should read and learn from this document as well (2:11).

And finally, John mixes in a liberal dose of *music*! There are thirteen hymns in this single book (4:8, 11; 5:9–10, 12b, 13b, 11:15b, 17–18; 12:10b–12; 15:3b–4; 16:5b–7b; 19:1b–3, 5b, 6b–9).

The literary complexity of the book of Revelation should keep alert readers on their toes from start to finish, requiring, as it does, a literary competency in at least four different genres: apocalyptic literature, prophetic literature, epistles, and hymns or poetry.

Reading "in" and "with" a tradition

Reading in and with a tradition is fundamentally not a method. Rather it is an attitude, mental framework or virtue we bring to the act of reading. Chapter Five will emphasize some of the mechanics of this form of reading, but for now we need to reflect on what we bring to this type of reading.

Reading "in" and "with" the body of Christ

Theologically the concept of the body of Christ, or the communion of the saints, emphasizes the importance of tradition in our life and reading. Through our faith in Christ and his sacrificial work we have become incorporated into a new community. The image of the body conveys the idea that we are a part of the life of other believers and they are of ours. Our very lives are organically knit together.

The body of Christ preserves our personal individuality in that it is composed of a multiplicity of members with a diversity of gifts. At the same time it contains an equal emphasis on the unity of the body. This unity has two axes in Paul's letters. Communion among the various members of a congregation can be represented along a horizontal axis (1 Cor. 12), while the relationship between Christ (the head) and the church (the body) corresponds to a vertical axis. The vertical axis also includes the unity between the church on earth and those in heaven above, where Christ is seated (Eph. 1:16–23).

I think we could also easily extrapolate a third axis and still remain faithful to Paul's thought one which represents the unity of the church across time. To be a member of the body of Christ is to say that we are members of the same body as the first believers in the early church. The doctrine of the body of Christ units individual members within a congregation, all the believers alive in "one holy catholic and apostolic Church" (*The*

> *To be a member of the body of Christ is to say that we are members of the same body as the first believers in the early church and with all believers across time.*

Nicene Creed, 325 AD), the church with Christ, and believers across time. If we see our organic relationship with and dependence on other believers (whether in a local congregation or across the globe) then we should also acknowledge our relationship with and dependence on those who have gone before us: those who, though absent from the body, are alive with Christ.

Paul's metaphor of the body conveys not only unity and diversity but also purpose: we are to grow in maturity in Christ (Eph. 4:1–14). Each member should be an active participant contributing their part according to how the Spirit has gifted him or her for the mutual growth of the body. In order for this to take place we must be rightly related to Christ and one another so that we might give and receive what others supply.

If we take seriously the idea that the church is a people on a journey and that we are growing into our maturity in Christ but have not arrived yet, then we need all the nourishment that a growing body requires. Most of our teaching and writing in this area asserts our synchronic unity – our interdependency among present-day believers. But we need a diachronic unity as well – what those in the past have given and still supply for our growth. Therefore, from a theological perspective the concept of the body of Christ underlines the importance of reading *in* and *with* a tradition.

Being grounded in a tradition does not necessarily imply that you can list all the relevant dates, names, places and people that shaped the Christian tradition or a specific denomination. While a general knowledge along these lines would be very helpful, and should be sought, it is not required. The ability to read the Bible in and with a tradition is something both the novice and the "card-carrying member" of a historical society can benefit from. Rather, what we need to bring to this form of reading is what I have been discussing in this chapter – that the biblical texts, the collection and canonization of these texts, the way the Holy Spirit has illuminated the church's understanding of the Bible in the past and present, biblical competency, and the doctrine of the body of Christ are all constituted and embodied within the Christian tradition.

Long before we consciously realize it, we belong to our tradition. We need to acknowledge and celebrate this rich heritage: how God has chosen to work in history, through people, and to preserve the results of those interactions. As a result, tradition is not something to be resisted or to be jumped over in an attempt to gain access to the pristine texts of the New Testament. Tradition is what we dwell within. And we need to cultivate our mindset of dwelling within a tradition.

Reading with Charity

If we are sincere about the idea that God has incorporated us into the community and tradition of the body of Christ, then we should approach this tradition in a charitable manner. All too often we tend to have a negative view of the history of the church, especially the Medieval period, with the exception of those aspects that involve people we consider to be heroes of the faith.

I have already discussed how our preoccupation with method has schooled us in this negative attitude. For some of us, it is the result of our pragmatic approach to the church or ministry. We think that we can do it better today than those who, from our perspective, seem to have set us on the wrong course in the past. The catch phrase *stuck in tradition* is often the rallying cry for this viewpoint. In contrast, we need to be open and receptive to the past. When we read Luther's comments on Jonah's fish we need to ask, "What can I learn about the book of Jonah from Luther? What insights does he have that I never considered? Why did he read the text this way? How does he apply the text to his audience's life and is this relevant for

> *When we read Luther's comments on Jonah's fish we need to ask what insights he had that I have never considered.*

my life or ministry?" We need to be open to Luther's claims
about the meaning of the biblical text and how it touches
our lives.

One of the blessings and difficulties contained within the
history of biblical interpretation is the diversity of readings for
any one verse or passage. Without exception, every passage
whose history of reception I have studied has surprised me
with the range of interpretations that have been preserved.
This may raise alarm bells for some. If this is the case for
you, hold on to those thoughts; in the next section we will
consider why this is not a problem in regard to the meaning
of a text. For the present I simply want to emphasize that the
different interpretations represent not a curse but a blessing.

Since this chapter opened with an illustration from the
world of art, allow me use another in an attempt to shed
some light on the question of how different readers can
perceive different meanings in the same text.

The Art Institute of Chicago owns four paintings by Monet
of the same haystack, from the same perspective, painted
at different times of the day. The result is four different
representations of the same object by the same artist. Having
the four of them together allows you to perceive more than
if you took them in separately. Since they are arranged side
by side in one room you can not only compare the paintings
with one another but also notice aspects of the scene that
you would not discern if only one was on display. Monet
has captured for us how the haystack inhabited the early
morning mist, stood in the afternoon sun, was drenched in
the rain, and retired in the dusk. The collective impact of
four artworks creates a much fuller appreciation for the scene
– much richer than only one work, or the four individually,
could convey. With the four we gain an understanding of the
passing of time, the changing of the weather, and how this
haystack stands sentinel in the field.

The same principle is operative in biblical interpretation.
Understanding a biblical text can be compared to an artistic
representation. Augustine paints one picture of what it means,
Gregory the Great another, and Calvin a third. By placing their
representations or readings alongside one another we gain a

much richer appreciation for the Bible than we would if we had only one. We see subtleties in the biblical text that we had never noticed before, intertextual references that we had not considered, the emphasis on different aspects of the narrative, how what was perceived as the meaning of the text has changed over time, and we grasp new possibilities for how the passage may be relevant to our lives. The goal is not to engage the past like a butterfly hunter collects his prey and mounts them in hermetically sealed cases. Instead of merely collecting facts about how the Bible has been interpreted in the past we want to engage this tradition of interpretation in an open and productive dialogue: How is our interpretation expanded, corrected, modified or reinforced by others' reading of the passage?

Openness

If we honestly engage the heritage of biblical interpretation it will be impossible to avoid being confronted with interpretations that are very different from how

> *The hermeneutical experience of tradition is characterized by a negation of our expectations or understandings.*

we understand the Bible. We could state this as a rule: *the hermeneutical experience of tradition is characterized by a negation of our expectations or understandings.* As opposed to the certainty which a methodological approach toward the Bible may promise us, the way our engagement with tradition negates our pre-understandings should develop and cultivate our openness to the views of others and our ability to learn from their insights.

In order for us to learn from the past and bring it into dialogue with how we read the Bible today we must approach the doctors of the church in an open manner. When I talk about openness to the claims of tradition I am referring to the same type of openness that is required in any sort of honest dialogue between two partners: I must be open to what the other person is saying. If an acquaintance of mine claims that such and such happened, then I must acknowledge that they might actually know more about the subject than I do and be willing to learn from them. The same is true when we engage tradition: we need to recognize that someone may possess knowledge of the text that is superior to our own.

The German philosopher Hans-Georg Gadamer summarized it in this way: "I must allow tradition's claim to validity, not in the sense of simply acknowledging the past in its otherness, but in such a way that *it has something to say to me*" (*Truth and Method*, Crossroad, 1989, p. 453). This is not easy, because approaching the past in an open manner does not culminate in a certainty about what the Bible may mean. In fact, it may raise more questions than it answers. When we experience in openness how others in the past read the Bible we grow and learn as individuals. We do not learn by reading the works of authors that agree with our views; rather it is precisely through our encounters with views and interpretations that are different from ours that our understanding of any issue expands. This is one of the more significant reasons for reading the Bible with the giants of the past: we need the insights of those in the past with whom we may disagree with the most, in order to mature in our own biblical worldview.

Self-discovery

The manner in which our thoughts and beliefs about the Bible are provoked by how others have read the Bible leads to self-exploration. As I've been saying throughout this book so far, whenever we read the Bible we bring a multitude of preconceptions and pre-understandings to the table. In most instances these background presuppositions are like the air we breathe: we rarely notice them. However, once we begin to examine interpretations and hermeneutical approaches that differ from, and may even challenge, our own, our preconceptions may be provoked. They come to the surface. When this occurs we need to pay careful attention. It is similar to those incidents when my wife asks me as I drive, "How long has that little red light on the dash been on?" There is a reason why that light has come on and I should give it some attention. The same is applicable when I find myself reacting, say, to Luther's idea that the fish that swallowed Jonah had huge, sharp, nasty, teeth and a throat the size of a cavern. Why would I want to dismiss his reading as ludicrous? What buttons is his interpretation pushing in my belief system about the world or the Bible?

In this respect, reading the Bible alongside the doctors of the church is as much a journey of self-discovery as it is about interpretations of others from the past. If I step back for a moment, what I discover is that my interaction with Luther is rubbing the beliefs and assumptions I hold about whales the wrong way. A converse argument could be made: if I do not find my thoughts, presuppositions and beliefs provoked as I read the Bible in light of how others in the past have interpreted it, then I should ask if I am dwelling within my tradition and if I am open to their claims about the meaning of the passage.

This is not to say that every encounter we have with the giants of the past will be a deep, traumatic, life-changing experience. Rather, it is to say that we need to be vulnerable and open to the past and that, as a result, we should experience this form of hermeneutical angst from time to time.

In *The Promise of Hermeneutics* Roger Lundin borrows a thought from C.S. Lewis that helps to clarify what I am trying to say.[7] In *The Four Loves* Lewis remarked on the difference between *eros* and friendship. With *eros*, the two parties concerned look intently at each other. Lundin notes how *eros* parallels the methodological approach, which is based on an observer objectively studying his or her subject: the interpreter stares intently into the scriptures trying to discern the intentions of the original author. But friendship involves a totally different manner of looking: friends stand side by side

---

[7] Roger Lundin, "Interpreting Orphans: Hermeneutics in the Cartesian Tradition" in *The Promise of Hermeneutics*, 55–56.

and look at the same thing from a similar perspective. We want to stand alongside the giants of the past – or better yet, on their shoulders – and look with them into the scriptures. To learn from them. And to enter into a dialogue with them about the meaning of the text and its ramifications for us today. For this to take place we must be grounded in our tradition, approach the giants of the past with openness, and be willing to learn from them as we engage in this process of self-discovery.

A Note on meaning

The question of meaning is a topic that has generated an immense amount of literature in the field of hermeneutics. Is there one correct interpretation for a text or does a form of hermeneutical anarchy reign, with each reader doing what is right in his or her own eyes?

With the rise of the natural sciences and the claims to objectivity in the universities during the Enlightenment the humanities came under increasing pressure. How does a field like theology, history or music validate its truth claims? One of the solutions put forward and widely accepted was that by means of some form of methodology the humanities could lay claim to a form of objectivity in their research. This would supposedly confer an objective standard by which they could arbitrate between competing claims.

In the field of biblical studies this has filtered down to us in various forms of the historical-grammatical method, whereby the interpreter attempts to discern the original author's intentions by means of a historical methodology along with a detailed grammatical analysis of the text. The work of E.D. Hirsch, Jr. has been popular among evangelical theologians for buttressing this approach (his most cited works are *Validity in Interpretation*, 1967 and *The Aims of Interpretation*, 1976).

Like any hermeneutical model it has its strengths and weaknesses. In regard to our discussion, this model creates numerous roadblocks when we attempt to engage in a three-way dialogue with the Bible. The Platonic ideal that a text such as Romans, for example, possesses one, timeless, unchanging meaning stands behind the goal to recover the author's intentions. It is a static conceptualization of meaning. The diversity of interpretations that have been historically offered for any biblical passage is explained away by making a distinction between *significance* and *meaning*. The *significance* of a text changes over time (e.g., the significance of the book of Romans was *this* for Augustine, and it was *that* for Luther, and so on) but its *meaning* (which is grounded in the author's intentions) never changes.

This is perhaps the most detrimental weakness in the way most of have been taught to regard the concept of meaning – it allows little or no ground to interact with or incorporate our tradition when we interpret or read the Bible. On the one hand, the split between meaning and significance does recognize the historical reality that the manner in which a biblical passage was read by the original author and audience (what is often referred to as *meaning*) is different from how it is read by subsequent generations (referred to as *significance*). On the other hand, to argue that the term *meaning* is restricted only to the original act of communication misses the fact that every generation of readers perceives *meaning* when they read the text. It does not take very long when reading the history of a verse's interpretation to realize that when someone comments on the text they are making claims about the *meaning* of the text, whether it was Augustine, Luther, or N.T. Wright.

We can conceive of meaning as a product of the interaction between a reader and the Bible, regardless of where that reader falls in the course of history, without claiming that every reading is equally valid. As an author I am concerned that the readers of my work understand what I have

> *If we define meaning as something that never changes we have little or no ground to interact with or incorporate tradition when we interpret the Bible.*

written in a manner that I would agree with. One of the most frustrating experiences for me as an author is when someone's criticism of my work is based on what I consider a misreading of what I wrote. So it is not that I disagree with the concept of the author's intention being a goal when interpreting a text. My concern is that we take a softer stance in regard to authorial intention and meaning as a whole so that we are able to learn from the doctors of the church. We need a concept of meaning that is able to incorporate the historically preserved diversity of readings for any passage but at the same time does not disintegrate into a *laissez-faire* anarchy of meaning.

> *We need a dynamic theory of meaning, but one that does not disintegrate into* laissez-faire *anarchy.*

Instead of conceiving of meaning primarily in static terms (one, correct, unchanging and timeless meaning) we need a dynamic theory of meaning. In order to help us shift to a dynamic model for meaning I am going to appeal to two different illustrations: music and historical trajectory.

Music and Meaning

A musical score is a type of text; only, instead of communicating by means of words it provides instructions as to how a piece is to be performed. Until a text is read or a musical composition is performed, the black marks on the page (whether they are letters/ characters or notes) are lifeless notations. Both the musician and the reader of literature must perform the "score" in order to bring the text/composition (back) to life, through a musical performance or by the reading the book. Each musical performance of a score will be different, even if the same musician performs the same piece on the same instrument in the same setting. No matter how skilled the performer is, each performance will vary in subtle nuances. Once we start comparing different performances by different performers against one another the differences become more distinctive. One only has to attend a musical competition to gain a first-hand experience of this.

To press this line of inquiry further, we should also ask about those performances where the musicians play instruments other than those the composer originally intended. "Silent Night" is a piece most of us should be familiar with. I cannot even begin to count all the various instruments that I have heard it played on. (On top of that, although it was originally written in German I can think of only a few occasions when I have not heard it sung in English.) Or consider the work of a classical composer such as Johann Sebastian Bach. Is it more correct to perform his work on sixteenth-century instruments or with a modern orchestra? (Dare we even attempt to include Wendy Carlos's synthesizer rendering of Bach's work, *Switched-On Bach*, in this discussion?)

What are the grounds that would allow us to judge between these different performances? A methodological approach may allow us to arrive at some conclusions regarding the technical merits of the performer(s). But this is only one facet of a performance. By contrast, if we engage in the practice of playing a musical instrument, not only do we learn how to play an instrument, but it should also instill within us the ability to make informed judgments about what constitutes a good performance on a basis that is very different from what a method allows us to make. When we learn to play a musical instrument we learn timing, hand positions, and other technical elements which are involved in playing that instrument. But we also learn about emphasis, feeling the music, how to bring out the different tonal qualities of an instrument. All those hours we spent as children practicing an instrument should have taught us a lot more than just the technical skills of how to read music or hand positions on the instrument. In particular, we should have developed an ear for musical excellence. By engaging in the practice of playing an instrument we should also have learned how to appreciate good music in ways we never could have if our parents had not made us take music lessons and sit down and practice each day.

In the same way, by engaging in the practice of biblical interpretation we should also develop an appreciation for what constitutes an excellent performance of the biblical score. As our biblical competency matures, our ability to judge what is an acceptable or appropriate reading expands. We understand how others have reached their interpretive conclusions, if they followed an appropriate hermeneutical path, to appreciate the fine nuances in the text that they observed, and also what counts as a legitimate or illegitimate interpretation. These are abilities that are caught more easily than they can be taught.

There is a second practice involved with music that informs our discussion of dynamic meaning: the practice of listening to music. As we are exposed to different performers, on different instruments, in different venues, our ability to make a judgment about what constitutes a good performance grows as well. A gifted artist's performance raises our expectations of what can or cannot be done with an instrument or a particular musical score. Our horizons are expanded and we now approach other performances from a different perspective: a revised and enlarged perspective. The analogy to reading the Bible is that by reading the great doctors of the past our understanding of what can and cannot be appropriately said about the text is developed. From the perspective of dynamic meaning, music allows us to see that while the musical score remains the same, every performance will differ from every other one. At the same time, we are still able to make judgments about how faithful the different performances are to that score.

In short, these three aspects to music – performance, practicing an instrument and listening to good performances – help us to grasp the concept of dynamic meaning. Each performance of the text will be different, but at the same time we can make informed judgments about the appropriateness of each of those performances.

Historical Trajectories and Meaning

The second illustration for dynamic meaning is that of trajectory. One of the fundamental themes of the Bible is that God is active in history: he initiated it, has been active in it, has a plan for it, and will see it through to the goal he has for history. The human side to this equation is that because of God's action in our lives we are now a people who are on a pilgrimage, sojourners on our way to a better place.

How we read and interpret the Bible should be seen in a similar light. How we understand the scriptures is part and parcel of this broader historical trajectory into which we have been grafted by grace. We are on a journey to a full and appropriate understanding of the scriptures; however, until we cross over from this age into the next we should view all of our interpretations as partial and provisional, open to correction and revision by those who will come after us.

Paul's view of the Christian life and how we comprehend God's revelation and his activity in the world coheres with the idea of dynamic meaning in terms of a trajectory:

> For we know only in part, and we prophesy only in part; but when the complete comes, the partial will come to an end. For now we see in a mirror, dimly, but then we will see face to face … Now I know only in part; then I will know fully, even as I have been fully known. (1 Cor. 13:9–10, 12)

Within the concept of a trajectory the impact and influence of an interpretation needs to be included. As I mentioned earlier, most contemporary evangelical hermeneutical models differentiate between the meaning and the significance of a text: meaning is fixed, but significance varies from situation to situation. However, the line between what an interpreter claims the text means and the significance of that interpretation for the believing community is a very hard line to draw. The separation between "What does the text mean?" and "What does the text mean for me?" is often an artificial one. Understanding and application are not either/or categories but both/and categories. In some instances the meaning that is perceived in a passage may be simply along the lines of, "this means x, y, and z." It merely helps us to grasp the sense, reference, or denotation of the terms or passage. In this case understanding, or meaning, and application are almost identical. In other instances the interpretation of a passage may inform, correct, declare or promise something, or commission the reader. It is best to see understanding and application as flipsides of the same coin.

Take 1 Timothy 2:12 as an example. The church has traditionally read this verse as a universal injunction that women are prohibited from holding a position of authority or teaching within the church. What I want to point out is simply that if we interpret this as a universally binding injunction forbidding women from positions of teaching or authority then the impact of that interpretation will be just that: women will be excluded from those offices in the church. What we claim the text means (objectively) and what the text means for us, especially for women, are not separate issues. What we claim the text means and what its significance is can be separated only at an abstract level, not in the real world. If we read 1 Timothy 2:12 as a universal command, then we need to take the proper stand in relation to that command. But if we understand 1 Timothy 2:12 as part of Paul's instructions to Timothy to address specific situations and challenges in the churches Timothy was pastoring, then the significance of this passage for our lives is very different.

When we consider the history of a text's interpretation one of the elements of any reading that we should watch for is what the impact of this interpretation was on the church of that day. How did their understanding of the meaning of the passage affect their worship, evangelism, mission, or their other practices? Would we say that their reading of the text and its impact on their practices was appropriate given their situation? In other words, we must be attentive to both interpretation and application, since these categories are interrelated and intertwined.

This naturally leads to questions about *influence*: How did that interpretation influence succeeding generations of readers? How was the influence of their reading of the text felt 100, 200 or even 500 years latter? What was the influence of their interpretation on the formation of the Christian tradition in other areas such as church practice, worship, art or music? And most especially, is the influence of how that person interpreted the text still felt today?

In a recent class on the parables a student who is a Presbyterian pastor was exploring John Calvin's exegetical approach to the parables. In his presentation to the class he remarked how surprised he was to realize how strongly Calvin had shaped his reading of the parables – almost 600 years later Calvin's influence is still being palpably felt. In this instance Calvin was influencing how the student understood the meaning of the parables, and the method by which he interpreted the parables, even though the student had never studied Calvin's work in this area before the class. By incorporating the influence of an interpretation into our study of the various historical trajectories of biblical interpretation we transform our study from an accumulation of facts about the past into a living dialogue with our tradition over the meaning of the scriptures in a manner that is relevant to our lives and ministries.

Impact and influence: William Tyndale

The impact and influence of one person's interpretation is clearly evidenced in William Tyndale's (1494–1536) translation of the Bible into vernacular English. It is almost incomprehensible to us that before this time an English version of the Bible was not readily available. In fact, there were laws, punishable by death, against even having a portion of the Bible in English in one's possession. As a result, Tyndale was forced to flee to the European continent in order to complete his translation of the New Testament, which was published in the Netherlands and smuggled back into England. The price he paid for his efforts was his life.

Tyndale had two aims in his translation. The first was *emancipation* – to break the bonds of how the Christian religion was practiced and taught in his day. Tyndale realized that in order to accomplish this, certain key terms needed to be translated differently from the way they were traditionally taught in the church in order for the reader to properly grasp the message of the New Testament. His second aim was *illumination*. John Foxe preserved Tyndale's famous line, "If God spare my life ere many years, I will cause a boy that driveth the plough, shall know more of the Scripture than thou dost" (Foxe, *Acts and Monuments*, V.117).

Tyndale's work was not based on a simplistic doctrine of the perspicuity of scripture. Rather, he clearly understood that the very words a translator employed could exercise a considerable impact on how the reader grasped the theological significance of the New Testament. To further assist the reader, Tyndale included translation glosses in the text of the Bible to help the reader understand the meaning of certain passages. In certain editions the publisher also included Tyndale's short treatise, *A Pathway into the Holy Scripture*, in which he attempted to provide the reader with a theological framework from which he or she could correctly enter into reading the Bible.

As a whole, Tyndale's New Testament was widely received and read in England. From 1526 (first printing in the Netherlands) to 1540 over 50,000 copies of his New Testament were in circulation in England. The fact that an average person could now read the message of God's love in their own tongue, not in Latin, was widely welcomed in England.

The impact of Tyndale's translation can be seen in two areas: his New Testament as a whole, and five specific words contained within it. The five terms Tyndale's translation is best known for are the ones that his opponent, Sir Thomas More, brought to the center of attention by pointing out how Tyndale had interpreted them differently from the manner in which the Roman Church had. In the debate between Tyndale and More, the latter also represents how institutions may defend or put forward a particular reading in order to support their status and authority. As such, some would claim that the Bible was being used for the purpose of domination. Tyndale's translation, sprang from his studies of the Bible in its original languages (based in large part on Erasmus's and Luther's work), represented an attempt to retrieve the original meaning of the Bible and convey that in a manner that spoke clearly in the vernacular of his day. It presented an implicit critique of the accepted reading of the Bible and called for a new understanding, teaching and application of its sacred message.

Among the terms that Thomas More called attention to were the following:

Greek term	Previous translation	Tyndale's translation
ἐκκλησία (*ekklésia*)	church	congregation
μετάνοια (*metanoia*)	penance	repentance
πρεσβύτερος (*presbyteros*)	priest	senior *(revised to "elder" in the 1534 edition)*
χάρις (*charis*)	grace	divine favor
ἀγάπη (*agapé*)	charity	love.

More realized that Tyndale's translation of these key terms subverted the teachings of the church. When Tyndale translated *ekklésia* as *congregation*, not *the church*, the meaning of passages that contain this Greek term shifted from a reference to the institutional Church of Rome to that of a local gathering of believers. *Presbyteros* was no longer translated as *priest* but as *elder* or *senior*. Tyndale's choice of *elder* instead of *priest* transformed the readers' understanding of church leadership. Both of these Greek terms played a significant role in how Tyndale's readers would have perceived the nature of the church. *Metanoia* was translated as the act of *repentance*, not the practice of *penance*. In place of *grace*, which was dispensed through the church via the sacraments, Tyndale preferred *divine favor* for *charis*.

But the term that Thomas More thought was most inappropriate was Tyndale's choice of *love* instead of *charity* for *agapé*. More objected to Tyndale's use of the verb *love* due to the sexual connotations this word held in that day. According to More, Tyndale had reduced *agapé* to "the lewd love that is between some worthless fellow and his mate" (*More, Dialogue concerning Heresies and Matters of Religion, 8.221–222*). *Charity*, by contrast, was the highest Christian virtue, greater than faith and hope (1 Cor. 13) and rightly played a prominent role in the teaching of the church and medieval society. Tyndale felt that the average person did not grasp the apostolic teaching on this term because of the preconceptions associated with the term *charity*. By replacing it with the vernacular term *love* he provoked his readers' thinking (as was clearly demonstrated in More's work) and opened up new vistas for how they understood the New Testament.

One could ask whether we do not face the opposite problem today. The word *love* is used in so many different ways and contexts that we need to ask whether the average reader today understands what Paul meant when he used the term *agapé* in 1 Corinthians 13. Perhaps if we were to revert back to *charity* the average person in the pew would have to pause for a moment and think, "Hmm, I don't remember reading it like this before. What exactly does it mean?" Maybe *charity* is not the best choice, but has the word *love* lost its distinctiveness to such an extent today that the force of Paul's argument is blunted?

William Tyndale discerned that many of the doctrines that the reform movement wanted to purge from the church were based on how biblical passages were read, and, even more fundamentally, on the very words in the text itself. His translation opened the reader to new possibilities of meaning. His New Testament introduced the English-speaking world to the core of Reformation theology and a recovery of the apostolic message. The combined effect of the new conceptual vocabulary in his New Testament undermined the Catholic Church's teaching, authority and practice in England. The body of Christ was portrayed as a local congregation, not as the Roman Church, led by an elder, not a priest, which removed the institutional claims of the Catholic Church. Salvation was now accomplished on the basis of God's divine favor toward us received through faith and repentance. This stood in contrast to the doctrine being taught that salvation was dispensed by the church, through the administration of the sacraments by priests, acts of penance, and the believer's faith.

The impact of Tyndale's translation was felt from the pulpits, in personal devotionals, in the university classroom, and as it was read publicly and privately. "So the Bible in English [Tyndale's] is not only a source of doctrine, a text for exegesis. It is itself an agent of the greatest change in national as well as personal life" (David Daniell, *The Bible in English: Its History and Influence*, 158).

One of the main reasons England swung Protestant so quickly was in large part Tyndale's translation. The lasting influence of his work is felt to this day in the English-speaking world. It is estimated that over 80 percent of the King James Version (1611) and almost 75 percent of the Revised Standard Version is based on Tyndale's translation. Many of the passages in our contemporary translations still bear the stamp of Tyndale's linguistic acumen. Phrases like *Give us this day our daily bread* (Matthew 6:11) are repeated almost verbatim in many or our translations. I remember explaining that the word *grace* in Ephesians 2:8–9, "for by grace you are saved," meant "God's unmerited favor toward us". In hindsight I now realize that I was unknowingly quoting Tyndale's definition when I did so. The influence of Tyndale's work has subconsciously shaped how I understand key Christian terms 500 years later. Tyndale's labor as a linguist and translator illustrates how one person's reading of the Bible can both have an impact on his or her generation and still exercise a powerful influence centuries later.

Four

Tradition as a Road Map of Interpretations

The tradition of biblical interpretation is similar in many respects to a road map. Instead of merely displaying the terrain and various routes this map is a record of the interpretive dialogue and debate over the meaning of the scriptures.

The emphasis in the previous chapter was on our relationship to our heritage of biblical interpretation. The direction of inquiry was from the present to the past. This chapter will take the opposite direction of travel and consider the Bible as the source from which rivers of interpretation flow.

The plan for this chapter will be as follows. First, we will consider how a book like the Bible functions authoritatively within a tradition and in turn shapes that tradition. The idea of the "classic" will be used in order to help us grasp some of the issues that surround this question. Second, we will examine how the interpretations that flow from the Bible form an ongoing dialogue and debate about its meaning. This extended dialogue to a large degree constitutes the Christian tradition. And finally, in the second half of this chapter we will turn our attention to a case study on a river of interpretive dialogue that the Great Commission (Mt. 28:18–20) has generated.

The Classical Bible

In *Attic Nights* (a text that is often considered a classic itself) the Latin author, Aulus Gellus, wrote, "A classical writer is someone of the upper class not of the rabble or proletariat." Many modern authors attribute our definition and use of the term *classic* to Gellus. A classic is a text that has been passed down over multiple generations and has been judged over the course of that history to stand above the rest; it is above "the rabble or proletariat." In this sense, phrases like *classic rock* and *classic car* are oxymorons. In order for something to be considered a classic it needs to have some history behind it.

Contemporary humanities and literary studies define the term *classic* in three different ways. First, it is used to designate works from a specific period of literary history, most often in reference to the classics of Greek and Latin literature. Second, the term *classic* is used to designate the great works of literature or those that are accepted as being the best representative works from a particular period. The works of Plato, Cicero, Augustine, and Shakespeare would fall into this category. Texts that have passed the test of time and are now looked upon as the best and the brightest from a particular period. Finally, *classic* refers to those texts which are considered part of the reading curriculum in an educational system – texts chosen for their value to teach morality, good taste, and the values of a tradition. Plato's *Republic*, to cite an example, is a text that is used in many college level ethics and government courses to introduce the students to some of the primary issues in those fields to this day.

It is the second and third definitions that are of particular interest to us, and there are two questions that I hope I can answer if we consider the Bible in terms of the concept *classic*. The first question is, "Why does the Bible continue to be read, generation after generation?" The second is, "How does the Bible continually produce new and divergent readings within and across countless generations?"

One of the unique features of a classical text is that we do not consider it an artifact or relic from the past. Plato's *Republic* is not studied because historical information about the government of Athens around 450 BC is preserved within it. Rather, we consider it worthy of attention because Plato has something significant to say to us. One of the primary characteristics of a classic, therefore, is that successive generations of readers have found it to be compelling and deserving of attention. Or to put it another way, classical texts constantly prove themselves by the way they are able to address new generations of readers. They retain their normative role in a tradition despite the constant reinterpretation to which they are subjected.

This seemingly timeless quality of a classic, the way readers through time have found it to be compelling and relevant, arises from two characteristics that a classic possesses. The first is that classical works address issues or questions that concern human existence. As a result, the themes of these works resonate with readers through the centuries. Consider the classical tragedies of Greece, for example. They were originally performed in Greek theaters for certain festivals. But their power to endure meant they were performed in new and different situations, until today they are no longer experienced as theatrical performances but are most commonly read as books. One reason why they have endured is that the original questions they sought to answer were not limited to ancient Greece but have persistently demanded answers from their audiences throughout many centuries: questions about things like honor and shame, death and immortality, loyalty and love.

The second characteristic of a classic involves a concept that picks up and moves forward the discussion of meaning as a dynamic concept from the previous chapter, namely this: a classical text possesses a surplus of meaning. By this we mean that if one of the traits of a classic is the way it is able to address each generation with its truth claims in a relevant manner, then the meaning of the classical text is not exhausted by one generation of readers, or even a few (and some would argue that potentially it will never be exhausted).

To put it differently: the truth claims of a classic are not monovocal (i.e. do not have only one correct meaning) but polyvocal (i.e. have more than one possible meaning or interpretation) – different readers will find different aspects of the text applicable or significant. Saying that a classic has a surplus of meaning indicates that its meaning of is open for new disclosures in every reader's horizon. The classic not only possesses an excess of meaning, but actually encourages

> *The truth claims of a classic are not monovocal but polyvocal, different readers will find different aspects deserving of attention.*

different readings through its reception. In other words, the more interesting and significant we perceive a text to be, the more we will want to read and interpret it in ways that are not just merely mouthing what has already been said about it but in ways that are relevant to our situation. A text is not a classic just because it can lay claim to a long pedigree. It must also be perceived by its readers as relevant and as addressing the questions they are asking before the status of classic is conferred on it.

These two qualities of the apparently timeless relevance of a classic are easily documented in the reception history of the Bible. Questions concerning human finitude, sin, mortality, the meaning of life, and reconciliation with God and humanity are examples of timeless questions the biblical authors addressed. The experience of Christians for the past 2,000 years of realizing new possibilities for life, faith and worship which have arisen from their reading the scriptures would, according to the quality of the surplus of meaning, firmly categorize the Bible as a classic. The only disclaimer I would make at this point in regard to considering the Bible a classic is that we attribute a unique authority to the scriptures, in contrast to other classic texts. For example, while Augustine's or Calvin's works are often considered theological classics, since they have proven themselves through history, the degree of authority that has been attributed to them is significantly lower than that accorded the Bible. Therefore, while the concept of a classic helps us to grasp how the Bible has functioned within the Christian tradition we should also view the Bible in a different light from other classical works.

These two traits of a classic – that it is polyvocal and addresses human questions – imply an elevation of the reader's or interpreter's role. If the timelessness of a classic is experienced by the way it addresses successive generations of readers, then its historical survival is dependent, to a large extent, on how its readers handle the text. Once we introduce readers into the equation, the timeless quality of a classic is destabilized. A text is recognized as a classic only as readers interact with that work over time. In any given period in recorded history a great deal was written. But only a few texts survive beyond the historical horizon in which they were written. And it is the rare exception that is recognized as a classic by later generations. To declare a book a classic soon after it is published (as is often the practice today) is presumptuous, since no one knows whether the next generation will appreciate it or not, let alone those generations one hundred years hence. Often a book that is immediately and widely acclaimed is closely aligned with the expectations and beliefs of its original audience. As time passes, that book can quickly become irrelevant as the next generation of readers' expectations change and they no longer find it message meaningful. A classic is recognized only in hindsight. The passing of time allows the surplus of meaning to shape and expand the expectations of future readers so that they are able to appreciate the text more fully, to appreciate folds in its meaning that the original audience may have not appreciated, and to recognize it retrospectively as a classic.

This definition or description of what makes something a classic dovetails with the discussion in the previous chapter about the formation of the canon. Over time the

> *To declare a book a classic soon after it is published, as is often the practice today, is presumptuous.*

church recognized that certain texts were trustworthy, authoritative and useful for worship, theology, teaching and devotional life. As the church realized the surplus of meaning inherent in certain texts they elevated them above other writings until they achieved canonical status.

However, the passing of time is a double-edged sword. While it is needed to recognize and appreciate a classic, it can also reduce a classic to an obscure corner of a tradition's heritage. As a tradition progresses, the way previous readers interpreted or taught a classic shapes the pre-understanding of the next generation of readers. On the one hand, this gives the next generation a point of entry for reading a classical work. On the other hand, if these interpretations become so widely accepted, or are taught as dogma, then certain generations of readers may look for nothing new when they read it. In such an instance, the text has lost its provocative power and potential for disclosing new folds in its meaning and the old proverb that "familiarity breeds contempt" thereby proves its truth. If the classic is not presented to a new generation of readers in a manner that protects its "otherness", then it is in danger of being swallowed up into the readers' pre-understanding. The readers naively projects their pre-understanding onto the classic as they read it. As a result, their understanding of the text is not enlarged, provoked, or corrected in this type of an encounter with a classic. The text is read in a way that only confirms the readers' prejudices, pre understanding, and practices.

In such cases, we must ask if this text should be considered a classic any longer. While it may function authoritatively in some situations it stands in danger of being dismissed as intellectual fast food, perhaps containing some good ideas but nothing special. In fact, just the opposite is true: the reader thinks that everything it has to say is obvious. In other instances a tradition may shift in the opposite direction and the questions that the text originally sought to answer are now so foreign to the readers that the text is perceived as obscure or obsolete. In either case, what once enjoyed the privileged status of a classic is now relegated to the back shelves or dustbin of history.

Each generation of readers must perceive the text as relevant to them and their situation if it is going to maintain its status as a classic and be passed on to the next generation of readers. Simply repeating how previous interpreters have understood a text like Paul's epistle to the

> *Each generation of readers must perceive the text as relevant to them if it is going to maintain its status as a classic and be passed on to the next generation.*

Romans, for example, does not constitute an active engagement with it. To do so is to miss the disclosive potential of Paul's letter to address the church, and to restrict its meaning to that particular historical or cultural context. Each generation must enter anew into direct dialogue with the text. Literary or other qualities alone do not make a text a classical one; equally important, if not more so, is a text's reception by successive generations of readers.

Both an insight and a challenge are presented to us when we apply these thoughts to biblical interpretation. The insight is that the diversity found in the history of the Bible's interpretation is not a curse but a blessing. If there was one agreed upon meaning for a book like the Gospel of John from the day it was penned until today, then its role within the life of the church would have ceased or, at the very least been greatly diminished, a long time ago. This definitive meaning would have been widely accepted and considered obvious by successive generations of readers, extinguishing any need for further study or reflection by the church on the fourth gospel. The church would not have found the text a rich source for theological reflection and art over the centuries. Nor would Christians have found the Gospel of John providing relevant answers to the new questions addressing them as culture changed. It is the living history of debate and dialogue over John's meaning that is partly responsible for maintaining its authoritative status within the church. The challenge the history of the biblical interpretation presents us with is: How will we engage the Bible? Will we merely repeat what we have been taught? Or will the laborious work that is needed in order to engage the text is a relevant manner and allow it to speak to us afresh today be undertaken?

The Road Map of Tradition: The Dialogue and Debate over Meaning

As a teenager I had a fascination with maps. Just about any map I could lay my hands on found its way into a drawer in my desk where my collection lived. Some of my favorites were the *National Geographic* maps depicting the topography of the bottom of the ocean, and reprints of antique maps rendered by explorers.

One of the things that I learned while poring over my treasure was that a map can tell you a great deal more than just how to get from point A to point B. For example, a map of Colorado can show you how to go from Colorado Springs to the old mining town of Cripple Creek. Even though Cripple Creek is only twenty miles west of Colorado Springs there is no direct route between the two. At 14,000 feet plus spare change Pikes Peak presents a formidable piece of geology between the two locations.

Looking closely the map I can see that I have three basic options for how to circumnavigate this unruly pile of granite. The shortest route is Old Stage Road. This road follows an old stagecoach route over the southern shoulder of Pikes Peak. Unfortunately it has not been improved much since the days of horse and carriage and is often not passable in the winter. But if you don't mind driving slowly and enjoying nature along the journey it can be a rewarding adventure.

The quickest way is to take Highway 24 northwest out of Colorado Springs to Woodland Park and then go south down the west side of the mountain to Cripple Creek. For almost half the journey you are on a four-lane highway and there are plenty of services along the way in case you need to stop for fuel or food. All told, you can easily do this trip in less than an hour.

Finally, I could go southwest to Canon City and then north to Cripple Creek. Not many people I know take this route, since it adds about two hours in driving time over the Woodland Park route. However, once you turn north from Canon City you are driving up through Phantom Canyon. It may take longer, but you would catch the real attraction of this route: its incredible scenic beauty. Three ways to get to Cripple Creek, each different and with its own drawbacks and merits.

The tradition of biblical interpretation is similar in many respects to a road map. Instead of merely displaying the terrain and various routes this map is a record of the interpretive dialogue and debate over the meaning of the scriptures. Alongside the more direct routes to the meaning of a text the less traveled scenic byways are often revealed. We might learn about an avenue of interpretation that navigated through some very scenic terrain: the Christological reflections of the early church, the devotional readings of the medieval theologians, or the pietistic meditations of the church. Footpaths that need to be reworked, hermeneutical dead ends that should be avoided and avenues that look promising at first but lead off in the wrong direction are often revealed. This is not just a map that records the facts and details of various interpretations but it also includes the history and formation of the Christian tradition as a whole. Church history and biblical interpretation are organically interrelated, just as the road map is related to and overlaid on a geographical map of Colorado.

One of the features of many traditions (whether religious traditions like Judaism or Christianity, or secular traditions like the American government that is based on the Constitution or the impact of the Magna

> *The shape and direction a tradition takes is determined to a large degree by how its foundational texts are read and applied.*

Carta on British law) is that they are based on an authoritative text. Such traditions are partially constituted through an extended argument over the meaning and significance of those authoritative texts. The shape and direction a tradition takes is often determined to a large degree by how its foundational texts are read and applied. In order for this extended debate over the meaning of an authoritative text to take place, two seemingly contradictory ideas need to be held in tension. On the one hand, the meaning of the text on which a tradition is founded needs to be perceived as fairly stable. If it was seen as being open to any possible reading then it would be difficult for any sort of consensus or communal identity for that tradition to form. Imagine the situation if the early church had accepted all interpretations of the Bible as equally valid. Instead of laying a foundation for the rise of the Christian tradition it would have floundered in a morass of competing views about God, the deity of Jesus, salvation, the church and so on. On the other hand, a foundational document also needs to be applicable to each generation and thus, as we saw when discussing the concept *classic*, open to new disclosures of meaning over time. If a tradition reaches a point in time where its foundational documents are no longer accepted as relevant or meaningful it is doubtful if that tradition could continue to maintain its identity or coherence.

The tension between these two poles is resolved through the extended debate over the meaning of a particular tradition's foundational texts as that tradition progresses. The ongoing process of critical interpretation and reinterpretation shapes a tradition. At the same time, we can measure the health of a tradition by means of this critical dialogue and debate. When a tradition merely reiterates the views of the past then we could say that it had stagnated in certain respects. Or a new question may arise for which it may not be able to find an appropriate answer based on either previous or new interpretations of its foundational texts. In a situation like this we could say that tradition had entered into a form of intellectual crisis. Debates over genetic testing of fetuses, in vitro fertilization and stem cell research are examples of contemporary questions the church has had to address that have never been asked before (at least not in the particular way the issues are currently being presented). In order to answer these questions we have to draw upon the Bible in ways that the church may have not done in the past. Divorce, remarriage, women in ministry, abortion and homosexuality are older questions that have been raised in a new ways because of our current cultural context, but for which we have a rich heritage of biblical interpretation to draw upon as a resource to help in the process of finding appropriate resolutions. The fact that there is a great deal of dialogue taking place over these issues is not something we should be discouraged about, but is an indication that the Christian tradition is vigorous in this respect. How these debates are resolved will then become part of the church's interpretive heritage. Whether we reach a healthy or unhealthy resolution remains to be seen. In either case these solutions will become part of the historical road map for how the next generation will read the scriptures.

The metaphor of a road map also communicates that there is a connection between where we are and where we want to go. The interpretive debate over the meaning over the Bible creates connections between us and the early church. At an unconscious level the truth claims of a biblical text enter into the memory of the Christian tradition through previous readers or interpreters. How the fourth-century church interpreted the Sermon on the Mount played a significant role in practices of the church of that day. However, their interpretations of the Sermon on the Mount are not limited to their historical situation but went beyond that context: they have entered into the memory of the church's tradition. Before someone reads the Sermon on the Mount the history of how the church has received it through the years has already influenced and shaped how that person will read the text.

These influences may be felt consciously or unconsciously. In some instances our encounter with the Bible will be indirect, through second- and third-hand sources such as art, music, movies or other literature. I don't know how many times when I have taught on the gospels that the students have been surprised to learn that Mary Magdalene is not described as a prostitute in the New Testament. This is a particular reading that entered into the interpretive memory of the church almost 1,800 years ago and operates at an unconscious level when people read the gospels. And recently Mary Magdalene's reputed scandalous past was reinforced with the release of the film by Mel Gibson, *The Passion of the Christ*.

> *Students are often surprised to learn that Mary Magdalene is not described as a prostitute in the New Testament.*

What I am trying to communicate at this point is that there is a living connection between the Bible and us. The history of interpretation, secondary sources, references, and allusions in other texts or works of art all constitute the connective tissues that link present readers with the ancient biblical texts.

Summit Dialogue

At a conscious level the reception history of the Bible actively contributes to the Christian tradition's continuity through what Hans Robert Jauss terms the "summit dialogue" of authors. The metaphor of a summit dialogue evokes an image of the undulating profile of a mountain range that we can trace across the horizon. There are two reasons why the summit dialogue level is often the most significant level for researching the history of a text's interpretation. The first is obvious: this is the level where the defining moments of a tradition are often located. The peaks, or high points, represent the most significant interpreters because of the impact they had on their contemporaries and the influence they exerted on later readers. These are the works that set direction for those that follow, that subsequent readers cite approvingly, disagree with, or engage in a dialogue over regarding how a biblical passage is read, for example, how Augustine read Romans and then how Aquinas read Romans in light of Augustine, and then how Luther read Romans through Aquinas and then through Augustine.

Not every reading of a biblical text is received equally within a tradition. Some readings are found to be more productive for the practices of the Christian community at that time, for theological reflection, for artworks; or are judged better at explicating the meaning of that text. Luther's exposition of Romans 1:17 is one example of a reading that has been widely recognized as one of the defining points in the Protestant tradition. His interpretation of Romans 1:17 became one of the focal points of interpretive debate within the Christian tradition in his day and helped to set in motion one of the most defining turning turns in Christian tradition, the Reformation.

The second reason why the summit dialogue is significant is that most of the textual evidence is preserved and accessible at this level. It is at the level of the summit dialogue that the most open and conscious conversation with a tradition takes place. One of the lamentable effects of history is that the events and developments on the grand scale are passed down, while the records from everyday life are often forgotten. As a result, what has been passed down to us represents only the tip of the iceberg: a great deal of material has been lost or forgotten in the history of biblical interpretation. Nevertheless, there is still a vast quantity of material that has accumulated over 2,000 years, much of this in the form of sermons, homilies, theological treatises and commentaries. It is through these preserved works that we can trace the various trajectories of interpretation through history. Given the overwhelming amount of interpretive material on the Bible that has been preserved, our primary consideration should be given to the most influential interpretations. This is especially true if you have only a limited amount of time to invest in this type of study.

> *We are connected to the Bible
> through the history of its
> reception and interpretation
> within the church.*

This textual record is a witness to the manner by which we are connected to the Bible through the history of its reception and interpretation within the church. Commentaries, theological treatises, sermons, devotional writings have all kept the Bible alive by continually demonstrating the relevance of the scriptures to everyday life for that past 2,000 years. If this interpretive debate about the Bible's meaning had been suspended the Bible would have ceased to function in any meaningful way within our tradition.

This heritage also allows us to check our understanding of the Bible against that of others. At the contemporary level, we can check our interpretations against the wider perspective of our peers by reading their works. At a historical, or diachronic, level we can test our reading of the Bible in light of tradition. If my interpretation is corroborated by my contemporaries and the doctors of the church then I can feel fairly secure that I am reading the passage in an appropriate manner. At the same time, as I engage the history of a text's transmission I may realize some theological, ideological or cultural presupposition that has crept into my understanding of the text. I may not agree with everything about how Luther reads the story of Jonah, but his understanding of the story challenges many of my assumptions. As I read his provocative (from my perspective) view of Jonah's fish my understanding of the book of Jonah is transformed.

In other instances the history of interpretation can offer needed corrections to contemporary readings. Whether the post-history of the biblical text confirms or corrects our interpretations, these readings have the potential to open us to the provocative and transformational message of the Bible in ways we may not have considered.

By way of review, allow me to summarize several points:

- First, the authoritative status accorded the Bible is related to the history of its reception and its function as a foundational text for the Christian and Jewish traditions.
- Second, the timeless relevance of the Bible is related to its surplus of meaning. The Bible addresses questions about human existence and our relationship to our creator in ways that we have found relevant and provocative down to this day.
- Third, the "summit dialogue" of commentators constitutes an interpretive debate that has contributed to the formation of the Jewish and Christian traditions and also forms a living connection between the Bible and contemporary readers. The summit dialogue is not primarily an interesting collection of historical artifacts but has also preserved perspectives on the text that can confirm, enlarge or correct how we read the Bible.

We need to realize how these historically constituted interpretations have shaped our tradition, contributed to our pre-understanding of the Bible, and form a living link, bridging 2,000 years between us and the Bible.

Case Study on How the Great Commission has been Read by the Church

When I joined the staff of Campus Crusade for Christ in 1983 I attended my first seminary courses as part of staff training. One day as I sat in my New Testament class the professor confidently explained that the mandate found in Matthew 28:18–20 to "go and disciple all nations" had been fulfilled long ago. Now I am not sure if anyone had bothered to tell him that he was lecturing the staff of an organization whose founder, Bill Bright, signed everyone of his letters, "Yours for the fulfillment of the Great Commission." As we shall see in this section, this professor's interpretation of Matthew 28 was not as innovative an insight he seemed to think it was, nor has it had a good track record in the history of the church.

I have chosen the reception history of the Great Commission as found in Matthew 28:18–20 as a case study for two reasons. First, this passage has played a significant role in regard to how the church defines its goals and purposes in relation to the rest of the world. Second, Matthew 28:18–20 occupies an area of middle ground between an open, poetic style of text and a closed text with little connotative meaning. It is neither a poetic text like a psalm or parable that is open to a great deal of latitude in meaning, nor is it a closed text like Paul's instruction to Timothy to "bring the cloak that I left with Carpus at Troas" (2 Tim. 2:13). At the same time there are a remarkable number of folds in the meaning of the conclusion to Matthew that are revealed in the history of its interpretation.

From Jerusalem to the Council of Nicea, 325 AD

This case study starts out on a surprising note, as we find that the early church did not view the closing verses of Matthew's Gospel as a command to evangelize and make disciples of the nations and that, in fact, most of the fathers who discussed this text viewed the command to "go and make disciples" as being directed primarily at the apostles and not at the church of their day. For them, the main thrust of the passage centered on the sacrament of baptism.

> *The early church did not view the closing verses of Matthew's Gospel as a command to evangelize and make disciples of the nations.*

Given the persecution which the church experienced during most of this time, their hermeneutical interests in this passage may be understandable. The questions that confronted them concerned issues involved with conversion – who should be admitted to the church and what was the proper manner by which they were to be admitted. Persecution is not a time when the church has the luxury of concentrating a conscious effort on missions but is, rather, a time of survival. Yet in spite of the persecution and a lack of teaching on the command to "go and make disciples" the church spread rapidly during this period.

There were three primary exegetical themes the various commentators noticed during this period.

The first theme that is visible in many of the homilies and lectures on Matthew 28:18–20 reflects their concern for protecting orthodoxy (correct teaching), especially regarding the deity of Christ. They clearly saw Christ's divinity affirmed in the statements "all authority has been given to me" (28:18) and "lo I am with you always." Tertullian cites this text in conjunction with John 1:1 to argue that the Son has been an equal partner with the Father not only in creation but in all the actions of the Godhead:

> Whence it is written, "From the beginning the Word was with God, and the Word was God;" to whom is given by the Father all power in heaven and on earth. "All authority has been given to me on heaven and earth." For when He speaks of all power and all judgment, and ways that all things were made by Him, and all things have been delivered into His hand, He allows no exception (in respect) of time, because they would not be all things unless they were the things of all time. It is the Son, therefore, who has been from the beginning administering judgment, throwing down the haughty tower, and dividing the tongues, punishing the whole world by the violence of waters, raining upon Sodom and Gomorrah fire and brimstone, as the Lord from the Lord. (*Against Praxeas*, ch. 36)

The second exegetical theme is their concentration on the use of the Trinitarian formula in the sacrament of baptism, thus also showing their concern for orthopraxis (correct practice). This is not surprising, since the Trinity was one of the most debated theological issues of the early church. The triune name of God in the baptismal clause (28:19) was seen as the norm indicating the proper manner in which one was to be baptized. This theme is found in the *Didache* (7.1), one of the earliest Christian documents preserved (written between 70 and 150 AD) and many of the church fathers during this period. Hippolytus, for example, used the baptismal clause of Matthew 28:19 to show that God was a Trinity and that all three persons of the Trinity are to be worshipped in the act of baptism. In his reading of this passage he combined the twin concerns of orthodoxy and orthopraxis:

> For indeed the Father is One, but there are two persons, because there is also the Son; and then there is the third, the Holy Spirit, the Father decrees, the Word executes, and the Son is manifested, through whom the Father is believed on. It is the Father who commands, and the Son who obeys, and the Holy Spirit who gives understanding: the Father who is above all, and the Son who is through all, and the Holy Spirit who is in all ... The Father seeks to be worshipped in none other way than this, gave this charge to the disciples after He rose from the dead; "Go ye and teach all nations, baptizing them in the name of the Father, and of the Son, and of the Holy Ghost." ... For it is through this Trinity that the Father is glorified. For the Father willed, the Son did, the Spirit manifested. The whole scriptures proclaim this truth. (*Against the Heresy of one Noetus*, 14)

The person who put an authoritative stamp on this reading of Matthew 28:18–20 in regard to baptism was Tertullian. For him, for baptism to be effective it depended upon the name into which a believer was baptized. It made "no difference whether a man be washed in a sea or a pool, a stream or a fountain, a lake or a trough" (*On Baptism*, ch. 4). This passage contained not only the commandment to baptize believers but also a "formula prescribed, 'Go' He says, 'teach all nations, baptizing them in the name of the Father, and of the Son, and of the Holy Ghost'" (*On Baptism*, ch. 13). Tertullian so advanced the doctrine of baptism that for several centuries little was added to his teaching on this sacrament. As such, he represents an early peak in the summit dialogue of authors in the history of how this passage has been received by the church.

The final theme that runs through many of the writers of this period was that the command to "go and make disciples" has been fulfilled. This fulfillment has taken place in one of two ways. Many of the leaders in the early church felt that this command had been literally fulfilled by the apostles. It is not clear exactly what criteria they used in gauging the fulfillment of this commission, except that they felt that the gospel had been taken by the primitive church to "all the nations." This may have been a hyperbole on their part for homiletical purposes. Or it may have reflected their world view that the Roman Empire comprised the known world and that since the church had made fairly good progress spreading throughout the Empire, then it may have been assumed that all the nations had heard the message. We cannot say much beyond this as they do not specifically comment on what they considered to be the extent of the inhabited world.

The geographic spread of the gospel among the Gentiles was also understood in terms of the fulfillment of prophecies in the Old Testament concerning the rule of the Messiah over the entire earth, not just Israel. Ignatius (died 109 AD) argued that the church's propagation of the gospel fulfilled Genesis 49:10 (that the scepter will not depart from Judah until all the peoples obey him), while Hippolytus felt that Daniel's vision of the Son of Man (Dan. 7:13–14) provided a better intertextual reference. In both of these instances the fulfillment of the Great Commission by the apostles was seen as the fulfillment of the Old Testament promises and thus bolstered their arguments for the orthodox teachings on Christ's deity.

From the Council of Nicea until the Middle Ages

Constantine's Edict of Milan (313 AD) ended the persecution of the church and by the end of the fourth century Christianity had become the official religion of the Roman Empire. Freed from persecution the church turned its energies to formulating its faith. This was an age of great church councils which defined the orthodox position on many doctrines. During this period Matthew 28:18–20 was primarily interpreted along four exegetical avenues.

First, the church continued to interpret the baptismal clause in 28:19 according to Tertullian's teachings, with some minor clarifications made along the way. Augustine clarified what had become the church's position regarding the correct practice of baptism in his debates with the Donatists. In response to the Donatists, who argued that baptism was efficacious only when administered by a priest that was holy and in communion with the church, Augustine asserted that it was the faith of the baptized person and Jesus Christ's authority which made baptism effective. "Baptism in the name of the Father and of the Son and of the Holy Ghost has Christ for its authority, not any man, whoever he may be; and Christ is the truth, not any man" (*In Answer to the Letters of Petilian, the Donatist, Bishop of Cirta*, ch. 24).

Second, the Trinitarian formula in Matthew 28:19 continued to be used to defend the orthodox position on the Trinity against various heretical teachings during this period. Their arguments and appeals to Matthew 28:18–20 reiterate many of the early church's interpretive uses of this passage to put forward or defend the deity of Christ.

Third, as in the preceding period, most interpreters felt that the Great Commission had been fulfilled by the primitive church. As before, this involved a double fulfillment: through the apostolic proclamation and also in relation to Old Testament promises. As Athanasius argued, "But now, unto all the earth has gone forth their voice, and all the earth has been filled with the knowledge of God, and the disciples have made disciples of all the nations, and now is fulfilled what is written, 'They shall be all taught of God'" (*Four Discourses Against the Arians*, Discourse 1, ch. 13). Even the early historian Eusebius claimed that the missiological element of Matthew 28:18–20 had been discharged by the apostles after they were driven out of Israel:

> And finally James, the first who had obtained the episcopal seat in Jerusalem after the ascension of our Saviour, was slain in the manner before related. But the rest of the apostles, who had been

harassed in innumerable ways with a view to destroy them, and driven from the land of Judea, had gone forth to preach the Gospel to all nations, relying upon the aid of Christ, when He said, "Go ye teach all the nations in my name." (*Ecclesiastical History*, book III, ch. V)

Fourth, during this period there was the lone voice of Gregory the Great (540–604) who broke with previous interpretations of Matthew 28:18–20 when he taught that the command to "go and make disciples of all nations" was still binding on the church. Like those who came before him he read the closing section to Matthew's Gospel as a fulfillment of Old Testament prophecies that the gospel would cover the earth, but in contrast to those before him, his knowledge of regions and peoples outside the sphere of the church and the Roman Empire enabled him to see that Matthew 28:18–20 had not been fulfilled by the early church. There is a well-known story that illustrates his heart in this area. It is related that one day (before he became Pope) while passing through the market he saw English people being sold as slaves. Upon seeing them he remarked, "*non Angle, sed angeli*" (not Angles, but angels). Shortly after this he set out as a missionary to England but was intercepted only a few miles outside of Rome by a delegation who persuaded him to return to the city in order to aid the ailing Pontiff. Later, when he was Pope, he was responsible for planting the church on English soil when he sent Augustine the missionary there. From his papal office Gregory commissioned Augustine and by means of correspondence he monitored his progress, answered questions, and sent further instructions. In doing so Gregory not only launched the Medieval mission of the church to present Christ to all nations, but also established the norm by which Matthew 28:18–20 was read and applied for the next millennium.

What is interesting is that the same passage which was now read as a mandate to evangelize the various peoples was also read by those who followed Gregory the Great as a summary of their primary message and their mode of operation. Wilfrid (also known as Boniface, 634–709) followed

Tertullian's Trinitarian baptismal formula in Matthew 28:19, that they must be baptized in the "name of the Father, Son and Holy Spirit", when he preached to the South Saxons in France. Hucbald of St Amand (late 900s) displayed a similar use of Matthew 28:19 when he recorded an evangelistic message given by the missionary Lebuin:

> God, the only good and righteous Being, whose mercy and truth remains forever, moved with pity that ye should be thus seduced by the errors of demons, has charged me as His ambassador to beseech you to lay aside your old errors, and to turn with sincere and true faith to Him by whose goodness ye were created. In Him you and all of us live and move and have our being. If ye will truly acknowledge Him, and repent and be baptized in the name of the Father, the Son, and the Holy Ghost, and will obediently keep His commandments, then will He preserve you from all evil, and will grant you the blessings of peace here and in the life to come the enjoyment of all good things. (*Vita Lebuini*; quoted by James Addison, *The Medieval Missionary*, 148-149)

The methodology employed by many of the Medieval missionaries was to admit groups of people for baptism. In many instances no changes in their lifestyle or beliefs were required before baptism. The converts' willingness to be baptized was taken at face value as evidence of faith. It was only after they were incorporated into the church that they were taught the doctrines of the Christian faith. This strategy appears to reflect the chronological order found in Matthew 28:18–20. "Go and make disciples of all nations" by "baptizing" (the sacrament that washed away the stain of original sin) and then "teaching them to observe" Jesus' commandments".

During the Middle Ages (especially the late Middle Ages) the church expended a considerable amount of missionary effort, in large part due to Gregory's teachings on Matthew 28. The monasteries often functioned as centers for training, sending, monetary support, and the development of indigenous leadership. During the early 1500s the Jesuits grew to become one of the greatest missionary movements ever.

Both the popes and the monarchs during this period often saw it as their duty spread the Christian faith. In 1493 (one year after Columbus sailed the Atlantic) Pope Alexander VI divided the New World between Spain and Portugal for trade and missions in his bull *Inter Cetera* that required all monarchs to spread the Catholic faith in their colonial ventures.

When the Reformation erupted, Roman Catholic theologians claimed that the missiological mandate in the final verses of Matthew could be carried out only by the Catholic Church. They based this argument on the claim that the Roman Church was the only church established by Jesus Christ. In contrast to the Protestant churches, the Roman church defended its legitimacy as the true church because it could trace its present instantiation back to Jesus through what they claimed was an unbroken line of apostolic succession. Since the church of Rome was the legitimate heir of the apostolic church, the command to go and make disciples of all nations, and the authority to carry this out, rested only in the Catholic Church. This doctrine was one reason why the Catholic Church took offensive actions towards Protestant missions once they were started (actions that continued until the twentieth century).

> *Roman Catholic theologians claimed that the missiological mandate in the final verses of Matthew could be carried out only by the Catholic Church.*

At the same time they also used Matthew 28:18–20 as an apologetic argument against the Protestant movement. Catholic theologians asserted that theirs was the true church since they were obeying the command to "go" in Matthew 28:18–20. Because there was a great disparity between the efforts made by the Catholics and Protestants in missions from the time of the Reformation until the 1800s the Protestant churches were extremely vulnerable to this line of argumentation.

The Reformation: 1517–1600

Given this history, what is surprising is the amazing lack of theological or practical emphasis on the missiological element in Matthew 28:18–20 among the early Reformers. There are several factors that may explain this, at least in part.

> The absence of theological or practical emphasis on the missiological element in Matthew 28:18–20 among the early Reformers is surprising.

Firstly, Protestantism was struggling for its survival. During the first century or two, Protestant nations did not have access to the New World. The Protestant churches' rejection of monasticism meant that they also lacked an institutional structure from which to prepare and send missionaries. At the same time the Reformers' return to the universality of the gospel of Christ paved the way theologically for the adoption of Great Commission by later generations.

Martin Luther (1483–1546) is an interesting case study in himself. On the one hand, he taught that the evangelistic element in Matthew 28:18–20 had been fulfilled by the apostles, much as Eusebius of Caesarea and Athanasius had done 1,000 years earlier. On the other hand, he knew this had not taken place. For example, Luther urged Christian rulers to resist the spread of Islam and urged Christian prisoners to bear witness to their Muslim captors. In contrast to the Catholic position there is no clear teaching in the works of Luther, or his successor, Phillip Melanchthon, that the church was responsible for those outside Christendom.

At the other end of the spectrum stood the Anabaptists. They saw the history of the early church until Constantine as the Golden Age of the Church. After the Edict of Milan the church fell into the dark ages as heretics corrupted the church. The Anabaptists attacked Luther because they saw him as a halfway man and criticized him for not introducing a thorough Reformation into the church (i.e., infant baptism was retained). The commanding theme of the Anabaptist movement was a desire to re-establish the primitive apostolic model of the church. Perhaps no other passage of the New Testament received as much attention from them as did Matthew 28:18–20.

The Anabaptists saw two primary implications in this text. First, the command to "Go and make disciples" was binding on all believers. However, their itinerant evangelists were perceived as a destabilizing influence in their society and were violently persecuted by the other Reformation parties. Second, following the way the text was read by medieval interpreters, they saw in the text not only a mandate, but a pattern to be followed:

> When Christ sent out his apostles to gather his church he spoke to them and gave them this commandment: Go and teach all nations, baptize them in the name of the Father, the Son, and the Holy Ghost, and teach them to observe everything that I have commanded you. The first teaching is that they present to them the basics of God's will in Christ. If then they accept the teaching and wish to become disciples of Christ they shall baptize them so that they may put on Christ and be incorporated in his holy church. Finally, in order that they may remain friends of Christ, the ones baptized should be taught everything that Christ commanded. All this can be clearly seen in the apostolic writings. (Bernhard Rothmann, *Restitution 1534*, quoted in *Anabaptism in Outline, Selected Primary Sources*, edited by Walter Klaassen, 106)

The most influential leader of this movement was Menno Simons (1496–1561), who taught that all believers were obligated to preach the gospel to the whole world according to Matthew 28:18–20. Simons courageously defended this view and survived only by moving about. Severe persecution of his followers, the Mennonites, is most likely responsible for undermining a sustained missionary effort on their part for several centuries.

John Calvin (1509–1564) represents a middle ground position between the Anabaptists and other Reformers. His commentary on Matthew 28:18–20 is a very significant work because of his importance theologically, ecclesiastically and exegetically. Because Christ's rule was not yet fully realized in the world the command to "go and make disciples" was of the utmost importance. The goal of this mandate was that "all nations" would be brought to the obedience of faith. This was to be accomplished through pastors teaching their congregations to "observe all" that Jesus commanded. Calvin never directly stated that the commission to go and make disciples still applied to the church. But there is indirect evidence that leads us to believe he thought this. From 1555 to 1560 he helped to form a pioneering mission work to Brazil, which unfortunately ended tragically.

While Calvin did not come to a full recognition of the missionary obligation of Matthew 28:18–20, his commentary provided clear insights into what this would involve. However, in light of the teachings and activities of the Roman Catholic Church his commentary, while clear and concise, merely retreads familiar territory in this regard. The most important contribution Calvin made to this historical debate over the meaning of Matthew 28:18–20 was his theocentric concept of the expansion of God's kingdom, a kingdom that was inaugurated by Jesus, was spread by the apostles, and was still being spread through Jesus' followers. Calvin's view of the kingdom, coupled with a clear emphasis on the universality of the gospel, laid the groundwork for future Protestants to read this passage missiologically.

Post-Reformation debates over Matthew 28:18–20: 1600–1800

From 1600 to 1792 there was a great deal of debate within the Protestant communities over the missionary mandate in Matthew 28. The Heidelberg Catechism (1563) and the Synod of Dort (1618–19) provide an introduction to how this passage was read in the Calvinist churches during this period.

The Heidelberg Catechism was the most popular of the Reformed statements during its day. Biblical references in the Heidelberg Catechism are made to book and chapter, not specific verses. Questions 22, 25, 31, 46, 47, 48, 50, 53, 54, 65 and 71 appeal to Matthew 28 to reinforce Calvin's position on baptism and the sacraments. The Heidelberg Catechism included only one minor reference to missions: "... so that by our godly living our neighbors may be won over to Christ". While the Heidelberg theologians did not see the mandate to "go and teach" as binding on the church, they did not teach that the Great Commission was fulfilled by the apostles.

The Synod of Dort was called due to controversy over the teachings of Arminius in the Netherlands, which it did by reaffirming the central tenets of Calvinistic theology. As in Calvin's work, there is a strong theological understanding of the universality of the gospel in the Canons of Dort. What the Canons of Dort did not contain was any form of statement teaching that the church was under obligation to the mission command in Matthew 28:18–20, but its theology was open to missions.

The Heidelberg Catechism and the Canons of Dort stand in contrast to the teachings in the Lutheran theological communities. In 1651 the theological faculty at Wittenberg attacked Count Truchess's teaching that Matthew 28:19 was still binding on the church. They appealed to Luther's teaching that the apostles had fulfilled the requirements of Matthew 28:18–20 to take the gospel to the world. Therefore pastors and laymen could not possibly be involved in missions, since the job was already accomplished. The presence of non-Christian nations was explained by the failure on the part of those who had either forgotten or did not to respond to the message. For many seventeenth-century Protestants the commission in Matthew 28:18–20 was read as applying only to the apostles. When the apostles died, Christ's mandate died with them. From the death of the apostles onward the expansion of the church took place through witnessing to those in the immediate community or resulted from those instances when the church was scattered due to persecution.

Born in the Netherlands and later forced to England due to political persecution, Hadrian Saravia (1561–1613) was one of the first Protestant teachers to advocate, in his book *De Diversis Gradibus Ministrorum Evangelii* (1590), the view that the Great Commission in Matthew 28:18–20 still applied to the church early in the seventeenth century. Saravia argued that the Great Commission extended to all generations even until the end of the world and that its scope was to every nation.

His argument rested on four points. First, the command to "go and make disciples of all nations" was connected with the promise, "Lo, I am with you alway, even unto the end of the world." Just as the promise applied to all believers, so did the command. Second, because the apostles chose successors in their work, they saw their efforts as only the beginning of the spread of the church. Third, the scope of Matthew 28:18–20 was far too great for the apostles to have accomplished it within their lifetimes. And fourth, a long history of missions proved that the church has traditionally been involved in missions.

Unfortunately, Saravia's reading of Matthew 28:18–20 was not favorably received, and actually attracted criticism from some of the biggest names in the church during his day: Theodore Beza (1519–1605) and Johannes Gerhard of Jena (1582–1637).

In his booklet *Upon the Tract by Hadrian Saravia, Belgian, concerning the orders of the Gospel Ministry*, Beza attacked Saravia's position. Beza agreed with Saravia's reading that the command to "go" and the promise that Christ will always be with us were linked to each other, but at the same time maintained a distinction between them. Following the pattern set by previous interpreters in the Protestant tradition Beza claimed that the command to "go" had been fulfilled by the apostles and was no longer binding on the church. However, a general call for the church to preach the gospel within its culture still carried over.

Johannes Gerhard, in his theological compendium *Loci Theologici*, combined Beza's criticisms with Luther's teaching that through the apostles the gospel had gone out into the whole world. For example, Beza believed, and taught, that there were more Christians in the Great Tartary (Muslim Asia Minor) than in all Europe, that Ethiopia was a Christian nation, and that America and the distant islands were once Christian. While he taught that the church was still responsible to preach the gospel and administer the sacraments, he also taught that it no longer had the authority to take the gospel to other lands. This authority had ended with the apostolic generation to whom Christ had given it. Johannes Gerhard defended his position by quoting Tertullian, Jerome, Chrysostom and Augustine as witnesses from the early church. And finally, if the command to "go" and the promise of Christ's presence were linked, as Saravia claimed, then every believer was responsible for sharing the good news with the pagans. This was a logical absurdity in Gerhard's mind. Nevertheless, his reading of Matthew 28:18–20 won the day and dominated Lutheran thought up to the eighteenth century.

During the Reformation the control of the high seas by the Spanish naval power kept Protestant countries from engaging in colonization or considering missions in the New World as the Catholic church was able to do. With the defeat of the Spanish Armada in 1588 access to the rest of the world was opened to northern Europe. Shortly thereafter, Puritan teaching in England began to produce a national awakening in regard to the church's obligation to obey the command to "go and make disciples of all nations."

This sentiment was reflected in the original Westminster Confession, which was written in 1643 at the request of the Long Parliament to combat tyranny, Catholicism and Arminianism, and was in line with most of Calvin's teachings. Section X, "Of the Gospel," discussed the implications of the doctrine that God desired all men to be saved and the implication that those who freely chose to reject this offer brought condemnation upon themselves. In Article 4 of Section X the church's obligation to obey the missiological mandate of Matthew 28:19 was clearly laid out:

> Since there is no other way of salvation than that revealed in the gospel, and since the divinely established and ordinary

method of grace, faith cometh by hearing the word of God, Christ hath commissioned his church to go into all the world and to make disciples of all nations. All believers are, therefore, under obligation to sustain the ordinances of the Christian religion where they are already established, and to contribute by their prayers, gifts, and personal efforts to the extension of the kingdom of Christ throughout the whole world.

(What is most surprising is that this section was edited out of the Larger [1648] and Shorter [1647] Catechisms based on the Westminster Confession. These works share the same authors and theology as the Confession and no explanation for this editorial decision is given.)

The impact of this reading of Matthew 28:18–20 was felt almost immediately. In 1648 a group of about seventy clergymen petitioned the Long Parliament about the need for the Christian message in America and the West Indies. This elicited from Parliament a manifesto in favor of missions which was to be read in every church and called for the necessary contributions to be collected, and in 1649 the Corporation or Society for the Propagation of the Gospel in New England was founded. John Owen (1616–1683) reiterated the Westminster Confession's teaching that the church was obligated to fulfill the command to "go and make disciples of all nations" in his academic teaching at Oxford and in his sermons. At the same time, he also acknowledged that the Catholic theologians were justified in their criticism of the Protestant churches for their lack of missions.

Meanwhile, back on the continent German Lutheranism was laboring under many burdens at the end of the seventeenth century. Theological wrangling had taken precedence over pastoral care, resulting in a weak church. The Thirty Years War (1618–1648) had created a wariness about religious causes. However, as in England, the growth of colonization and international trade made the previously held assumptions about the universal diffusion of gospel untenable. This forced the German church leaders to make adjustments in the older Lutheran expositions of Matthew 28 and interpretations of church history, such as those which had been put forward by Johannes Gerhard.

Lutheran interests in missions first arose in the Pietist movement, not in Lutheran orthodoxy. Phillip Jakob Spener (1635–1705), who is regarded as the father of German Pietism, emphasized the Reformed concept of a union between faith and works in contrast to seventeenth-century Lutheran theology, which stressed doctrine. Spener broke from the accepted Lutheran teachings of his day when he taught that the command to "go and make disciples of all nations" in Matthew 28:19 was still binding upon the church. Because there was no hope of salvation outside of Jesus Christ the church ought to spare no expense in taking the gospel to the heathen.

August Herman Francke (1663–1727) inherited the leadership of the Pietist movement from Spener and believed that the world was in dire need of the Christian message. The Protestant churches of Europe were responsible for meeting that need according to the command in Matthew 28:18–20, and "Yea, herein the zeal of the Papists puts us to shame, for they by their missionaries and envoys have more earnestness for the spread among the heathen of their religion, … than we manifest for our pure evangelical truth" (Sermon on "The Feast of Ascension").

One of the students whom Franke profoundly influenced while he taught at the University of Halle was Count Zinzendorf (1700–1760). Zinzendorf went on to found the Moravian church which sent over 2,170 missionaries by 1880. While much of the enthusiasm of German Pietism died off after 1850 the influence of their teachings and the missions of the Moravian church are still felt today.

In England, John Wesley (1703–1791) broke the superficial morality that had set into the British church of his day by calling for a return to

> *Count Zinzendorf founded the Moravian church which sent over 2,170 missionaries by 1880.*

a full biblical message and practical Christian living.

In regard to Matthew 28, Wesley felt that the commands to baptize and teach were the two central ideas of this passage. If the church was accomplishing these two duties then it would be fulfilling the command to "make disciples of all nations." By means of itinerant preachers who were, ideally, to fan out over the entire world under Christ's authority and preach the gospel wherever they may gain an audience, the Great Commission could be fulfilled:

> Yes, yes, "Go into all the world"; and though I will not pretend to say, that this enjoins ministers to go into every part of the world; yet I insist upon it, and by the grace of God, if I were to die for it, I will say, that no power on earth has power to restrain ministers from preaching, where a company of people are willing to hear (Sermon on "The Gospel a dying Saint's Triumph").

His ideas were similar to Calvin's view of the expansion of God's kingdom. Wherever the gospel was preached the "kingdom of God is at hand" and was manifested through God's reign in the hearts of those who believe in him. Wesley's vision for Matthew 28:18–20 involved awakening and reviving the Christian communities in England and in America and the other colonies. An ever-expanding sphere of humanity would come under the preaching of the gospel from these reinvigorated communities of believers.

On the other side of the Atlantic, Jonathan Edwards was reforming Calvinism in America which emphasized the sovereignty of God to the point where the believer's responsibility to present the gospel to others was obscured. The depth and importance of Jonathan Edwards's works have earned him the appellation of "America's greatest theologian". In his work *A History of Redemption* he spelled out three elements he felt were central to Matthew 28:18–20:

> The next thing was Christ's appointment of the gospel-ministry, by commissioning and sending forth his apostles to teach and baptize all nations. Of these things we have an account in Matthew 28:19–20. "Go ye therefore, and teach all nations, baptizing them in the name of the Father, and of the Son, and of

the Holy Ghost; teaching them to observe all things whatsoever I have commanded you; and lo, I am with you alway, even unto the end of the world." There were three things done by this one commission. 1) The appointment of the office of the gospel-ministry. For this commission which Christ gives to his apostles, in the most essential parts of it, belongs to all ministers ... 2) Something peculiar in this commission, viz. to go forth from one nation to another, preaching the gospel in all the world ... 3) Here is an appointment of Christian baptism. This ordinance indeed had a beginning before ... but now especially by this institution is it established as an ordinance to be upheld in the Christian church to the end of the world. (III.2.3.3)

By way of summary: The period following the Reformation reflects an extended dialogue and debate over Matthew 28:18–20. It took the Protestant church 100 years before they began to seriously consider the missionary mandate in this text. The accepted reading of Matthew 28 during the Reformation held that the command to "go and make disciples of all nations" had been fulfilled during the apostolic age and only applied to the early church. The theological soil for reading this passage as binding on the contemporary church was laid in Calvin's works. The Heidelberg Catechism and the Synods of Dort both contained the seeds which would later germinate into a full acceptance of the command to "go" in Matthew 28:19. Once the domination of the high seas by the Spanish and Portuguese ended, the New World was opened to England, Germany and other nations. Contact with the New World opened the eyes of the churches in northern Europe to the need for missions. This created the need for a sound theology to support mission ventures. It was the Puritans in England and the Pietists in Germany who hammered out the necessity of obeying this command. In America, Jonathan Edwards was the man who modified the hyper-Calvinism of his day so that the church could once again hear the need to obey this passage and then teach the necessity to heed that message.

William Carey to the Present

As European colonists and explorers fanned out around the world, European knowledge of the world exploded, which continued to arouse an interest among the churches of Europe in missions. The clearest illustration of this is seen in the life of William Carey (1761–1834), whose interpretation of Matthew 28:18–20 is one of the most significant for this study. While William Carey labored as a cobbler, schoolteacher and Baptist preacher he studied the *Journal of Captain Cook's Voyages* and compulsively collected any geographical information from around the world he could find. He recorded this on a map that he had made from scraps of leather and which hung in his schoolroom. Carey's conviction that the church should be involved in missions was based on his geographical and biblical studies.

Another formative factor which stimulated Carey's interest in missions came from his readings of Jonathan Edwards's works. The dissenting Baptist church in England that Carey belonged to was known for its hyper-Calvinistic theology. Based on the arguments of Theodore Beza, Johannes Gerhard and others they believed the command of Matthew 28:18–20 was no longer binding on the church. Missions could not seriously be considered, because according to their theology God had not yet chosen to convert the heathen. At a pastors' conference at Olney in 1786, Carey tabled the question "whether the commandment given to the apostles to teach all nations in all the world was not obligatory on all succeeding ministers to the end of the world, seeing that the accompanying promise was of equal extent?" The president, Dr Ryland, reacted strongly to Carey's question. "You are a miserable enthusiast, to propose such a question. Nothing certainly can come to pass in this matter before a new Pentecost accompanied by a new gift of miracles and tongues promises success to the commission of Christ as in the beginning" (*Memoirs of the Life and Writings of the Rev. Andrew Fuller*, by J.A. Morris).

In order to counter the theological presuppositions of his community, Carey had to present a very articulate and strong argument for them to reconsider the implications of Matthew 28:18–20. It may have been the strength of the resistance he had to overcome that contributed to the thoroughness and force of his argument. As a result, the impact of his tract was felt much more widely than by his original audience, his denomination. This took the form of *An Enquiry into the Obligation of Christians to Use Means for the Conversion of Heathens* which he penned in 1792.

In his booklet Carey presented an extended argument to show that the mandate of Matthew 28:18–20 was binding on all churches at all times. He opened his tract by citing the long history of missions within the church. He then advanced a three-point argument based on Matthew's text. First, if the command to "go and make disciples of all nations" in 28:19a was restricted to the apostles, then the command to baptize in 28:19b should also be restricted to the apostles. If the command did not apply, then those who continued to practice baptism were in grave error.

The second point was a corollary to the first: if the command to "teach all nations" was limited to the apostles, then all those who have taken the gospel to the heathen have overstepped their bounds. His hyper-Calvinistic opponents argued that it would take a new Pentecost or commission from Christ before the church could obey Matthew 28:18–20. However, the respect which the Moravian movement and Jonathan Edwards held within the church presented a dilemma for them. Carey exploited this dilemma. The leaders of his denomination either had to admit that they were wrong or maintain that these evangelists were misguided in their attempt to reach out to the "heathen".

Carey pressed his argument further in the third point. The command in 28:19 was inseparable from the promise of Christ's presence in 28:20, he said. If the church was to deny the command then it could not claim the promise. The command of Matthew 28:18–20 was still binding because the church still practiced the sacrament of baptism, believers continued to obey the command to "go", and the command was linked to the promise of Christ's presence. Therefore, Carey concluded, Christ's mandate in Matthew 28:18–20 remained in effect and required the obedience of Christians.

Carey's *Enquiry* was warmly received by churches of various denominations on both sides of the Atlantic and its impact is still felt today. Because of his *Enquiry* and his own personal commitment, demonstrated by his serving in India until his death, William Carey is known as the father of modern missions. Written by a shoe cobbler and part-time schoolteacher, *An Enquiry* in effect ended the debate within Protestantism about the responsibility of the church to obey the command to "go and make disciples of all nations."

> *The debate within Protestantism about the responsibility of the church to obey the command to "go and make disciples of all nations" was ended by a shoe cobbler and part-time schoolteacher.*

The main exception to the influence of Carey's work is found in the liberal theological traditions. With the rise of the Enlightenment in Europe a change in biblical scholarship took place that is persists until today. Scholars began to apply the historical-critical method, based on anti-supernatural presuppositions, to investigating the Bible. The books of the Bible were often viewed as the result of a number of editors who wove various sources together into a narrative. As a result many denied that the words in Matthew 28:18–20 came from Jesus, claiming that they were, instead, the result of an insertion by an editor as late as 200 AD.

To cite one example from this trajectory: Adolf Harnack (1851–1930) used the historical-critical method to separate the "kernel" of the gospel from the "husk." According to Harnack the kernel of Jesus' teaching was "the fatherhood of God and the brotherhood of man." Jesus' entire ministry was focused on Israel and he never commanded the apostles to go to the Gentiles. The commission in Matthew 28:18–20 was put on the lips of Jesus and reflected the developments in the second-century church. The Christian community invented the Great Commission to explain and validate the universal spread of the gospel and the existence of the Gentile church.

This reading of the conclusion to Matthew resulted in a shift in how the mission of the church was perceived. Liberal churches turned their attention more towards the social aspects of missions as orthodox Protestantism continued to focus more upon the soteriological aspect of missions.

Other than this exception, William Carey's *Enquiry* has had a profound impact among different denominations and Christian organizations. The great British preacher Charles Spurgeon (1834–1892) followed Carey's reading of the Matthean text in both the pulpit of London's Metropolitan Tabernacle and his pastors' college. Hudson Taylor (1832–1905, China Inland Mission, now Overseas Missionary Fellowship), John Raleigh Mott (1865–1955, Student Volunteer Movement) and Bill Bright (1921–2003, Campus Crusade for Christ) are all examples of founders of Christian mission organizations who read Matthew 28:18–20 primarily as a mandate for outreach rather than a repository of teaching on the Trinity or baptism.

What is remarkable is that the level of recent debate over the meaning of this passage has been very limited compared with the scope and nature of the debate before William Carey. In fact, the two most significant points of debate over the meaning of this passage now center on lexical and grammatical issues: the meaning of the phrase *all nations* and the use of the participle *go* (literally *going*).

One of the products of the Student Volunteer Movement was Donald McGaveran (1897–1991), who began his long career as a missionary to India and returned to the USA only to start the Church Growth movement and the School of World Mission at Fuller Theological Seminary after the age at which most people retire. He is one of the most influential men in the field of missiology in recent history. His most significant contribution concerning how this passage is read today involves how we understand the phrase *to all nations* in 28:19. He maintains that *nations* does not refer to political nations or countries, but to ethnic groups: the Greek term usually translated *nation* is *éthnê*, the root of our English word *ethnic*). Instead of thinking that India was evangelized if there was a thriving church in that country, said McGaveran, we should ask instead if there was a church among the different language groups, among the different castes and among the Hindu and Muslim populations in India. Instead of seeing India as a monolithic whole McGaveran wants us to see India as a mosaic of hundreds of ethnic groups, each of which needs to hear the gospel in a viable manner in its culture. That is what the phrase *all nations* in Matthew 28:19 referred to, rather than political entities. McGaveran's thought on this one phrase has helped the modern church to redefine the scope of the Great Commission.

> *Donald McGaveran wanted us to see countries like India as a mosaic of hundreds of ethnic groups, each of which needs to hear the gospel in a viable manner.*

The second feature of Matthew 28:18–20 that receives a fair amount of attention among contemporary writers concerns the Greek grammar behind the phrase *go and make disciples*. In the Greek the verb *go* is a participle and some argue that it should, therefore, be translated as a participle, i.e. as *going*. *Make disciples* is literally one verb in Greek and is in the form of an imperative or command.

Those who argue that the Greek word for *go* should be translated into English as a participle reduce the force of Jesus' commission. Those who hold this position contend that we should translate this clause along the lines of *as you go, make disciples*. In other words, the Greek participle should be interpreted as a reference to our journey through life, not to pulling up stakes and relocating to another geographic location in order to make disciples.

On the other hand, the command to *make disciples* is located in the middle of three participles: *going, baptizing, teaching*. In Koine Greek a participle can take the force of its verbal action from a main verb (in this case the main verb is the command to "make disciples"). Now all this can get rather complicated and I have enough trouble trying to explain it to my Greek students, but the short explanation is that the participle *going* should be read as an imperative as well. In fact, this type of grammatical construction is common in Matthew (see, for example, 2:8,13; 5:24, 6:6, 11:4, 17:27, 21:2 and 28:7, where the participle that precedes the imperative is almost always translated as a command). Contextually, since the scope of the command "make disciples" is "all nations" it is best to read the preceding participle *going* as having an imperatival force. This is by far the most common reading of Matthew 28:18–20 among commentators today. Two of the best-known representatives of this reading are Donald Carson's commentary on Matthew in the *Expositor's Bible Commentary* and Donald Hagner's two-volume work in the *Word Biblical Commentary*.

The history of the interpretation of this passage can be compared to a river which began as a small stream and grew in depth and breadth as additional sources contributed to its flow. The early church focused on Christ's deity, the promise of his presence, and the sacrament of baptism. Tertullian's use of the Trinitarian name in the baptismal formula is still widely used today, especially in liturgical churches. By contrast, most commentators today do not focus on the Christological or Trinitarian aspects to this passage (though they may touch on them) but on the command to "go." The early church's claim that the Great Commission was fulfilled by the apostolic church served an apologetic purpose in that context, but proved to be a troublesome reading of the passage that resurfaced several times during the history of the church, including in my experience when I first joined the staff of Campus Crusade. Gregory the Great's understanding of the mandate to "go and make disciples of nations" set in motion the missionary societies of the Catholic Church for the past 1,400 years.

One would have expected the Reformers, with their focus on salvation by faith and the authority of the Bible, to have read the Great Commission as a mandate to propagate their new perspective on the message of the New Testament and salvation abroad. However, the early Reformers' denial of the church's responsibility to fulfill the mission command of Matthew 28:18–20 held the Protestant church back from missions for over a hundred years. The Anabaptists were a lone voice of dissent during this period. While the Reformers denied the command to "go and make disciples," their theology, especially Calvin's, paved the way for future generations to adopt this command.

During the 1600s and 1700s the Protestant church debated whether the church was obligated to obey the missiological commission in Matthew 28:18–20 and the issue was not resolved until a shoe cobbler and schoolteacher from the middle of England, William Carey, wrote his tract *An Enquiry into the Obligation of Christians to Use Means for the Conversion of Heathens.* With the exception of some of the liberal interpretations the obligation of the church to fulfill this command is no longer debated. Donald McGaveran's recent contribution to help us grasp the scope of the command to "make disciples" of all ethnic people groups is perhaps the most significant contribution made to how we read Matthew 28:18–20 since William Carey sailed for India 200 years ago.

We have an incredibly rich heritage in this one text alone. I cannot help but think that we shall be held responsible for our stewardship of this heritage in the future. At the same time, given such a rich history it would also be premature to close the history of how the church understands and has received this passage with our contemporary reading.

Appendix

Guidelines for Tracing a Text's Historical Road Map

The following are a set of guidelines that I have found helpful when excavating the history of a passage's interpretation and the impact and influence of those interpretations. These are not hard and fast rules, nor are they designed to be done in order (step one, then step two, etc.). Rather, they are more reminders or lines of questioning I try to keep in mind as I engage this type of research.

Relationship to the Biblical Text

Any time we are reading a text that offers an interpretation for a passage of Scripture we should do so with our Bible open on the side. There are two aspects we should examine when reading someone's references to, or comments on, a biblical passage.

First, do they quote the entire verse (or verses) or only a portion of it (them)? Often times this will clue us into where they placed the emphasis when they read the passage. In the study on the Great Commission the emphasis that different commentators perceived on the deity of Christ, the Trinity, the baptismal formula or the command to "go and make disciples" indicates what they thought were the most significant clauses in Matthew 28:18–20.

Secondly, the wording between their quotation and the biblical text should be closely compared. Ideally, this comparison should be made from the original languages. If they wrote in Latin then compare the Latin text of their work with the Vulgate; or if they knew Greek or Hebrew, those editions of the Bible. As long as our goal is not an academic research paper, then a fair amount of progress can made by comparing the English translations (of both an interpreter's work and the Bible) with each other. Differences between the biblical passage and their citation may reveal a translational decision made by the interpreter. He or she may have felt that the meaning of the passage could be more clearly conveyed by using a different word in their citation (translation) of the passage. If you suspect that this is the case then you should start to ask questions about how this change in vocabulary affects the passage's meaning or their interpretation of it. Or these linguistic changes may reflect the version of the Bible they are working from. How a reader visualizes Jonah's fish will depend to a certain degree on whether they are reading the original Hebrew, the Septuagint, or the Latin Vulgate.

Intertextual Biblical References

Because the biblical canon provides the most immediate and natural context within which a reader will understand any of the individual texts within the Bible, careful note should be taken of any secondary biblical texts the writer appeals to in order to expound the passage under question. There are any number of ways that an interpreter can make a connection between various biblical texts. Does the interpreter appeal to the secondary passage because it reinforces their interpretation of the passage? Does the reader perceive that one passage is a prophetic fulfillment of the other? What type of theological connection is the commentator making between the two passages? Or is the commentator making a connection based on similar words or ideas in both passages?

When we read the early church fathers or the Medieval theologians this guideline takes on even greater importance. For the early church the Bible was seen as a comprehensive system of truths. Any one passage could be understood only in light of the larger whole of the entire Bible.

Because the methods of biblical interpretation have changed over the centuries the rules by which we construct intertextual relationships have transformed over time as well. Since it would not be appropriate to impose our rules on earlier readers we need to give careful consideration to the intertextual relationships they are making and how they are making them.

Exegetical Themes

Any given reading of a biblical text often contains several exegetical themes that overlap and are related to one another. In most cases it is possible to break down a commentator's exposition into several constituent exegetical themes. The study on Jonah's fish in chapter 2 involved reading the various interpreters and then extracting from their larger discussions of the passage what they specifically said about the sea creature in the book. It was one exegetical theme among many in their comments. If you were to go back and examine some of the quotes I included in that case study you may notice that most of them touch on a much wider diversity of issues than I dealt with in the discussion. In their original contexts an even greater array of exegetical issues were involved in how each commentator read the passage.

Once you have read and reflected on someone's exposition the next step would be to try to identify what they considered the primary exegetical theme to unlock the passage's meaning. What did they claim was the primary thrust of the passage? What were the key terms that they felt needed defining and how did they define them? What features in the biblical text did they find enigmatic or obscure and how did they resolve these questions? We can learn to become better readers by carefully reading their expositions and identifying their exegetical themes. The questions they asked may open our eyes to consider lines of interrogation that we have not been trained to ask.

The historian R.G. Collingwood compared the role of a historian to that of a nature guide. As a tourist naively hikes through the forest taking in the beauty of the trees and foliage. Without warning, their guide stops them in mid-step and silently motions. "'Look,' says the woodsman, 'there is a tiger in the grass'" (*Autobiography*, 100). Just as the naturalist can bring to the attention of the untrained eye aspects of their surroundings they would not have seen, so also the doctors of the church can act as our guides as we explore through the Bible. The various exegetical themes can also help us to shape the contours of a biblical text's passage through time. Some exegetical themes will be pursued by only a few interpreters and are then forgotten. Others, however, set the playing field for generations to come. We can learn a great deal through the various methods we use for interpreting the Bible today, but there is still a great deal those of the past can teach us.

Gaps in and Omissions from the Text

> *Every text has gaps that the reader must fill in.*

Related to the idea of exegetical themes is that of additions or expansions the interpreter contributes to the biblical text. One aspect of any text is that an author cannot include every detail or piece of information in his or her writings. If they were to attempt this they would quickly get bogged down and their work would never progress beyond the first scene or idea they were trying to communicate. As a result, every text has gaps that the reader must fill in. Obvious examples of such gaps are found in the gospel accounts, where Jesus is said to be teaching in one location and then in the next scene we find him in another town or location. How did he get there? How much time elapsed? What took place between the two stories? Another form of omission commonly found in the Bible is details about a character's physical description. Have you ever noticed how little we know about the characters we meet in the Bible? David was short and ruddy, Saul was tall, and Zaccheaus was short. Beyond that we really know very little about most of the other Bible characters. How a reader fills in these gaps and omissions in the biblical text often provides insightful information about what they thought was important for reading the text properly. Interpreters often fill in these blank spaces in the biblical record with a word, phrase, or entire passage so that their audience will have understood the text in the same manner they did. This is why music, drama and artwork are often so significant in the history of how a passage has been read. The very medium by which these arts communicate require that the gaps and omissions in the biblical text are filled in. It would have been impossible for Da Vinci to portray the *Last Supper* without depicting the table, seating arrangement, and physical traits of the various apostles and Jesus.

Relationship to non-Biblical Authorities

Non-biblical sources are often cited to provide insight that enables the reader to understand some facet of the biblical passage. These sources can range from the text of an earlier commentator to a text that is recognized as authoritative on that particular topic. In many cases the commentators will indicate when they are quoting someone else. The most obvious indication is either quotation marks or some variation of "as Chrysostom says ..." However, in some instances the text may lack any sort of indication that an author is quoting or referring to someone else's thought (what we call plagiarism) was not an issue but a virtue at some periods in history or in certain cultures. As you become familiar with the views of the different authors you will hopefully begin to notice similarities between the various interpretations or ways in which a later writer is dependent on an earlier one. These may be thematic dependencies (where the later reader takes the same approach or uses the same exegetical themes as their predecessor), or they may agree word for word. In either case, what we are looking for are the references and/

or authoritative texts the commentator thought was relevant in their explication of the passage. Do they appeal to other writers for linguistic, historical, cultural, philosophical or theological insights? What does this extra-biblical authority contribute to their interpretation of the Bible?

In many instances the intertextual biblical and non-biblical references that a commentator cites plays a significant role when we begin to ask if there is a summit dialogue taking place in the history of this passage's interpretation. The intertextual connections that an earlier reader realized may be adjudged particularly insightful by later readers and thus become associated with what is considered a proper reading of that passage. For example, Augustine may cite an Old Testament verse in his explanation of a parable. When we stumble upon a later interpreter whose reading of the parable parallels Augustine's and he or she mentions the same Old Testament verse (especially if the connection between the two passages is not self-evident), then we can be fairly certain that Augustine's exposition influenced his successor's reading.

The same can be said when non-biblical references enter into the trajectory of a passage's history of interpretation. A major turn in how Jonah was read occurred when Calvin introduced Rondelet's work on marine biology into the question about what type of fish swallowed Jonah. Instead of this story being read through the lens of the Medieval bestiaries or the *Philologus*, it was subsequently read from a scientific perspective. This was not only a shift in how Jonah was read, but also involved an exchange regarding which extra-biblical texts were considered authoritative resources to use when interpreting the Bible. Rondelet replaced the dominant texts of the Medieval church and was cited as the authoritative source for resolving this question by many who followed Calvin.

Shifts in Word Meaning

Language changes over time and words are about as stable as sand. A sandy beach is solid enough to walk on, but if you were to return in a year you would find that the tides and the wind have completely rearranged the configuration of the

> *Language changes over time and words are about as stable as sand.*

sand dunes or curve of the beach. Do not assume that a particular author used words the same way you do. Watch for clues in the context as to how they used certain words with possible connotations or denotations that we do not recognize today. Grammar school children are taught try and determine a word's meaning from its use in a sentence. The same skill needs to be practiced when we research the history of how a biblical passage has been read. Pay careful attention to how *this* author is using *these* words in *this* particular context.

Since the ideas behind this guideline has already received an entire chapter's worth of attention it is unnecessary to spell them out any further. However, if you still have questions about this guideline, please refer back to chapter two.

Recognized Authorities

As a historical map for the reception history of the text you are studying begins to take shape, keep a sharp eye out for those commentators that the church has recognized as authoritative on this passage: the summit dialogue of interpreters. Not every interpretive insight is significant or will enter into the memory of the Christian tradition. But those that have received this recognition deserve special attention. Whether it occurred because others recognized that those particular interpreters' readings unfolded the meaning of the passage in a profound manner, or whether others cited them because their name carried clout, we need to pause and give their work deliberate consideration because it has played such a defining role in the history of that text's interpretation.

This is especially true if they introduced a major turn in how that passage subsequently came to be read. William Carey's reading of Matthew 28:18–20 is one such example. To this day his tract is seen as one of the most influential works that shaped how we understand this passage.

Elements of Domination and Distortion

In a perfect world we would not have to ask questions about whether the Bible was ever used in a particular manner to repress individuals, teachings or institutions. However, the use of the Bible to support the slave trade in the Confederate States is one of many examples that could be cited as an inappropriate reading and application of the Bible. Related to the idea of domination is the question of distortion. Distortions may be unintentional or intentional, as in the instances where a text is misappropriated in order to support a heretical teaching. In many instances elements of domination or distortion have been identified and rectified with the passing of time through the collective judgment of the universal church. However, this does not diminish our responsibility to watch for these elements in how the text has been read historically.

William Tyndale's translation is a case in point, where the church in England was using the Bible to support its institutional authority and practices. When he presented an alternative reading of the New Testament through his translation, he not only subverted the established understanding of the Bible but also undermined particular teachings that were used to buttress particular teachings and institutions within the church.

Engaging in a study on a text's impact and influence may make us aware of issues of domination or distortion in how we read that passage. On the one hand, we may realize that we are repeating a misreading from the past and learn why it is wrong and what an appropriate correction would be. On the other hand, the doctors of the church may provoke our thoughts in ways that raise our subconscious attitudes and beliefs to consciousness. In this process we may become aware of how our readings and teachings need to change. Prophetic lessons like those from the past are too valuable for the church to ignore.

In all of these guidelines the underlying question is that of impact and influence. What was the impact of this or that interpretation or reading upon the audience the author wrote for? And how did this or that reading then influence subsequent interpreters? These guidelines are meant to help identify various features and themes of the different interpretations so that we can discern how they enter into the history of a text's interpretation and also help us to be more attentive to the text and notice folds in the meaning of the text that we may not have noticed before.

Five

Reading and Tradition

We move from one understanding of the text to the next, constantly shifting, expanding and revising how we read the Bible. The history of the Bible and the church is, to a large extent, a record of the hermeneutical spiral since the original authors finished their work, and this spiral will continue until we are ushered into the new age which awaits us.

Jewish and Christian believers have been labeled for centuries as the "People of the Book." For the past four chapters we have considered how we can read this Book, the Bible, in sympathy with those who have read it before us. To learn from them as we read the Bible today. To stand on their shoulders and thus gain the vantage point of their insight and wisdom. Now some attention needs to be given to reading in general.

There are two aspects of reading the Bible in light of this abundant heritage of interpretation that will be discussed in this chapter. In the first half we will survey three different levels or manners of reading. The second half will focus on a discussion of a handful of guidelines I have found useful when reading the Bible with the giants of the past.

> *Until we pick up a book and read it, it is impotent. It requires a reader to realize its potential meaning.*

Reading is highly rewarding and very demanding at the same time. It is not a passive pastime but requires active engagement on our part as readers. It requires us to construct meaning from the black marks on the page so that we can understand and enjoy the message. Until we pick up any text and read it, it is impotent. It requires a reader to realize its potential meaning, and in the process the reader is affected by how they read the text. In the past thirty years a great deal of attention has been given on both the text's and the reader's side to this endeavor that we call reading. Rather than review the various theories about what occurs in the act of reading, the first half of this chapter will focus on different strategies for reading the Bible.

Some texts seem to spell out their meaning clearly, while others carefully guard theirs, slowly dispensing insights into their mysteries one precious morsel at a time to those who labor over them. So different texts require different approaches when we read them. At the same time, we do not want to read a written work the same way every time. We will want to ask different questions of the text so that we can experience more of the richness that it promises to offer if we do so.

With this in mind I would like to suggest three levels or strategies when we read the Bible. The first is pleasure or devotional reading. The second is reading the Bible with an eye to its literary structure and composition. And the third level involves engaging with the detailed studies that look at the nuts and bolts of the text: the words the author used, the historical background to the work, and considerations of theological themes embedded in the passage.

First Level of Reading: Pleasure or Devotional Reading

Reading the Bible for pleasure or devotional purposes is the ground on which all other levels of reading and interpretive activities are based. What do I mean by this? First, pleasure or devotional reading is not characterized by consciously asking questions about grammar, word meanings or theology. Rather, we are primarily seeking an answer to the question:

"What does the Bible say to us?" Second, it is characterized by an active engagement of our imagination through which we respond to the words in the text and recreate those scenes, images, dialogues or dramatic encounters in our minds. Consider the following passage from Ezekiel 1, for example:

In the thirtieth year, in the fourth month, on the fifth day of the month, as I was among the exiles by the river Chebar, the heavens were opened, and I saw visions of God. On the fifth day of the month (it was the fifth year of the exile of King Jehoiachin) ... the word of the LORD came to the priest Ezekiel son of Buzi, in the land of the Chaldeans by the river Chebar; and the hand of the LORD was on him there. As I looked, a stormy wind came out of the north: a great cloud with brightness around it and fire flashing forth continually, and in the middle of the fire, something like gleaming amber. In the middle of it was something like four living creatures. This was their appearance: they were of human form. Each had four faces, and each of them had four wings. Their legs were straight, and the soles of their feet were like the sole of a calf's foot; and they sparkled like burnished bronze. Under their wings on their four sides they had human hands. And the four had their faces and their wings thus: their wings touched one another; each of them moved straight ahead, without turning as they moved. As for the appearance of their faces: the four had the face of a human being, the face of a lion on the right side, the face of an ox on the left side, and the face of an eagle; such were their faces. Their wings were spread out above; each creature had two wings, each of which touched the wing of another, while two covered their bodies. Each moved straight ahead; wherever the spirit would go, they went, without turning as they went. In the middle of the living creatures there was something that looked like burning coals of fire, like torches moving to and fro among the living creatures; the fire was bright, and lightning issued from the fire. The living creatures darted to and fro, like a flash of lightning. (NRSV)

When you read this passage from Ezekiel, can you envision yourself beside a river in the midst of the Mesopotamian desert? Imagine an expanse of parched land meeting the river's flow; the sound of wind-blown sand and lapping water intermingling. To the north there is an ominous storm gathering. Glowing with unrestrained power and lightning constantly flashing forth like arms desperately seeking something to grasp and pull inside the tempest it is something from an apocalyptic dream. It is coming your way ... it is upon you.

What I find troubling is that so little attention is given to reading the Bible for pleasure in our churches or theological institutions today. This may be partly due to

> *What I find troubling is that so little attention is given to reading the Bible for pleasure in our churches or theological institutions today.*

our preoccupation with a text having one, static, correct meaning. The idea of actively engaging the scriptures with our imagination may be just a little too uncontrolled for many of us and as a result we are uncomfortable with the idea. It may also be the result of how we train clergy in the seminaries and universities. In most cases the focus of their education revolves around the means and methods for exegeting the text and little, if any, attention is given to reading devotionally.

However, if we believe that the Bible is inspired by God, trustworthy and authoritative, then we need to give attention to how we as readers should respond to its message. St. Augustine argued that if someone expounded the text in the most precise manner but their message did not build up their audience's love for God and others then they have interpreted the scriptures incorrectly. His point is not that precision in exegesis is wrong. Rather, his point is that transformation needs to take place. And if we are going to see transformation take place in our lives when we take up the Bible we need to learn how to listen to it. And that is the whole idea behind the first level of reading – listening to what the text has to say.

As stated above, this level of reading is fundamental, as it is the ground from which the more in-depth levels of reading will take place. Through devotional reading we become familiar with the stories, poetry and letters that make up the Bible. We come to know the whole of the Bible, from Adam and Eve to the marriage feast of the Lamb. With a text as complicated as the Bible a firm grasp of the big picture is not something that comes easily or in one or two readings, but requires a habitual engagement with the text.

Devotional or pleasure reading provides much more than just a grasp of the big picture. This type of reading is not a mindless, autopilot form of reading activity. It requires a conscious effort in order to bring our imagination into play. But it is not the same type of cognitive interaction that we employ when doing a word study, for example. The difference between these types of reading depends on who has the upper hand. When I am doing a word or background study I am the one asking the questions and deciding which direction the study will go (making a decision to pursue this line of inquiry rather than another). When I am reading devotionally the Bible has mastery over me. Allow me to make an analogy. It is like dancing. In this instance the Bible is the partner that is leading and I am the one following its steps.

To follow where the Bible leads with our imagination requires concentration and receptivity. Every act of reading requires a great deal of mental effort as we construct words, sentences and entire narratives from the little black marks inscribed on the page. An even greater degree of concentration is needed if we are going to enter imaginatively into the dialogues, social interactions and world that those little black squiggly marks signify. This holds true whether we are reading Ezekiel, a psalm, or one of Jesus' parables. To be able to sit on that hillside under the bright Palestinian sun and listen to Sermon on the Mount requires an amazing feat of mental re-production. As we dwell in this re-production of the various biblical accounts we may experience pleasure, uneasiness, comfort or fear, depending on the story and how we approach it. But it is through these experiences that we may experience new possibilities for understanding the story and its significance; new ways of relating to God and others.

In John 11 we walk with Mary and Martha to the tomb of Lazarus. Jesus is with us and he is mourning with the sisters. As I vicariously take my place in this solemn procession I realize that Jesus is not some far-off God, a distant creator. He is beside us, walking with the sisters in one of life's dark valleys, and he feels their sorrow and loss.

Or perhaps I may put myself in the position of Lazarus lying there in the cold and dark. The stillness and silence of the rock tomb is broken by my name – more real, powerful and personal than I have ever been addressed in the past. It calls me up from death and out into the bright light of day to the cries of joy and astonishment from friends and family. In my imaginative engagement with John 11, I am struck by the realization that some day, when all grows dim and quiet and warmth slowly ebbs out of my body, I too will hear the Shepherd call my name – like I have never heard it before – and I will have no choice but to cross over from death to life.

We realize possibilities for how we live in this world through our encounters with the biblical text. The experiences we have reading devotionally have the potential to break through the ordinary

> *I am struck by the realization that some day, when all grows dim and warmth ebbs out of my body, I too will hear the Shepherd call my name ... and I will have no choice but to cross over from death to life.*

and mundane perceptions of everyday life. Almost any form of literature has this potential. By reading about the lives of others (whether in fiction or in non-fiction) we have the opportunity to see the world through their eyes. We may never trek the jungles, but we can follow in the footsteps of explorers through their biographies. For the believer, the characters we relate to when we read the Bible can have a significant impact in our lives, for at least two reasons. First, because the biblical narratives are based on the lives of real people and thus have a greater relevancy for our lives. Second, because these stories were specifically incorporated into the scriptures because of their significance for our faith and/or daily practice.

> *Our perception of the text opens up to us new possibilities for life.*

Our perception of the text opens up to us new possibilities for life. What we learn from this first level of reading is closely related to the concept of edification. Edification is the building up of the individual through the teachings, lives and ministries of others. It is not a purely subjective process of growth, but is based in the communities to which we belong. Likewise, we are edified, built up, through our active, imaginative, devotional reading of the Bible.

Because others read the same Bible, and we are co-members with them in the body of Christ, there is also an intersubjective element to devotional reading. We are not reduced to a solipsistic "This is what it means to me." Just as we learned to read in an intersubjective setting (e.g. in school), so our devotional reading is also open to intersubjectivity. We can test, correct, and expand our understanding against that of others.

The rich history of how others have read the Bible in the past intrudes into this level of reading because our aesthetic reading experiences of the Bible are intersubjective and not purely personal. How these readers experienced the Bible has been concretely recorded for us in their works. These texts often give us a glimpse of how they imaginatively reconstituted the text. The Medieval views of the great sea monster, often associated with the devil, rising up out of the churning black and green sea to swallow Jonah, calls to mind a totally different re-enactment of Jonah's story than my contemporary perspective on whales.

If my Christian imagination is (to use a metaphor) the creator of my aesthetic, or devotional, experience of the biblical story, then the work of someone like Luther can serve as a co-creator.

Mel Gibson's film *The Passion of the Christ* illustrates how previous readers can function as co-creators of an aesthetic experience together with contemporary readers. *The Passion* is an attempt by Gibson to re-present the suffering and death of Jesus. One the one hand, this film is a product of Gibson's artistic and theological imagination to portray the final events of Jesus' life on film. On the other hand, there are two co-creators (at minimum) that play significant roles in the form his movie takes, and the influence of the past is seen in Gibson's choice of events and how certain scenes are depicted. One of these co-creators is the Stations of the Cross.

The practice of the Stations of the Cross originated in Medieval Europe so that the dedicated believer who could not make a pilgrimage to Jerusalem and retrace Jesus' steps could re-enact Jesus' arrest, trial and crucifixion where they lived. Like Gibson's movie, the Stations were not intended to be approached from a historical perspective: "Is this how it really happened?", but are a self-involving practice to be experienced prayerfully and devotionally. The goal was that as I prayerfully proceed through the Stations I should feel something of the depth of Jesus' love for me and experience the meaning of his sufferings and crucifixion. The basic outline of the second half of *The Passion* follows the fourteen Stations of the Cross from the moment Jesus is condemned to die until he is laid in the tomb (and depending on which version of the Stations of the Cross is involved, Jesus' resurrection also). In fact, the entire narrative plot for this portion of the movie follows the Stations very closely.

The second co-creator is Sister Anne Catherine Emmerich (1174–1824), a German nun who was known for her acts of service and charity. Towards the end of her life she was bedridden. It was during this period that she had a series of very detailed visions about Jesus' passion and death. These visions were later published in 1828 as *The Dolorous*

Passion of Our Lord Jesus Christ. Gibson admits that her work had a profound influence on his spiritual life and on the movie. In particular, Emmerich's visions fills in gaps in the narrative accounts found in the gospels. The opening scene in the movie, where Jesus is in the garden and questioned by the devil, "Is it possible for one man to bear the sins of the world?", is taken from Emmerich's work. The same holds for the discussions Pilate has with his wife, Claudia. While these scenes help fill out the narrative flow and the character development they are not found in the Bible but are taken from Emmerich's *Dolorous Passion*.

Now I doubt that many of us are going to transcribe our devotional readings and find a major financial backer so that we can put them on the big screen. But Gibson's movie demonstrates how those who have gone before us can contribute to and shape how we recreate the biblical drama in our imaginations, how they can function as co-creators with us at this level of reading. In the same way *The Passion* will most likely play a formative role in how readers in the future envision the passion accounts in the New Testament.

Previous to the advent of cinematography, artworks often performed a significant role in shaping the expectations that readers brought to biblical texts. Sculptures, frescos, mosaics, paintings and stained glass artwork in churches were designed to instruct the faithful in images, especially if the congregants were not literate. With the advent of the printing press, not only was the printed Bible widely available but it often included artistic renditions of famous biblical stories. In the earlier editions of printed Bibles these depictions were in the form of engravings and woodcuttings. These depictions preserve an important dimension to how the Bible has previously been read, as this was the form of art that was most widely available to the common reader. As such, these engravings and pictures not only preserve how the artist understood the text but also give us an indication of how the readers of these Bibles would have pictured the biblical scenes and encounters.

There are numerous books that are part of our biblical heritage that can be read in conjunction with the first level of reading that will aid our reading imagination. John Bunyan's *Pilgrim's Progress*, and almost anything by C.K. Chesterton or C.S. Lewis would be worthwhile pursuits. Devotional literature such as Thomas à Kempis's *The Imitation of Christ* focuses less on the imagination and more on a spiritual or contemplative reading. The homilies and sermons from the church fathers are one form of literature that I find very helpful for this level of reading. These are often just about the right length to consume in one sitting. They offer excellent food for thought. And there are various collections of them, from the time of the earliest church down to the present.

Since the subject of this book is how to read the Bible in conjunction with the long tradition of interpretation I would recommend that if you decide to read a devotional or a more creative retelling of a biblical theme you should consider a work by an author who has been tested and approved by the collective consciousness of previous generations. Contemporary works suffer from two handicaps in respect of this form of reading. First, a recent publication may line up so closely with our network of beliefs that it does not provoke our thoughts or imagination. Second, a contemporary work has not yet undergone the test of time. This is not necessarily a bad thing, as it may truly turn out to be a book that our generation and those that follow us find to be an excellent explication of the gospel or some other biblical theme. My point is that it has just not yet undergone this test, and as a result we should look to those works that have passed this examination.

In terms of practical considerations, there are two suggestions I would like to make before moving to the second level of reading. One of the best pieces of advice I ever received on how to read the Bible was to approach it as I would any other good book. Find a comfortable location that is conducive to reading. Set aside a block of time equivalent in length to what you would set aside for any other type of literature. For example, some people are able to engage a text almost immediately and can a have great reading experience in just a few minutes. I, on the other hand, tend to waste the first five or ten minutes just getting settled. Find a time and place that works best for you.

My second suggestion is to possess a quiver full of different Bible translations. If you read from just one translation all the time you may find yourself getting bored with the text. If, for example, you usually read the New International Version, try the King James Version every now and then for a change, just because the words and phrases it uses are so different from what you are used to reading. Consider, for example, the renderings on page 167 of the story of the woman who is healed in Mark 5:24–30 in the King James Version and New International Version (italics have been added to accentuate some of the key differences).

Is the perspective the same in the two translations? When the KJV records that "the fountain of her blood was dried up; and she felt in her body that she was healed of that plague", does this paint a different picture of the scene in your mind than the NIV's "her bleeding stopped and she felt in her body that she was freed from her suffering"? Or you may want to add Phillip's translation or The Living Bible to your library since they tend to use more vivid descriptions. The simple act of reading a different translation can produce a very different reading experience.

At this point we need to shift from pleasure reading to a literary level of reading. But as we shall see, the different levels of reading are not hermetically sealed off from one another. There is some degree overlap between the different levels, and, most importantly, a great deal of communication between them.

Second Level of Reading: Literary Reading

The second level of reading is characterized by a literary approach to the text. But isn't that what we were talking about in the first level? No, and one of the most significant ways that the two levels differ can be illustrated by returning to the analogy of dancing. When we are reading for devotional purposes we may come with our own needs to that act of

King James Version (KJV)

And Jesus went with him; and much people followed him, and thronged him. And a certain woman, which *had an issue of blood* twelve years, And had *suffered many things of many physicians*, and had spent all that she had, and was nothing bettered, but rather grew worse, When she had heard of Jesus, *came in the press behind*, and touched his garment. For she said, If I may touch but his clothes, *I shall be whole*. And straightway the fountain of her blood was dried up; and she felt in her body that *she was healed of that plague*. And Jesus, immediately knowing in himself that *virtue had gone out of him*, turned him about in the press, and said, Who touched my clothes?

New International Version (NIV)

So Jesus went with him. A large crowd followed and pressed around him. And a woman was there who had been *subject to bleeding* for twelve years. She had *suffered a great deal under the care of many doctors* and had spent all she had, yet instead of getting better she grew worse. When she heard about Jesus, she *came up behind him in the crowd* and touched his cloak, because she thought, "If I just touch his clothes, I *will be healed.*" Immediately her bleeding stopped and she felt in her body that *she was freed from her suffering*. At once Jesus realized that *power had gone out from him*. He turned around in the crowd and asked, "Who touched my clothes?"

reading, but it is the text that leads the dance. In the second level the text still plays an important role for how the dance will proceed, but the reader exercises greater control over the flow of the dance. At times both partners, text and reader, may be cooperating in harmony, and at other times the lead will switch back and forth between the two.

When we read devotionally we want to bring the text to life, imaginatively engage it, vicariously experience the situations, story and message contained in the letters on the page. The second level of reading, by contrast, is less imaginative and more investigative. It asks questions about the literary features of the text,[8] about features such as the overall argument found in the letter to the Romans, the narrative structure and flow of the Gospel of John, and wider questions such as how this or that book fits into the entire biblical canon.

At the same time, we cannot ignore the literary features that occur at the micro-level. This would include individual stories or events within a larger narrative, such as the healing of Jairus's daughter (Mark 5) which is located within the larger context of the Gospel of Mark; or perhaps a sub-argument about the experience of sin and conviction within a person's life (Romans 7) within the larger argument of the epistle.

Between the micro-level and the macro-level there is a middle level (for lack of a better name, but it makes for a nice alliteration!). Chapters 2, 3 and 4 of the Gospel of John form a nice unit within which they share several themes, as do chapters 9, 10 and 11 of Romans, where Paul discusses God's grace and election in regard to Israel and the Gentiles.

As I pointed out in the previous section, the customary manner in which most of us are exposed to the Bible in worship services or study groups is fragmented in character. We read only a few verses or a paragraph at a time and then consider the meaning and implications of that passage. Would you consider a talk based on only a few lines from a soliloquy

---

8   See the section "The original horizon of understanding: Inside the Text" in chapter one for a more thorough discussion of literary features and genres.

in Shakespeare's *Hamlet*
an appropriate presenta-
tion of the play's
message? Probably not,
yet how many of us
have heard a sermon
based on a reading of

> *Most of us are exposed to the Bible in worship services or study groups in a very fragmented manner, only a few verses at a time.*

the entire Gospel of John, the Epistle to the Romans,
or even the twenty-five verses of Jude's epistle? I
don't even need one hand to count the number of
times I have.

The central issues this level of reading revolves
around are: (1) What type of literature are we reading?
(2) What is the literary structure (at the micro-, middle,
and macro-levels) of the text?

Let's consider these two issues in order. While
it seems obvious, this point needs to be reiterated:
the Bible is not one book but a collection of books,
stories, poems, prophecies and letters. These different
genres vary in a number of respects. In order to read
any book in an appropriate manner we need to know
its literary genre and some of the basic rules for that
genre. If I begin a story with the line, "Once upon a
time …" you immediately know several things. You
know what type of story I am going to tell you – that
it is a fairytale. You also know that the purpose of the
story is not to convey a factual retelling of an event
or series of events. You may also be attentive to the
possibility that it may contain a moral lesson. The
reason why you immediately grasp these features in
the story I was about to tell is that you know the
"rules" relating to fairytales.

Let's apply this idea to a biblical example. In Luke
18:10 we read, "Two men went up into the temple
to pray, one was a Pharisee, the other was a tax
collector …" On the surface this story appears to be
about the experience of two actual men worshipping in
the temple. But because Luke tells us in the preceding
verse that "Jesus told this parable" we know that this

is not to be taken as a factual account, but as an illustration or extended metaphor to teach us something other than who was in the temple on that day.

The purpose of asking about genre is to help us determine what game is being played and thus know what the rules are. Or to use other terms, what genre is the text and which conventions does it employ. One of the genres found in the New Testament is letters. But we certainly do not want to read a book like Revelation according to the same rules we would use for a letter like Romans. No matter what book in the Bible you are reading, it is important to clarify what type of text it is.

The second area of concern under a literary reading is the macro-structure of the text. How do the individual *parts* of a text fit together into the *whole* of that book or letter?

The most straightforward way to gain the big picture is simply by reading and rereading a book. When I was a university student I was fortunate to be mentored in the basic skills of Bible study by someone who loved God's word. One of the rules that he etched deep into my psyche was to read whatever text you are studying once a day for fifty days. By the time you have finished this exercise you will know that book backwards and forwards. For a longer text, like Matthew or Isaiah, it may be necessary to divide the text up into readable portions. (As a side note: this method has a tradition behind it. As far as I can determine, this method has been handed down for over 100 years and originated with Harry Ironside, a well-known pastor and Bible teacher from the last century.)

Alongside repeatedly reading a book, use an outline – it is a very useful tool to gain a big picture for a book. If you read other books on biblical interpretation, or take a seminary course, you most likely will be cautioned not to look at someone else's outline before you construct your own. But isn't this precisely why outlines are included in commentaries and other reference works – to provide a big picture? Instead of following the majority opinion at this point I recommend looking at outlines at an early stage in your studies. Why reinvent the wheel when there is no need? And since the point of this book is to have you engage other readers and how they understand the Bible, what better way than looking at their outlines? By consulting the work of others we make better use or our time, we gain from their work and wisdom, and we are applying the idea of a three-way dialogue in a very practical manner.

Another genre of literature on the Bible that is extremely helpful for reading at the second level is the various introductory texts that spell out the main themes of a biblical text, its argument, or its theological contributions. They vary in length and style, from *Luther's Preface to the Letter of St. Paul to the Romans* (which is often found as an individual text today, about ten pages in length), to the one- or two-page introductions found before the various texts in a study Bible, to the lengthy introductory notes located towards the beginning of a good commentary.

In some instances such introductory texts have played a notable role in the history of how a book in the Bible has been read. An example of how significant a role introductions can play is the record of events related to Jerome's prefaces in the Latin Vulgate. When Jerome (325–420) translated the Bible into common (or "vulgar") Latin he included a brief introduction to each book. In his introductory notes to the Apocryphal books (such as Judith, Tobit or Maccabees) Jerome claimed that these texts should be read for the purpose of edification but should not be held at the same level as the canonical books or used to form or confirm doctrine. In doing so Jerome mediated the desire of some of his contemporaries to include the Apocrypha in the Bible but also remained faithful to his position that these texts were not canonical.

During the Medieval period his introductions were preserved in many editions of the Vulgate (the Bible used during most of this period) and his position on the Apocryphal books went largely unchallenged. However, with the debates over authority, tradition and truth that occurred during the Reformation this middle ground was abandoned in favor of either rejecting these texts outright or canonizing them. Protestant theologians excised the Apocrypha from their Bibles for theological reasons. In part, their argument was based on Jerome's position that the Apocrypha should not to be considered canonical.

Leaders of the Catholic Counter-Reformation took the opposite stance. They removed Jerome's introductions and in the process elevated the Apocryphal texts to the same authoritative level as the other canonical books. They then argued that since the Reformers' Bibles did not contain the Apocrypha, Protestants did not have full access to God's truth. The legacy of this debate continues to this day, as most Protestants are largely uninformed about the Apocrypha (which in many cases can shed background information on some New Testament passages).

The influence and impact that Jerome's introductions have had on Christian tradition demonstrates the significant role this type of text can play and why such texts should not be quickly pushed aside as we read the Bible in light of 2,000 years of biblical interpretation.

Third Level of Reading: Detailed Studies

Finally, we arrive at the level of reading that most people are familiar with when we speak about studying the Bible: the detailed, nuts-and-bolts research such as word studies, the grammatical analysis of a verse, or background studies. This is the level where most of the methods learned in Bible studies, information gleaned from a commentary, or training in a seminary reside. The problem is, as I have already discussed, elsewhere in this book, that – whether intentionally or unintentionally – we tend to establish this as the primary, and often only, level at which we study or read the Bible. We jump into the text and begin digging away at the original meaning of Hebrew or Greek words, or the history behind the text, in order to uncover what the text "really" means.

In order to get a handle on how the third level relates to the first two levels of reading, let's return to the analogy of dancing once again. When we read for devotional or pleasure purposes we are following the lead of the text. As we shift to a literary level of reading we and the text take turns leading the dance. But at the third level we, the readers, lead the dance. We decide which questions we want to ask of the text, how we are going to find the answers to those questions, what resources we will employ to get those answers, and how much time we have to devote to that question.

Indulge me for a moment longer. The three levels of reading can also be compared to viewing a work of art. Pleasure reading is similar to gazing at a picture: we appreciate its beauty and allow it to work its magic on us. We shift to the second level of reading when we consider the overall composition of the work: How is the scene composed? What color scheme did the artist employ? Is there a story or message embedded in this work of art? At some point our interest may be caught by a particular detail in the picture. What type of canvas, brush stroke, or technique did the artist use? How did the artist convey the impression of depth or lighting? Is there a story behind this work? Questions of this nature indicate that we have moved from asking questions about the big picture, the second level of reading, to questions that examine the finer details in the work, the third level of reading.

If we did not perform the critical, historical and linguistic studies, then the first two levels of reading would be lopsided in favor of our contemporary pre-understanding. We would naively read the text according to our worldview and assume that we understand the text as the author or original audience once did. The illustration from Psalm 121, "I lift up my eyes to the mountains, where does my help come from?" in the Introduction should have alerted us to this danger.

Thus, one of the goals for reading at the third level is to raise to consciousness some

> *One of the goals of interpretation is to raise to consciousness some of the historical, cultural and linguistic differences between our contemporary horizon and the original audience's.*

of the historical, cultural and linguistic differences between our contemporary horizon and the original audience's. As an example, consider Mark 13:44: "The kingdom of heaven is like treasure hidden in a field, which someone found and hid; then in his joy he goes and sells all that he has and buys that field." What aspects of this concise parable capture your attention? Which elements of the parable do you not understand? Perhaps you want to gain a better grasp of what Jesus meant by the term *kingdom of heaven*? What laws governed the purchase of property or recovered treasure in first-century Palestine? What is the literary structure of a parable and how does this particular parable fit that model? The list of questions that we could generate off this one passage could be quite extensive. But unless you are independently wealthy or a struggling seminary professor you most likely do not have the time to track down the answers to more than a few of these questions. This is where you must take the lead and decide which questions you are going to invest your time and effort in.

Two Primary Questions

There are two primary, and interrelated, questions we should ask at the third level of reading. The first question is, "How are the words, ideas and references in the text related to the beliefs and expectations of the historical horizon in which it was penned?" This includes studies such as what the word *whale* may have meant to Jonah's original readers. It also raises larger questions about the relationship between the literary style of the text and literary conventions of that culture.

For example, in the introduction to his gospel Luke cites a series of widely known events to fix the inauguration of John the Baptist's preaching (3:1–3). This has led some commentators to speculate whether Luke was trying to imitate a style of historical literature that Greek authors such as Thucydides and Herodotus had followed. When Luke writes that he "investigated everything carefully" and set out to "write an orderly account" (1:3) what does this mean in relation to the literary conventions in which Luke was educated? How do the literary conventions that Luke employed relate to the standards we use today? All too often we assume that the phrase *write an orderly account* indicates that Luke was composing a chronological account of the events of Jesus' life. But he could just as easily have been referring to a theological order or a rhetorical order. The only way we can be certain is by digging into the background of what a phrase like *orderly account* may have meant in Luke's time and day.

The second primary question at the third level of reading is, "How is the biblical text originally a response to a question, problem or need?" In some instances

> We need to inquire how the biblical text is originally a response to a question, problem or need.

this is a fairly easy question to which to discern the answer. For example, 1 Corinthians appears to be a response from Paul to reports about schisms (chapters 1 and 2), sexual immorality (chapters 5 and 6), and abuses of the Lord's supper (chapter 11). At other points in the letter Paul is answering questions they have written to him about. These include whether married couples should engage in sexual intercourse (chapter 7) and the nature of the resurrection (chapter 15). Paul also raises a concern of his own: his plan to make a collection for the church in Jerusalem. While 1 Corinthians contains numerous references that assist the contemporary reader, other texts make us work for the answers to this question. Once again, commentaries come to our rescue. A good commentary should include not only a detailed exegesis of the text but also an extensive discussion about the historical situation in which the text was composed.

Rationale behind the two questions

There are three reasons why it is important to answer the above two questions:

First, unless we realize something about the historical and cultural distance that separates between our world from the world of the original readers we will most likely naively claim to understand the Bible but will only be parroting the values of our own worldview.

Second, the transmission of the text from the author to us could have been broken with the passing of time. Our culture and network of beliefs may be so different from those of the original audience that the text means something completely different to us today than it did for them. Aspects of the text may be an enigma to us today because we no longer possess the background knowledge the author and his or her audience shared. I suspect that Paul's reference to angels in his discussion of whether women should wear a veil when they pray and prophecy in the worship service falls into this category (1 Corinthians 11:10). Either his readers shared this piece of information (about why angels should be taken into consideration) or they were as confused by this idea as we are today.

And third, because elements of unintentional distortion or deliberate domination (see point 8 in the appendix to chapter 4 for a fuller discussion of distortion and domination) have crept into how the text is interpreted these types of studies are critical. A few years ago I had the privilege to teach in Poland. The students were puzzled as to why the English translation of Colossians 4:15 read, "Give my greetings to the brothers and sisters in Laodicea, and to Nympha and the church in *her* house." Why was the feminine pronoun *her* used, they wanted to know, since this indicated that Nympha was a woman. The Polish translations rendered this pronoun masculine: *his*.

The textual notes at the bottom of the Greek New Testament indicated that in the earliest manuscripts the proper noun *Nympha* and the accompanying pronoun were feminine. However, this did not resolve the issue for them. On the one hand, the Greek name Nympha is normally feminine, but there is the remote possibility that it could be a man's name as well. The difference between the masculine and feminine forms of this name is where the accent mark falls: Νυμφαν for the feminine versus the masculine Νυμφαν. Without going into the details of textual criticism it is sufficient at this point to say that it would be very easy for a scribe copying the manuscript by hand to mistake the gender of *Nympha*, especially if you consider that the earliest manuscripts of the New Testament did not contain accent marks and so it would have been impossible to tell the difference based on how this name was written on the papyrus. The pronoun *her* is a different story, however, as there is a clear difference between *him* and *her* in Greek.

So we need to contemplate how this word could have been copied differently. What we have to remember is that the person copying the manuscript by hand was an active participant in

> *The person copying the manuscript by hand was an active participant in the process and did not just blindly copy it like a photocopier.*

the process – he (it was most likely a man) did not just blindly copy the manuscript like a photocopier. Perhaps when he came upon the feminine pronoun *her*, he thought that the person who had transcribed the manuscript he was working from had made a mistake by using the feminine pronoun. Therefore the latter scribe might have thought he was simply correcting the pronoun to its rightful masculine gender. If this was the case, then we would have an instance of unintentional distortion that should be corrected.

On the other hand, if the copyist was bowing to the patriarchal values of his culture and changed the pronoun to the masculine form (and possibly the accent mark on *Nympha* as well) because the idea that a woman could have been the patron for the church, and by implication a leader in the church, was not theologically acceptable to him (just as it is not accepted in many branches of the church today). If this was the case, then we have found a case of intentional domination.

Whether this is a case of distortion (a copying error) or domination (correcting the text to reflect patriarchal values) is a question that needs to be answered when we engage the history of interpretation at the third level of reading. The reason why the Polish Bible used the masculine was that the textual tradition the translators relied on (i.e. the manuscript they considered the most important) dated from the sixth century, and both *Nympha* and the pronoun are masculine in that Greek manuscript. Most of the English (and other Western European) translations now use earlier Greek manuscripts and have corrected the translation to the feminine form. With the fall of the Iron Curtain it is probably just a matter of time before a new Polish translation is completed, and it will be interesting to see whether Nympha is a man or a woman in that translation.

> *Every act of interpretation springs from what we already know – our pre-understanding, or preconceptions.*

Reading within the Hermeneutical Circle

One of the favorite terms that theologians like to throw around is the *hermeneutical circle*. The basic premise behind the concept of the hermeneutical circle is that every act of interpretation springs from what we already know – our pre-understanding, or preconceptions. It is our pre-understanding that gives us a point of entry or contact with a text, person or event. In order to understand something about the object of our enquiry we need some common ground between ourselves and the subject matter the text is addressing. If what we are attempting to read is totally foreign to us then we will need to find some point of contact before we will be able to understand anything about it. We always move from what is already known to what we learn through reading, study or interpretation. Anything new that we learn from reading is incorporated into our pre-understanding, which in turn sets the stage for our next encounter with that text.

Some authors prefer to speak in terms of a *hermeneutical spiral* rather than a *circle*, since each time we cycle through this circle our starting point changes. Every time I read the Gospel of John, I notice a new feature of the text, learn something new, or have my grasp of the text as a whole expanded. This means that I will understand the Gospel of John differently from before I had read it again. Each time I read through the text I learn something new, notice a facet of the story line I had not realized before, or pick up some of the fine points the author embedded in his work.

I can remember reading books to my children when they were young. Even if we had read that book everyday for a month (to the point where they even had the words memorized and would correct me if I deviated from the script by even a single word!) they would point out with great delight details I had not noticed on the page. As they did so I learned from their observant eyes something new about the book. In the same way, as you and I read and reread the Bible, our understanding of the whole is revised. And this may take place in ways that we may not realize in some cases.

The three levels of reading are related to one another in a number of ways in the hermeneutical circle. One of the easiest entry points to understanding how the hermeneutical circle binds the three levels of reading together is through the relationship between the parts and the whole. As I read a book I constantly keep assessing how the individual parts (sentences, paragraphs and chapters) might be contributing to the larger picture of the whole book. It is like putting a jigsaw puzzle together: as you fit the individual pieces together the whole picture begins to take shape, until you put the last piece in place and the entire picture is now in front of you. In a similar manner, as we read a book we construct a provisional picture of what the whole of the book is about. In the process of reading the book this provisional concept of what the book is about is constantly being revised and corrected as I progress through the book. One of the joys of reading is the reward that comes from having our expectations either fulfilled or subverted as new information is gleaned and twists in the plot unfold as we read.

The whole also provides the context to understand the parts. If we study one piece of a jigsaw puzzle it may be difficult, if not impossible, to determine how this piece is related to all the others or how it contributes to the whole picture. But once I have completed the puzzle I can now see the connection between all the various pieces and how they contribute to the overall picture. Likewise, after I have read a book I have an understanding of the whole that allows me to assess the meaning and significance of the parts.

In the third chapter of the Gospel of John, for example, we meet Nicodemus when he visits Jesus at night. As interesting as this story is in its own right, it gains greater significance from its location within the larger context of the gospel. The fact that we are told that Nicodemus comes to Jesus alone "at night" is a small detail that could be easily overlooked. But light and darkness, night and day are themes that John develops throughout his entire gospel. This theme starts in the prologue when we are told that Jesus is the light that has come into the darkness and that the darkness is not able to overpower or comprehend it (1:5). Nicodemus's encounter with Jesus needs to be understood within in this context, especially since he comes to see Jesus, the light of the world, at night and the conversation ends with Jesus chastising him for being a teacher of Israel but not understanding the subject matter of their conversation (3:1–10). In chapter 7 we meet him again when he asks his fellow members of the Jewish council if they shouldn't hear from Jesus personally as they attempt to come to a decision about him. He is silenced by one of his peers, who asks him, "You are not from Galilee too?" implying that he was also a follower of the wandering preacher, Jesus (7:50–52). The third time we meet Nicodemus is at Jesus' burial, with Joseph of Arimathea, providing an exorbitant amount of aromatic spices to prepare Jesus' body for the tomb (19:39).

Thus we see how John portrays Nicodemus as a man on a journey: from a private visit with Jesus at night, to taking a tentative stand before his peers, to publicly identifying himself, in the middle of the day, with the body of the dead miracle worker. Knowing something about the overall message of the entire gospel and some of the themes John develops in it we can perceive the significance of the parts. We see how the pieces fit into the big picture. In this manner, the "parts vs the whole" dimension of the hermeneutical circle ties the pleasure and literary levels of reading together with the nuts and bolts of the detail studies.

The Hermeneutical Circle and Tradition

The hermeneutical circle is grounded in tradition. As I wrote above, every time we approach a text we do so with some measure of pre-understanding that we have inherited from our tradition. In turn, a tradition also proceeds by means of the hermeneutical circle. This is especially true of religious traditions. As new generations of believers read, study, and apply how they understand the sacred documents of their faith they ask new questions about these texts. As a result, new folds in the meaning of those texts are realized. Thus they pass on to their heirs a richer understanding of their scriptures. This means that all three levels of reading are constituted by the reader's place within a tradition.

When it comes to reading the Bible this point cannot be overstated. Our pre-understanding of the Gospel of John, for example, or of the entire Bible, is part and parcel of what has been handed down to us through the Judeo-Christian tradition. More has been written about the Bible than about any other book (or collection of books) in history, and the stories and themes of the Bible has inspired more literature, artwork, music and messages than any other subject in history. This vast wealth of material within our tradition has contributed to the pre-understanding we bring to the three levels of reading.

> *The Bible has inspired more literature, artwork, music and messages than any other subject in history.*

At a personal level this means that when I am reading the scriptures I am approaching them from a position of strength. My preconceptions of what the Bible means has been shaped by the judgment of countless others who have read, written about, and taught these texts before me. I am part of the process of revising and transmitting that understanding to the next generation. I am not a passive vessel that passes on exactly what I received. Rather, I am part of a dynamic flow of the river of history. As I read, study and teach the scriptures I contribute to the revision and expansion of that inheritance. The questions that are being raised in my historical context are not the same as those that faced my parents. This requires that I faithfully study the sacred scriptures so that I can answer those questions in an appropriate manner. Every generation of readers is called upon to fulfill this same responsibility.

We move from one understanding of the text to the next, constantly shifting, expanding and revising how we read the Bible. The history of the Bible and the church is, to a large extent, a record of the hermeneutical spiral since the original authors finished their work, and this spiral will continue until we are ushered into the new age which awaits us.

> *"You mean to say that we will never arrive at a definitive understanding of the text?"*

For some, this can be a rather disheartening thought. "You mean to say that we will never arrive at a definitive understanding of the text? What point is there to studying the Bible then?" Instead of dwelling on what eludes us in the present, let us concentrate on the challenge this calls us to. The corollary to the previous idea is actually a point of great excitement. It means that we are fellow sojourners with all those who came before us and with all who will come after us in the pursuit of reading, interpreting, expounding and applying the Bible appropriately. We are called to be faithful stewards of God's word, to study it, to allow it to address our lives and the situations in which we find ourselves, and to help others to hear to its message more directly.

The question is not if we will adopt the idea of the hermeneutical circle, or if we will attempt to study the Bible in light of it. We are already on the merry-go-round. It is part of the very nature of what it means to be temporal beings. We all possess some form of pre-understanding about the Bible, whether we are first-time readers or a professor emeritus at a university. The challenge facing me as a reader is to try to determine where I am in the circle in regard to the text I would like to read. If I am not very familiar with Isaiah, then I may want to take my first spin around the circle by reading it devotionally. On the other hand, if I have read Isaiah before, then I would probably benefit more from a literary reading. If I am being called upon to teach the book of Isaiah to others, or have the time and energy, then digging deeper into one portion of the book may be the better place to start. In other words, how I engage a text should involve a careful negotiation between my needs, what I already know of the text, the nature of the text I want to read or study, and the three levels of reading. One size does not fit all.

Ten Reading Strategies

There are wide variety of reading strategies that can be interjected into the hermeneutical circle which allow us to engage the Bible in a three-way dialogue. Because everyone of us finds ourselves at different locations around the hermeneutical circle I would be grossly overstepping my bounds if I were to suggest that there was one particular approach for incorporating the history of interpretation into how we read the Bible. Rather, what I would like to do is suggest a number of different reading strategies. This should not be taken as an exhaustive list, but is meant to serve as a guide to stimulate your thoughts as to where you could go in your own explorations.

#1 Short and Sweet

It has been said that the most valuable commodity today is time. The average person really does not have a great deal of time to invest in a new project or activity. It is for this reason that I have placed this strategy at the top of my list of suggestions. The quickest form of reception study is simply to search for an interesting quote or insight from the history of a passage's interpretation that could be used to illustrate a passage. With the advent of various biblical software packages, a list of various theologians, preachers and commentators that have written on a biblical passage can be compiled within a matter of minutes. This type of study can also be done on internet sites such as the Christian Classics Ethereal Library (located at Wheaton College). Within ten to fifteen minutes I will usually have found two or three insightful observations or reflections on a passage.

Now I know what you are thinking: "This approach is shallow, superficial and vulnerable to all forms of abuse," and I do not deny that this is a possibility and does occur. However, the goal of this strategy is not a thorough study but to quickly locate an illuminating illustration from the treasury of tradition. The value of familiarizing ourselves with our heritage of biblical interpretation outweighs the criticisms that can be leveled against this approach. And we also have to admit that we resort to this type of study more often then we would care to admit.

#2 *Random Reading*

The method behind this strategy is exactly as it sounds. A great deal can be learned simply by poking around in the writings of the church fathers and reading for curiosity's sake during our free time. The random approach fits under the rubric of reading for pleasure. I don't know how many times I have happened upon a fascinating discovery while just reading randomly. This strategy is particularly useful if you are considering purchasing a work by an author with whom you are not well acquainted. Before giving your precious money to a bookstore for a second-hand copy of E.B. Pusey's commentary, for example, you may want to randomly sample some of his work. This strategy also serves the useful purpose of acquainting us with resources we may have not been familiar with.

#3 *Reading an Entire Text*

For those who are a bit more disciplined, the next suggestion would be to read through a commentator's work – through one of Calvin's or Luther's commentaries on Romans, for example. You could incorporate this form of reading into your daily devotions. The insights you gain from a commentator could be for personal, academic or ministry purposes.

Keeping a journal as you read is highly recommended. One lesson I have gradually learned is that my memory is not as strong as I like to imagine it is. The number of times I have had to go back and read the same material again because I did not keep a record of what I had read can be truly discouraging.

#4 *Reading the Collected Works of an Author*

One step up form the previous strategy would be to read a particular commentator's collected works. In the case of some authors this is a fairly easy task. For example, Clement of Rome wrote only one letter, 1 Clement, at the end of the first century (2 Clement was actually written by an anonymous elder) and provides rich insights into how the second generation of church leaders read the scriptures and taught them to their congregations. On the other hand, if you are reading Calvin or Augustine you may want to be selective due to the sheer quantity of their compositions. Instead of reading all of Calvin's commentaries you may want to see what you can find on how Calvin read the parables. For this you would need to look at his commentary on the gospels and also peruse his *Institutes* and sermons.

Other questions to ask could be, "How did Augustine understand and teach Romans 7?" or "What was Luther's view of the book of Romans?" If you are Lutheran, then reading Luther's commentaries not only exposes you to the history of interpretation but also places you in a better position to understand your denomination's history and theology.

#5 Reception History Commentaries

In the past few years a number of new commentary series have begun to be printed that aim at exposing the reader to the history, use and impact of how the Bible has been interpreted. *The Ancient Christian Commentary* (InterVarsity Press), for example, includes citations from the church fathers from 100 to 600 AD with little explanation. The *Blackwell Biblical Commentary* series examines the entire history of the Bible's reception from the time of the early church to the present day and covers a diversity of sources, including artwork. The *Evangelisch-Katholischer Kommentar zum Neuen Testament* (originally published in German but now appearing in English, thanks to Augsburg Fortress Press) and the *New International Greek Testament Commentary* (Paternoster and Eerdmans) are two technical commentary series that include relevant information from the post-history of the books on which they comment. While these commentary series lend themselves to the "Short and Sweet" or "Random Reading" strategies, their real strength comes when you are studying a chapter or passage and would like to have had the groundwork of sifting through and collating the history of interpretation done for you.

#6 Specialized Studies

Besides the historically oriented commentaries there are a number of books that are more specialized types of studies. For example, Richard Trexler has written an excellent study entitled *The Journey of the Magi* which traces how the magi in Matthew's Gospel have been understood through the centuries and in different cultures. Taking a slightly wider scope, *The Lord's Prayer: A Text in Tradition* by Kenneth Stevenson is a thorough study on the history of how this very significant passage has been interpreted, taught and practiced in the church's history. Ulrich Luz's study, *Matthew in History: Interpretation, Influence, and Effects*, is an excellent and concise study that touches on some of the key themes in Matthew but also surveys some of the wider questions involved with studying a biblical text from this perspective. Two recent books have looked at how the Bible as a whole has been received and read through history: *God's Last Words: Reading the English Bible from the Reformation to Fundamentalism* by David Katz, and David Daniel's *The Bible in English: Its History and Influence* are wonderful surveys that deliver what their titles promise.

#7 Reading Narrowly

Instead of reading one of the specialized studies mentioned in the previous strategy you could do your own research. The study I included on Jonah's whale is one example of taking one exegetical theme and following its twists and turns through history. This type of study will most likely require access to adequate research resources and may not be possible for everyone. But in reality, what really determines success in this type of study is a dogged determination on the reader's part, an ability to be creative in finding new lines of inquiry when others run dry – and to a certain extent, good fortune.

#8 Reading Widely

In an ideal world all of us would have an abundance of free time so that we could read widely from the doctors of the church and trace the history and significance of various concepts, passages or books of the Bible. Unfortunately we don't live in an ideal world. But for those times when you are fortunate enough to have the time and energy there is a great deal of unexplored territory in regard to how the Bible has been read, understood, and taught. Reading widely requires the use of the commentaries I mentioned above, specialized studies, the internet, and perhaps sleuthing around in a good library (or befriending a librarian who will work with you in gaining access to the primary texts). Perhaps best of all, this strategy gives you a wonderful excuse to add more books to your library.

#9 Sermons and Devotionals

In many instances the devotional literature or collections of sermons that have been preserved from the early church days till the present are more important than theological treatises or commentaries. The reason is that a good sermon has its feet firmly planted in two worlds: the world of the Bible and the world of the speaker's audience. A sermon preserves not only how the preacher read the Bible but how he or she perceived its significance for his or her congregation – interpretation, explication and application all rolled up into one neat package.

Devotional literature contains the same ingredients as a sermon but is more oriented, in most instances, to an individual reader rather than a congregation. However, the preconception that devotionals are more spiritually, or more internally, oriented, and sermons more applicational, often does not hold up. The collection of Oswald Chamber's devotions, *My Utmost for His Highest*, is one violation of this preconception. And many of the homilies and sermons by the early fathers are more spiritually oriented than what we would consider practical by our standards. Sermons and devotionals are not only a storehouse of valuable information on how particular texts were read, understood and applied but are excellent material for pleasure or devotional reading.

#10 Art and Music

Art and music, while not strictly a form of reading, are not last on the list because they are least important, but because I hope you will remember them precisely because they are the last strategy listed. Because art and music communicate through different media and make use of different manners of communication, they disclose different nuances of the Biblical text from those a commentary can. For example, Rembrandt introduced an element of his own complicity in Jesus' crucifixion when he portrayed himself as one of the soldiers at the cross. Van Gogh's *The Good Samaritan* or *Pietà* evokes our emotions through his bold use of color and form in his depictions of these well-known biblical stories. Salvador Dali's *Last Supper* discloses the spiritual and eternal dimensions of the communion meal. In their work these three artists all present us with artistic representations of how they read the biblical stories.

If there is one frustration I have had as an author it has been that the constraints of written communication do not allow me to incorporate art (in its true size, color and texture) or music into my manuscripts. Do not let the constraints I am working within lead you to conclude that art and music are less significant than written works. To do so would be to miss out on some of the richest treasures the tradition of biblical interpretation has to offer.

Six

Reception Theory, Teaching and Preaching

Every scribe who has been trained for the kingdom of heaven is like the master of a household who brings out of his treasure what is new and what is old.

Matthew 13:52

A challenge that constantly confronts anyone contemplating teaching or public speaking is how to create and sustain interest in the audience. Interest is one of those nebulous qualities that is linked to a number of factors – like how well rested the audience is, their personal involvement in the subject matter, and the personal presence of the speaker. Many of these factors are outside the control of the speaker, but two elements that *are* under his or her control concern how they address what the audience regards as relevant and the preconceptions that members of the audience bring with them.

Relevance is an interesting factor, in that it is like a double-edged sword. The audience needs to recognize the relevance of your material if you hope to keep their attention. However, if as a speaker you attempt to make every point relevant or applicable you run the risk of losing your audience. You would think that if almost every point in your speech was perceived as relevant it would generate a high degree of interest. And it may for a time. However, as your presentation progresses there is the very real possibility your material will be reduced to the level of a "to do" list in your listeners' minds. I once sat through a talk given by a respected speaker that contained over forty points of application. I do not remember a single one of them. What I do remember is losing interest in the presentation and counting the number of points instead. (If you want to test this principle for yourself, all you need to do is try reading one of those thick manuals that come with some software packages and see how long it holds your interest.)

On the other hand, if the speaker's content is too theoretical, the hearers may drift off because they don't see the relevance between the subject matter and their lives. Between these two poles lies a middle ground in which practical relevance and theoretical curiosity captures the audience's attention, and if carefully balanced, will sustain their attention.

> *A fine balance exists in relation to the preconceptions that members of the audience bring into the room with them.*

A similar balance exists in relation to the preconceptions that members of the audience bring into the room with them. If the content of your message lines up too closely with those preconceptions, there is a high probability that some in the audience will go to sleep – "been there, done that," they subconsciously check off as they seek out something else that will engage their minds a bit more or as they drift off in a daydream. On the other hand, if you violate too many of their preconceptions, all you will succeed in doing is alienating them. You may hope to capture their interest by being provocative, but all you may accomplish is to create the impression that you are rather absurd.

Once again there is a middle ground where interest is created and flourishes that lies somewhere between telling people what they already know and negating their preconceptions.

This is not just a theoretical consideration for me, but is a subject that is very relevant for what I do on a regular basis. Most of the students I teach are pastors or work for a parachurch ministry, or are moving in that direction. As a rule, they are an incredible group of people to have the privilege of teaching. The challenge I face is that they bring with them certain well-defined and well-developed preconceptions about the New Testament. Trying to teach a group of people who consider themselves already well informed on the subject matter can be rather intimidating!

I have found several ways to create an interesting and dynamic learning environment by employing reception history. What I hope to demonstrate in this chapter is how the rich heritage of biblical interpretation can be brought into play when teaching the Bible, and in particular, how reading the Bible with the giants of the past can generate interest along the axis of preconceptions and relevance. With a bit of tweaking to your particular situation these same concepts can be used in relation to a wide variety of speaking situations and subjects.

The Original Horizon

Chapter one opened with a discussion of Psalm 121. I had two goals in mind when I chose to start with that passage. First and foremost I wanted to capture your attention. Second, the manner in which I decided to accomplish that was by raising the question as to whether the way we understand this psalm today would have been shared by the author or the original audience. In order to answer this question I opened some aspects of the historical, cultural and linguistic distance that separates us and the historical context in which the psalm was originally communicated. As we began to realize how the original audience may have understood the Psalm, it became foreign to us. This should have set several cognitive processes in motion. When our reading of Psalm 121 was placed beside how the original audience may have read it, a tension was created that needed to resolved: Do I need to study the psalm more, correct my interpretation, or find some way to reconcile these two different readings? As we seek to resolve the tension between the two readings we find ourselves in transition – from one understanding to another, from how we used to apply the passage to our lives to how we see it applying now. How we used to understand the psalm has been challenged and we must now seek a different or more comprehensive way to read the text. We are forced to reevaluate its relevance to our lives and ministries.

> *When we realized how the original audience may have understood the Psalm, it became foreign to us.*

This is one of the simplest ways to use reception history for creating interest. The remainder of this chapter will examine three other pedagogical practices we can use to create interest when we speak, teach or preach.

A Snapshot in Time

Is Romans 7 about the non-believer's experience, the believer's experience, or Paul's own conversion in hindsight? This is a tough question to answer. If you were to line up all the contemporary theologians and biblical scholars you would find that they are fairly evenly divided over this question. The same percentages have held true in the classes I have taught – the students are more or less evenly split, depending on the their denominational affiliation. What makes Romans 7 so intriguing is that there are elements in the text that can be used to support each of the views. As a result, this passage from the Pauline corpus has generated several clear trajectories of competing readings through the ages.

However, our concern at this moment is not to trace the complete history of this debate over Romans 7. Rather, we want to take one cross-section from that history and look at how one particular person read the passage and examine how that information can be used to create interest; we want to focus on one person at one point in time. The difference can be compared to watching a movie (representing a diachronic study that looks at how a passage was understood over the centuries) versus looking at a photograph (representing a synchronic study that examines how a passage was understood at one period in history).

The person I will focus on in this snapshot is St. Augustine. Augustine's teachings on this passage are very illuminating in several ways. In his earlier work, Augustine understood Romans 7 in terms of the experience of the unsaved person, saying that the chapter portrays the inner struggle in the heart of a man or woman who agrees with God's law, but because of their unregenerate nature they are unable to fulfill their desire to obey God. In his *Confessions* Augustine often spoke from personal experience about how miserable this condition could be. This inner struggle should drive a person to cry out in desperation and throw themselves upon the grace of God, as Augustine thought Paul did toward the end of the chapter:

> And our experience gives abundant evidence, that in punishment for this sin our body is corrupted, and weighs down the soul, and the clay tabernacle clogs the mind in its manifold activity; and we know that we can be freed from this punishment only by gracious interposition. So the apostle cries out in distress, "O wretched man that I am! who shall deliver me from the body of this death? The grace of God through Jesus Christ our Lord." (Augustine, *Anit-Manichean Writings*, book XXII)

If this were all Augustine had to say about Romans 7, it would be a rather monochromatic snapshot.

However, towards the end of his life Augustine wrote his *Retractations* (1.23.1), in which he reviewed his writings and recounted how he had changed his stance on numerous biblical and theological questions. While Augustine's earlier views on Romans 7 are scattered widely through his writings, his revised reading of Romans 7 is located primarily in a series of sermons (151–156) that he gave towards the end of his life. He now read this chapter as an illustration of the believer's experience – a 180 degree turn from how he had originally understood it.

There are two explanations for why he changed his stance on this passage. The first involved his long struggle against the teachings of Pelagius and Julian, who taught that human nature was capable of initiating the process of salvation and living a virtuous life apart from the enabling of God's grace. Augustine may have reconsidered his teachings on Romans 7 because he felt his earlier views might be used to support his opponents' teachings.

The second reason why he may have changed his view is that he now read the passage in light of Plato and Cicero. Based on Plato's and Cicero's philosophical works, Augustine developed a perceptive view of the will. Human will was not a simple concept for Augustine, but consisted of three movements: suggestion, desire, and consent.

Let's look briefly at the concept of suggestion. As human beings we are assaulted with suggestions from every direction at all times, and we can exercise only a limited amount of control over them. The advertising industry is a prime example of this. The number of people that make their living devising new ways to place images, ideas and products before us on a daily basis is truly staggering. Suggestions enter our mind through the senses and exercise a powerful effect on our desires and thoughts, so these people know that if they succeed in placing the image of a new laptop before our eyes it may stimulate our desire to purchase a new one.

> *Desire is a fleeting movement, but it is always there, ready to be aroused.*

So the second movement of the will is desire. While desire is but a fleeting movement, it is always there, ready to be aroused. Augustine thought Paul was alluding to this when he wrote, "I do not do what I desire, but I do what I hate ... I delight in the law of God in my inner man" (Romans 7:15, 22). This, Augustine taught, could be uttered only by a person of faith – only someone who was regenerated could desire to follow God's law. The conflict between these desires reflected the struggle between the ongoing influence of sin (especially in regard to sexual desires) and the sanctifying work of the Holy Spirit. In fact, Augustine believed that the more we mature in Christ the more intense this conflict becomes.

The final movement of the will is consent: whether we decide to act upon our desires or not to do so. Consent raised the question of how someone obeys and follows God. For Augustine, consensual obedience did not spring from any merit found in human nature (contrary to what Pelagius taught). In Romans 7 Paul narrates a vivid description of the believer's inner turmoil and human inability to do the will of God. This inability forces the believer to trust in the enabling work of the Holy Spirit, who works in our hearts by influencing and transforming that middle movement of the will, desire, so that our inclination will be to obey God and thus to consent to follow him. Grace empowers us to consent to God's law. Our will is always influenced by something outside of it: either by the suggestions that enter our thoughts or by the work of the Holy Spirit. The more we consent to the lower, sinful desires, the more we are bound by them. Therefore the idea that we are free to make our own autonomous choices was an illusion for Augustine. But in order to for us to obey God's law our will must be enabled to do so by God's grace. This inner conflict begins at the moment of salvation and will end only at the resurrection. Until that day we are forced to rely on the assistance of God's transforming grace.

This then leads quite naturally into Paul's thoughts in Romans 8. A "snapshot" of Augustine's views on Romans 7 opens a transitional space in which we can reevaluate how we read the epistle. In this instance, this space is not based primarily on the distance between the contemporary reader and Paul's original audience. We have introduced a third element into the equation, Augustine's thoughts on this passage, which help us to notice folds in the meaning of the text that allow us to consider two different manners by which to read this section of Paul's work. As such, Augustine is an excellent example of a snapshot in time study, because he was open to changing how he read Romans 7, which raises the question whether we are open to change also. He helps us realize that there is a wider range of meaning to this passage than we may have originally perceived. A snapshot type of study will acquaint your audience with a portion of the rich heritage of biblical interpretation and provide them with a model for how to engage the Bible in a three-way dialogue.

Tracing a Trajectory of Reception

Is it possible to do justice to the reception history of even a single verse within the confines of a single teaching or speaking engagement? I am not sure, because the scope of material is so broad that it would be very difficult to cover it all adequately in one session or lecture. However, I have learned not to underestimate just how gifted and creative some teachers are. Having said that, I have found this line of attack better suited to a series of talks on one theme or passage.

I regularly use this approach when I teach a course on the parables. The course begins with how the early church fathers used Jesus' parables in their teachings, and we then work our way chronologically up to the present. In order to foster more class involvement I assign the students presentations on various interpreters from the different historical periods. It is at this point that I usually get one of two questions: "Can I write on something else?" (Translation: "I don't want to read one of these boring, old, dead guys.") Or, "I have no idea on whom to write; can you suggest someone?" (Translation: "Help, I know very little about how the Bible has been interpreted historically.")

The answer to the first question is simple: "No." But to answer the second I need to probe a bit about that student's personal background, denominational affiliation and ministry experience. Usually, I am able to point them in the direction of several commentators who mesh well with their background and spirituality in a meaningful manner. Their initial reservations quickly fall away as the course progresses. Frequently during their presentations they interject a comment along the lines of, "I had no idea Gregory the Great was so interesting to read. Not only did I learn a great deal about the parables from his work but he spoke to my life as well."

Instead of exploring the hermeneutical distance between our contemporary situation and the original context in which the parables were uttered this approach

> *A tradition of interpretation should not be ignored or jumped over in an attempt to access some pure, pristine, timeless meaning encoded in the text.*

demonstrates how 2,000 years of history is filled with a living dialogue and debate over the meaning of the parables, a tradition of interpretation that should not be ignored or jumped over in an attempt to access some pure, pristine, timeless meaning encoded in the text. By actively engaging tradition the students begin to realize just how connected they are to those who have preceded them – that they truly are dwarves standing on the shoulder of giants. How Calvin, after 500 years, still speaks so powerfully. Why they interpret a parable allegorically – or don't. Even down to why they interpret the meaning of a particular parable the way they do. (For example, why, so often, is only half of the parable of the prodigal son taught and the half about the older son ignored?)

As we trace the history of how the parables have been read and taught, we learn not only why we read them the way we do, but how to read them in alternative yet appropriate ways. Instead of looking

> *When we engage we begin to realize just how connected we are to those who have preceded us – that we truly are dwarves standing on the shoulder of giants.*

though a telescope at a distant object on the horizon we are now surveying a vast panorama of readings.

Tracing this living and ongoing dialogue over the parables should produce some secondary benefits in our lives. First, as we study the history of the use and impact of a parable we become conscious of our place in that tradition – not just passively, but recognizing that just like all who have come before us, we too now have the responsibility to read and teach the parables in an appropriate manner. That what we do with the parables will enter into the collective memory of tradition.

Second, as a result of an educational exercise along these lines we should become more sensitive and attentive readers. As discussed earlier, reading is a very complex skill to learn, and the ability to read well should be highly prized. But how does one go from knowing *how to read* to *reading well*?

One way to do this is to sit at the feet of someone who is a gifted reader. When I was in university I spent a disproportionate amount of time skiing. (I even chose my university based on its proximity to major ski resorts!) Even though I grew up skiing, I learned more about the sport by watching and imitating friends of mine who skied professionally. As I imitated their turns and moves, my skills as a skier grew. In the same way, we can learn new ways to navigate a parable, make exegetical moves, and gain a deeper appreciation for just how rich a parable can truly be by following the lines of someone like Archbishop R.C. Trench or C.H. Dodd through a parable.

The third potential benefit from this type of study is the ability to make sound judgments about what constitutes a good reading, interpretation or application of a biblical story. This ability is directly linked to our development as readers and flows from that. As you trace how a text has been read historically you quickly realize the wide diversity of readings any single text can generate. But are all these readings and uses of the Bible valid? Throughout church history the resounding answer has been "No." At the same time, when we read the Bible in conjunction with tradition we realize that the other extreme, that there is only one, fixed, timeless meaning to a text, is not a suitable criterion to determine what constitutes an appropriate reading of a biblical passage. Between the two extremes there is a playing field of meaning which possesses a degree of latitude that allows for a number of readings but at the same time has boundaries or limits on what counts as an appropriate interpretation.

But who decides what the boundaries to this field of play are? The way we learn where the boundaries are and what constitutes an appropriate interpretation is by observing the doctors of the church at work. We learn by watching. Hopefully this will instill in us the ability to make sounder judgments about what constitutes a good reading of the text.

Tradition also presents us with certain boundaries. The ecumenical creeds from the first five centuries are perhaps the strongest and most universally accepted statements that can be appealed to when making a judgment as to whether a particular reading is orthodox or not.

Related to the ability to make sounder judgments, becoming more sensitive and attentive readers and open to how others have interpreted the text, is the virtue of humility. As we observe how others have wrestled with the text and come up with readings that may be very different from what seems to be natural to us, we should take a softer stance in regard to our own understanding of a parable. On the one hand, we test our readings of a text in relation to how others read it. On the other hand, in the process of reading how others in history have understood the Bible, we realize that there are a number of ways that almost any passage can be read, and as a result, our understanding of the text should be informed and broadened by the readings of others. Reading the Bible in conjunction with tradition serves as a preventative and remedial medicine against the attitude of claiming that we possess the definitive meaning of the Bible, or a passage within it. This is a cure that is sorely needed in many circles today.

Monumental Moments

To rephrase a line from George Orwell's *Animal Farm*, "All interpretations are equal, but some interpretations are more equal than others." This has been true in the post-history of every biblical text I have studied.

There seem to be two traits that make some interpretations "more equal" than others. There are those readings that offer

> *All interpretations are equal, but some interpretations are more equal than others.*

a fresh perspective on a passage, that introduce a paradigm change in regard to how a passage is read. Then there are those commentators that put their reading of the passage across so clearly, or in such a forceful manner, that it has a profound and persistent influence on how a biblical passage is read and taught. In some instances this may be due the fact that the commentator is so highly recognized by the church that anything he or she writes is accepted as authoritative.

In either case, what this means is that there will most likely be four or five significant historical moments in the history of how a biblical passage has been received that stand out above the rest. Hans Robert Jauss refers to these definitive readings as "summit dialogues" between authors. Living in Colorado, I find the image of the rise and fall of a mountain ridge which this metaphor evokes helpful when trying to grasp Jauss's thought on this topic. The peaks that protrude above the rest form the distinctive backbone of a range and correspond to those authors or readings that define or shape the history of a text's reception. Jauss cited the way Lévi-Strauss was a reader of Rousseau, who in turn was a reader of Augustine, as one example of this type of summit dialogue between philosophical thinkers. By examining the turning points, or peaks, in the reception history of a text we find that the dramatic twists and turns in how a passage has been understood are brought into sharper relief.

Let me provide an example of how I have used this approach when teaching on the epileptic boy in Matthew 17. I assigned selections from Origen's and Calvin's commentaries and a fairly recent article by John Wilkinson for the class to read and prepare to discuss the next time we met. In order to keep the class discussion focused I had them pay particular attention to how the different authors interpreted the affliction of the child who was brought to Jesus. There were several learning objectives in this assignment. On a surface level I hoped to introduce the students to several shifts in how this passage has been read historically. At a deeper level, this assignment served as an introduction, by way of case studies, to the complex interaction between the Bible, the reader, his/her place in history, and the language involved in every act of interpretation. In order to illustrate how these objectives would play out in a lecture hall, allow me to summarize three different interpretations of the boy's calamity.

In Matthew 17:15 the boy's father kneels before Jesus and implores, "Lord have mercy on my son, for he is an *epileptic* and suffers terribly; he often falls into the fire and often into the water" (NRSV). The Greek word which is translated as *epileptic* is *seleniazomai* and literally means "to be struck by the moon." (For the sake of simplicity I will refer to the boy's ailment as epilepsy without intending to endorse one particular view.) The King James translation *lunatic* is perhaps closer to the Greek than the NRSV's *epileptic*, although the term has largely fallen out of use in recent history.

In the early church there was no consensus over how the boy's ailment should be interpreted. Some of the early church fathers argued that the boy suffered from demonic possession. Others claimed it was an illness brought on by the influence of the moon, a view not only supported by Greco-Roman conceptions of this affliction but also found in the writings of the rabbis, who wrote that if a man and woman conceived a child under the light of the moon their child would be an epileptic. Both views were widely taught in the church until around 300 AD.

It is easier for us to sympathize with the view that the boy suffered from demon possession rather than that he was being harmed by the moon. After all, doesn't the text tell us that Jesus rebuked the boy and a demon left him (17:18)? Whether we believe in the existence of demons or see this text reflecting primitive superstitions we can agree to some measure with this interpretation, whereas the idea that the boy was "moon-struck" may be rather foreign to us.

> *Because the moon is composed primarily of moisture, exposure to it has the potential to create an imbalance in the moist humors that compose the human brain, resulting in epileptic seizures.*

As the church spread and moved from Palestine to the broader Roman Empire the beliefs of Greco-Roman culture became part of the framework within which the boy's affliction in Matthew 17 was interpreted. According to Hippocrates and Galen, two of the most respected Greek medical authorities from antiquity, the moon exercised a powerful effect on the brain. Because the moon was composed primarily of moisture, exposure to it had the potential to create an imbalance in the moist humors that compose the human brain. Epileptic seizures were the body's attempt to restore balance to the four humors that made up the human body. Galen wrote that the froth that appeared in the mouth at the end of an epileptic fit indicated that the imbalance between air and moisture in the body had been restored. As further evidence, Galen also noted that the effects of epilepsy were weakest at half-moon and strongest during the full moon.

It is against this backdrop that Origen's comments on this passage must be situated. His commentary on Matthew 17 is significant for the three reasons. First, it was written between 245 and 250 AD and is one of the earliest commentaries on the Gospel of Matthew. Second, he specifically interacts with many of the preconceptions that readers in the early church inherited from their culture. And third, his commentary on Matthew exercised a profound influence in the early church up to and including the Reformation.

Origen's comments on the boy's ailment centered on what he considered two very important misconceptions his contemporaries held (see book 13 in his *Commentary on Matthew*). While he acknowledged that the Greek term *seleniazomai* was etymologically related to the "Moon" (*Selene*) he said one should not make the mistake of assuming that the moon was the cause of the ailment concerned. This was the error that the magicians and the physicians fell into. The magicians thought that the heavenly bodies possessed semi-divine attributes, some of which (such as the moon in this instance) affected our lives in a malevolent manner, while others affected our lives in a benevolent manner. Beliefs such as these had to be rejected by the believer, according to Origen. The scriptural teachings on creation did not allow room for such thinking. "No star formed by the God of the universe" could work evil. The moon, along with the other created heavenly bodies, performed the significant and positive role of participating along with all creation in giving praise to the creator. The physicians, on the other hand, erred in that they denied spiritual influences in cases like this and would attribute the child's illness to the result of "the moist nature in the head being moved in sympathy with the light of the moon." Thus, both the magicians and physicians slandered God's creation in their diagnosis of this affliction.

In response to these beliefs, Origen claimed that the true nature of the boy's sickness should be clear to those who believed in the gospel: the boy was possessed by an "unclean and dumb spirit." Origen hypothesized that a demon, by carefully observing the phases of the moon, deceived those who observed the boy's suffering into attributing its cause to the moon.

Chrysostom's homily on this passage reflects the influence of Origen's interpretation of this story. Chrysostom followed his predecessor's reading of the passage almost point by point. Because his comments are more concise than Origen's I quote him:

> For the evil spirit, to bring a reproach upon nature, both attacks them that are seized, and lets them go, according to the courses of the moon; not as though that were the worker of it; — away with the thought; — but himself craftily doing this to bring a reproach on nature. And an erroneous opinion hath gotten ground among the simple, and by this name do they call such evil spirits, being deceived; for this is no means true.

(Chrysostom, *Homilies on the Gospel of Saint Matthew*, Homily LVII.3.)

While not every interpreter followed Origen's comments, his interpretation set the direction for how the boy's illness was read for over 1,000 years and was followed by many of the most influential theologians during this period.

By the time of the Reformation a lot of water had passed under the bridge in regard to how an illness like the boy's was understood.[9] Leading up to and during the Reformation an increasing emphasis was placed upon the study and reinterpretation of classical works. This led to a rediscovery of Hippocrates's and Galen's writings. By Calvin's time, Galen's diagnosis was once again widely accepted and epilepsy was attributed to the lunar phases. Evidence of this is seen in Calvin's comments on the use of this term in Matthew 4:18–25:

> Lunatics ... is the name given to those, in whom the strength of the disease increases or diminishes, according to the waxing or waning of the moon, such as those who are afflicted with epilepsy, or similar diseases.

Common experience and observation proved that the child's illness in Matthew 17 was caused by the phases of the moon, in Calvin's opinion. As a result, Calvin specifically rejected Chrysostom's (and by extension Origen's) argument and based his interpretation on the prevailing medical paradigm of his day:

> Matthew describes a different sort of disease from what is described by Mark, for he says that the man was lunatic ... The

---

9   One example was the rather gruesome procedure that was developed during the Medieval period to treat epilepsy. In many places in Europe a common treatment for epilepsy was to cut a small hole in the person's skull so that the "surgeon" could search for and supposedly remove a small stone from the sufferer's brain. Oftentimes these surgeries were carried out in a stall in the market place. Artistic depictions of these procedures often include the image of stones hanging from strings in the healers' stalls advertising their ability to cure this illness.

term lunatic is applied to those who, about the waning of the moon, are seized with epilepsy, or afflicted with giddiness. I do not admit the fanciful notion of Chrysostom, that the word lunatic was invented by a trick of Satan, in order to throw disgrace on the good creatures of God; for we learn from undoubted experience, that the course of the moon affects the increase or decline of these diseases. And yet this does not prevent Satan from mixing up his attacks with natural means. I am of opinion, therefore, that the man was not naturally deaf and dumb, but that Satan had taken possession of his tongue and ears; and that, as the weakness of his brain and nerves made him liable to epilepsy, Satan availed himself of this for aggravating the disease. (John Calvin, *Commentary on a Harmony of the Evangelists, Matthew, Mark, and Luke,* translated by W. Pringle.)

It was obvious to Calvin that the child suffered from an illness triggered by the phases of the moon. Calvin reconciled the demonic references in the text by arguing that Satan has taken advantage of this poor boy's state and even exacerbated his condition. Origen's reading of the passage was overturned and Calvin's commentary signals a shift in how Matthew's reference to this illness would be read from then on.

What was obvious to Calvin may strike most modern commentators and readers as anything but that. It is particularly ironic that William

> *What was obvious to Calvin may strike most modern readers as anything but that.*

Pringle, a modern translator of Calvin's *Commentary on a Harmony of the Evangelists,* had so much difficulty with Calvin's interpretation at this point that he felt compelled to include a footnote on Calvin's comments on epilepsy in Matthew 4:24. According to Pringle, Calvin's comments reflected superstitious beliefs that had been dispelled by advances in scientific knowledge:

Till lately, mental derangement was universally believed among ourselves to be influenced by similar causes; if indeed there be not some who still defend that opinion by plausible arguments ... The term *seleniazomenoi*, in this and similar passages, does not imply, that the sacred writers supported the common opinion, any more than the English word lunatic, used with equal freedom by philosophers and by the unlearned, countenances an exploded theory,– any more, in short, than the popular use of the phrases, the rising and setting of the sun, expresses a belief that it is the motion of the sun, and not of the earth, that produces the succession of day and night. (Pringle's translator's note in *Commentary on a Harmony of the Evangelists* by Calvin)

Why do we find Calvin's and Origen's interpretations so peculiar? Primarily because the network of beliefs we hold in regard to this illnesses have radically changed over the years. What Origen read through a theological lens and Calvin according to Medieval medical knowledge we now read according to the presuppositions of modern medical science.

In 1967 John Wilkinson submitted an article to *Expository Times* entitled "The Case of the Epileptic Boy" which represents the third reception moment I would like to touch upon. While his article has been cited in several respected commentaries, I would not place it at the same level of the summit dialogue as the work of Calvin or Origen. Rather, I have chosen this article because it represents a view shared by many contemporary commentators, and by extension readers.

Wilkinson analyzed Matthew 17 and the parallel passages in Mark 9 and Luke 9 in order to construct a medical history the boy's affliction (the onset, progress and present symptoms of the illness). Matthew's use of the term *seleniazomai* was dismissed because it seemed to "imply that the fits came every month, but we cannot be certain since the word probably embodies a superstition rather than accurate observation." In this statement we can clearly discern that the criteria he used to reach a conclusion about the boy's illness are not those shared by the evangelists. Matthew's understanding reflected a primitive superstition, while Wilkinson's diagnosis reflects a more accurate conclusion.

The same attitude is taken in regard to the parallel passages in Mark and Luke. Mark says the boy was demon-possessed and then mentions that he was thrown to the ground, foamed at the mouth, ground his teeth and became rigid (Mark 9:17, 20, 25 and 28–9) as indications of this. Wilkinson disagreed with Mark's conclusions, saying these were clear symptoms of epileptic seizures. He read every indicator of the boy's illness mentioned by the evangelists in light of our contemporary medical understanding of epilepsy.

However, the manifestations of the boy's suffering recorded in the gospel accounts were not overlooked or ignored by Calvin or Origen, and they clearly arrived at very different appraisals of the situation than Wilkinson. Neither Wilkinson nor Pringle shared Origen's or Calvin's beliefs about the influence of the moon on the human brain. As a result, they did not count an interpretation that pointed to the moon or to demonic activity as the source of the child's torment as a valid reading. Instead, both of these contemporary authors inform us that such views reflect prescientific, superstitious beliefs and that we know better today.

Why do these four commentators interpret the boy's affliction in three different ways when reading the same text? Which of the three is closer to how Matthew, and the church he was writing to, would have understood the story? Which interpretation should we go with? These are the types of questions that I hope will be raised in the class discussions.

During these discussions, I see my role as being primarily to guide the discussions, not to provide answers. I try to help the students explore how the com-

> *The network of beliefs we bring to the act of reading is part of the matrix that determines what we will count as a valid interpretation.*

mentators' respective historical horizons shaped their preconceptions and pre-understanding of the text, how the network of beliefs a reader brings to the act of reading is part of the matrix that determines what he or she will count as a valid interpretation. As they engage these three moments in the history of how this boy's illness has been understood the students should begin to look at biblical interpretation in a more sophisticated manner. Reading the Bible is not simply an act of communication that takes place between a reader and the text. It is a complex interaction between the Bible, the reader, and his or her language, culture and tradition. Looking at these three moments in the reception history of the story of the epileptic boy we are afforded a glimpse into how the questions, methods, criteria and vocabulary internal to the practice of biblical interpretation have been modified and at times radically transformed over the years.

Sinking a Mineshaft

The mountains of Colorado are littered with abandoned mineshafts from the late nineteenth and early twentieth centuries. When you come across one of these old mines while hiking you are immediately impressed by the amount of time and effort the men who dug them invested in their dream of striking it rich. Most were not fools, and sank their mines in particular locations because of the promising geological indications or because other mines in that area were producing valuable ore.

In a similar manner, if there is a particular biblical text, interpreter, school of thought, or reading of a biblical passage that seems to possess the potential for digging a lot deeper, then it may be worth taking the time and energy to mine it.

This pedagogical approach of "sinking a mineshaft" shares some similarities with the "snapshot in time" method. But while both may concentrate on one interpreter or historical period, there are significant differences between the two approaches that warrant separate considerations.

The Snapshot in Time approach focuses on how a biblical passage was read at one point in history so that an audience can engage that reading in a sympathetic and productive manner. At the same time, the Snapshot in Time is not meant to be an in-depth study, but is more suited for a talk or sermon. It can be compared to examining the geological evidence that is visible on the surface of the ground. By contrast, the goal of the mineshaft approach is to dig deeper in order to explore the underlying hermeneutical strata that in most cases will require a great deal more time and effort. And finally, this type of study is much more appropriate for an upper-level course in which the students are already familiar with the necessary research tools, with church history, and possibly with the biblical languages.

Why did Origen find the idea that the moon may be the cause of the boy's affliction so troubling? How could those he argued against hold such a view? Perhaps other issues involved in his comments on this illness may come to mind. For example, the fact that several of Origen's predecessors mentioned that this type of condition was very difficult to heal by prayer may have played a role in Origen's considerations. Origen's debate with the Greek philosopher Celsus may require some exploration as well, especially since Origen was concerned about correcting Celsus's misapprehensions of Christian and Jewish beliefs in regard to the sun, moon, planets and heavens.

Expanding the scope of our investigation we find that there are several Greco-Roman authors who described epilepsy and what life was like for those who suffered from it. These writers provide additional insight into the preconceptions that Origen's readers brought to the text and which he wanted to dispel in his commentary. The impact and influence that his comments on Matthew 17 had on his successors should also play a role in a study on how Origen interpreted this story. And finally, some attention should be given to a critical appraisal of Origen's interpretation.

The answers to these and countless other questions could fill a book. This is why I liken this learning exercise to sinking a mineshaft. The goal is not to traverse a great deal of historical territory, but to dig deeply in one location.

There are two ways I have managed this type of study in the classroom. One way has been to photocopy selections

> *The goal is not to traverse a great deal of historical territory, but to dig deeply in one location.*

from a number of primary sources (such as Galen's writings on epilepsy, those of other church fathers, or Origen's writings against Celsus) for the students to examine outside of class. The other way has been to assign a short research paper examining the issues we have been discussing in regard to Origen's reading of Matthew 17. In the first case I tell them where to dig and hand them the shovel. In the second, I point them in a general direction and wish them luck in their mining venture. In both cases I reserve a significant amount of time in class to discuss their findings.

Sinking a mineshaft into Origen's commentary should not be reduced to an exercise in the history of interpretation. Rather, one of the learning objectives I have for an exercise like this is to raise students' appreciation of how complex every act of interpretation is and to help them uncover some of their subterranean assumptions and expectations about how they study the Bible.

Origen's and Calvin's beliefs about epilepsy stand in stark contrast to our understanding of this illness. As we study their works the preconceptions we bring to the passage concerned should be provoked: How does Origen's allegorical method of interpretation conflict with our values about what constitutes the meaning of a passage? Does the linguistic and cultural background of being "moon-struck" correct, expand, or conflict with what we perceive the boy suffered from and how we understand its cause and proper treatment?

In other words, a study like this should provoke and bring to consciousness the unexamined presuppositions we bring to Matthew 17. By placing Origen's comments alongside our own we should get a clearer understanding as to why we read the text the way we do; why we "count" one interpretation as appropriate but wrestle with others. Our engagement with tradition should not be a tidy affair, but should stir things up. Raise questions that lead to further discoveries of how Origen read the text, the tradition of biblical interpretation, the text of Matthew 17, and we learn something about ourselves in the process.

Summary

You can create interest among the members of your audience in a number of different ways. Drama, music, art and illustrations are all useful tools and should be included in our teaching methods.

From a hermeneutical perspective, one of the most effective elements for creating interest is distance. By *distance* I am referring primarily to one or a combination of three concepts: temporal distance, cultural distance, and linguistic distance.

Temporal distance involves the recognition that the Bible is the product of a time very distant and different from ours.

Cultural distance is the result of the ways of life, customs, reality of daily life, and religious beliefs and practices that separate us from the lives of the biblical authors and their audiences.

And finally, there is a linguistic distance that separates contemporary readers and the original readers of the biblical books.

In this chapter I have discussed four exercises that I have found useful for incorporating reception history into my teaching. Each of these exercises employs at least one form of hermeneutical distance in order to create interest in my students. When readers are alerted to the cultural, linguistic and temporal distance between them and the Bible a gap is opened between them and the biblical text that they once found very familiar. Once this gap is opened the natural desire is to restore the text to a position of familiarity, to close that distance that has been opened between them and the text.

Resolving this tension is a constructive learning experience. On the one hand, interest is generated because some of the presuppositions of the readers have been challenged ("Maybe Paul did not mean what I always thought he did in Romans 7 …"). On the other hand, the tension that this hermeneutical distance has raised addresses the need for relevance, since the readers are forced to wrestle with the problem or challenge of closing the distance between them and the text, to reconfigure how they read the passage and perceive its relevance to their lives.

And all of this takes place as we engage the rich heritage of biblical interpretation of which we are the privileged and responsible heirs.

Resources for Further Study

I. Reception Theory

Holub, Robert C., *Reception Theory: A Critical Introduction.*
Terence Hawkes (series ed.), *New Accents* (London
and New York: Methuen, 1984)
A critical and comprehensive introduction to the
literary and philosophical concepts behind reception
theory. While Holub does not address issues of biblical
interpretation his work serves as a comprehensive
introduction to Reception Theory.

Holmes, Stephen R., *Listening to the Past: The Place of
Tradition in Theology* (Grand Rapids and Carlisle:
Baker and Paternoster, 2002)
Grounded in a doctrine of creation, Holmes
articulately argues that we cannot just read the Bible
without understanding our place within a tradition.

Iser, Wolfgang, *The Implied Readers: Patterns of
Communication in Prose Fiction from Bunyan to Beckett*
(Baltimore: Johns Hopkins University Press, 1974)
Iser collaborated with Jauss at the University of
Constance (Germany) in developing Reception
Theory and is perhaps the better known of the two
within English-speaking circles.

Jauss, Hans Robert. *Towards an Aesthetic of Reception.*
Timothy Bahti (tr.). Edited by Wlad Godzich and
Jochen Schulte-Sasse. Vol. 2, *Theory and History of
Literature* (Minneapolis: University of Minnesota
Press, 1982)

A collection of some of the earlier and more seminal articles Hans Robert Jauss wrote on Reception Theory. This is the single most important book in English on the philosophical and literary theory behind Reception Theory.

Rush, Ormond, "Living Reception of the Living Tradition: Hermeneutical Principles for Theology" in Neil J. Byrne (ed.), *Banyo Studies: Commemorative Papers to Mark the Golden Jubilee of Pius XII Seminary* (Banyo, Queensland: Pius XII Seminary, 1991), 242–90
Ormond Rush presents a clear discussion of Reception Theory and its application to the development of doctrine from a Catholic perspective. (Not widely available.)

Thiselton, Anthony C., Roger Lundin and Clarence Walhout, *The Promise of Hermeneutics* (Grand Rapids and Carlisle: Eerdmans and Paternoster, 1999)
The three chapters in this work are all relevant to the study of how the Bible has been interpreted and taught throughout history. Roger Lundin's contribution discusses how the traditional historical-critical method divorces the reader from the text. Clarence Walhout examines the relationship between narratives, readers and truth claims. Anthony Thiselton's article draws the first two chapters together and shows, among other things, the significance of these ideas for Reception Theory.

───────────

The following works touch on several ideas and concepts that are central to what is discussed in the book in regard to how language and theories change over time.

Barbour, Ian G., *Myths, Models and Paradigms: The Nature of Scientific and Religious Language* (London: S.C.M. Press, 1974)
Considers the implications of Thomas Kuhn's idea of paradigm changes for theological studies.

Gutting, Gary (ed.), *Paradigms and Revolutions: Appraisals and Applications of Thomas Kuhn's Philosophy of Science* (Notre Dame, Indiana: University of Notre Dame Press, 1980)
A collection of scholarly articles that appraise the appropriateness of Kuhn's concept of paradigm shifts.

Kuhn, Thomas S, *The Structure of Scientific Revolutions* (Chicago: University of Chicago Press, 1970)
Kuhn's pioneering study on how scientific theories are advanced or replaced by newer theories that placed the idea of paradigm changes on the intellectual map. In particular Kuhn shattered the idea that knowledge advances by means of a steady accumulation of facts and correction of theories.

II. Literary Theory and Biblical Interpretation

Alter, Robert, *The Art of Biblical Narrative* (N.Y.: Basic Books, 1985)
Alter's work on the literary structure of Old Testament stories laid a solid foundation for the adoption of literary and narrative approaches in biblical interpretation.

Briggs, Richard, *Reading the Bible Wisely* (Grand Rapids: Baker, 2003)
Since Richard is a good friend I had to include his book! Fortunately, I can also sincerely recommend it as the first book someone should read if they are just beginning their study of the Bible.

Caird, George B., *The Language and Imagery of the Bible* (Oxford: Clarendon Press, 1980)
Unfortunately George Caird died prematurely after publishing this excellent inquiry into how metaphorical language functions in the Bible functions.

Fee, Gordon D. and Douglas Stuart, *How to Read the Bible for all its Worth* (Grand Rapids: Zondervan, 1993)

A solid introduction to the various literary genres found in the Bible and how a reader should approach them.

Frei, Hans W, *The   Eclipse of Biblical Narrative: A Study in Eighteenth and Nineteenth Century Hermeneutics* (New Haven and London: Yale University Press, 1974)
Examines the negative impact of the historical-critical method on how the biblical narratives are understood. Frei argues that the power of a biblical story to transform our lives dissipates when meaning is grounded in some reference outside of the text itself, such as historical facts.

Hirsch, E.D., Jr., *Validity in Interpretation* (New Haven, CT.: Yale University Press, 1967)

——, *The Aims of Interpretation* (Chicago: University of Chicago Press, 1976)
These are the two works are often cited by conservative theologians in defense of a split between what the author intended (meaning) and how the church has read the Bible (significance).

Kermode, Frank and Robert Alter (eds.), *The Literary Guide to the Bible* (London: Collins, 1987)
A book by book discussion through the entire Bible by a team of international scholars who explore the richness of the literary elements found in the Bible.

Klein, William H., Craig L. Blomberg and Robert L. Hubbard, *Introduction to Biblical Interpretation* (Dallas: Word Publishing, 1993)
Covers most of the most widely accepted and practiced contemporary methods of biblical interpretation taught in seminaries today.

McQuilkin, Robertson, *Understanding and Applying the Bible: An Introduction to Hermeneutics* (Chicago: Moody Press, 1983)
Covers much of the same territory that the previous book does, but is easier to digest. Filled with lots of solid

advice for interpreting the Bible when using the historical-grammatical approach.

Osborne, Grant R, *The Hermeneutical Spiral: A Comprehensive Introduction to Biblical Interpretation* (Downers Grove: InterVarsity Press, 1991)
Written for university or seminary level, this book dives deeper into some of the philosophical issues behind the various methods of biblical interpretation. Osborne largely follows E.D. Hirsch's views on meaning.

Patzia, Arthur G. and Anthony J. Petrotta, *Pocket Dictionary of Biblical Studies* (Downers Grove and Leicester, England: InterVarsity Press, 2002)
One volume in InterVarsity's concise dictionary series on various theological fields. Like the others in this series, this dictionary contains concise, clear and useful definitions on topics such as *sensus plenior* (in case you were curious about what that referred to).

III. Resources for Researching the History of How a Biblical Passage has been Read by the Church

Daniell, David, *The Bible in English: Its History and Influence* (New Haven and London: Yale University Press, 2003)
A very well written, 900-page *magnum opus* on the history of English translations of the Bible and their impact on the church and culture.

Jeffrey, David Lyle (ed.), *A Dictionary of Biblical Tradition in English Literature* (Grand Rapids: Eerdmans, 1992)
Nice concise articles that discuss not only biblical texts found in English literature but also various aspects of English literature itself and how it has been influenced by the tradition of biblical interpretation.

Katz, David S., *God's Last Words: Reading the English Bible from the Reformation to Fundamentalism* (New Haven and London: Yale University Press, 2004)

Almost a companion volume to Daniell's work. Whereas Daniell focuses on the history of the various English translations, Katz turns his attention to the expectations and questions English readers have brought to the Bible for the past 400 years.

Lampe, G.W. and S.L. Greenslade (eds.), *The Cambridge History of the Bible* (Cambridge: Cambridge University Press, 1969)
A three-volume standard reference work by some of the most respected scholars on the historical development of the Bible and its impact on Western civilization.

IV. The Church Fathers

Perhaps the most widely accessible collection of the church fathers from the second century until the early medieval period is the following collection of thirty-eight volumes in three series (ten volumes were edited by Roberts & Donaldson and twenty-eight volumes by Schaff and Wace). This collection can be found in many libraries, is available on the internet and can be purchased in several different software packages.

As far as it was possible all the quotations from the early church in this book were taken from this series.

Roberts, Alexander and James Donaldson (eds.), *The Ante-Nicene Fathers: Translations of the Fathers Down to A.D. 325.* 10 volumes (Grand Rapids: Eerdmans, 1979)

Schaff, Phillip and Henry Wace (eds.) *A Select Library of the Nicene and Post Nicene Fathers of the Christian Church.* 14 volumes (Grand Rapids: Eerdmans, 1965)

——, *A Select Library of the Nicene and Post Nicene Fathers of the Christian Church: Second Series.* 14 volumes (Grand Rapids: Eerdmans, 1979)

This series is available online at: Christian Classics Ethereal Library:
http://www.ccel.org/

Calvin, John, *Calvin's Commentaries*. 22 volumes (Grand Rapids: Baker Book House, 2005). Also available online at: http://www.ccel.org/ccel/calvin/calcom.html

Luther, Martin, *Luther's Works*. 55 volumes. Jaroslav Pelikan et al. (eds.) (St. Louis and Philadelphia: Fortress Press and Concordia Publishing House, 1955)
See volume 19, *Lectures on the Minor Prophets II: Jonah, Habakkuk*, for Luther's comments on Jonah.

St. Pachomius Library.
This site contains a wide selection of Orthodox theologians and writers from the early church till the present.
http://www.voskrese.info/spl/index.html

Internet Sites: The following internet sites are also excellent sources to access some of the treasury of authors who have written on the Bible and related material.

Online Books Page at the University of Pennsylvania:
http://digital.library.upenn.edu/books/
The goal of this massive site, maintained by John Mark Ockerbloom, is to make books freely readable over the internet.

Perseus Project:
http://perseus.mpiwg-berlin.mpg.de/
The strength of this site is its extensive collection of Greco-Roman authors from Homer down to around 500 AD. Many of the texts are available in both their original language and English.

Project Gutenberg:
http://www.gutenberg.org/
Over 17,000 books available to download. Since copyrights vary from country to country persons accessing the site are responsible for determining if they have the right to download a particular text.

History Sourcebooks
Maintained by Fordham University these sites contain invaluable historical reference works and primary sources. There are also links to a number of other sourcebooks on various other historical topics.
The Ancient History Sourcebook:
http://www.fordham.edu/halsall/ancient/asbook.html

The Internet Jewish History Sourcebook:
http://www.fordham.edu/halsall/jewish/jewishsbook.
html

The Medieval History Sourcebook:
http://www.fordham.edu/halsall/sbook.html

Medieval Texts:
Great site listing all the various types of medieval literature with examples, illustrations and explanations and links.
http://medievalwriting.50megs.com/word/categories.htm

Representative Poetry Online
An online collection of over 3,000 works of poetry by over 500 different authors from the Medieval period till the present.
http://rpo.library.utoronto.ca/display/index.cfm

Other Primary Sources cited in this book:

Carey, William, "An Enquiry into the Obligation of Christians to Use Means for the Conversion of the Heathens" in Ralph D. Winter and Steven C. Hawthorne (eds.), *Perspectives on*

the World Christian Movement (Pasadena: William Carey Library, 1981), 227–36
Carey's short work that launched the modern missionary movement among Protestants.

Descartes, René, *Discourses on Method and the Meditations.* F.E. Sutcliffe (tr.) (New York: Penguin Books, 1968)

Emmerich, Sister Anne Catherine, *The Dolorous Passion of Our Lord Jesus Christ*
http://www.sacred-texts.com/chr/pjc/index.htm
The spiritual visions of Sister Emmerich that influenced Mel Gibson's reading of the passion narratives in the gospels and how he framed those accounts in his movie *The Passion of the Christ.* Also available in print (El Sobrante, CA: North Bay Books, 2004)

The Heidelberg Catechism, Canons of Dort and the 1646 Westminster Confession:
http://www.reformed.org/documents/index.html

Physiologus and Bestiaries:
http://www.abdn.ac.uk/bestiary/bestiary.hti
This site is worth visiting just to look at the beautiful photographic reproductions of the illustrations and text of a Bestiary alone. An English translation and commentary are included on one side of the photographic reproduction of the *Physiologus.*
Project Gutenberg's copy of an Early English *Physiologus.*
http://www.gutenberg.org/etext/14529

A downloadable version of a *Physiologus* can be accessed at the following site:
http://bestiary.ca/etexts/rendell1928/rendell1928.htm

The Talmud: Epstein, Isidore (ed.), *The Soncino Hebrew-English Talmud.* 30 volumes (New York: Soncino Press, 2001)
The Soncino translation of the Talmud into English completed in 1952 is the standard version used today. The

printed form is especially valuable since the format of the Hebrew text clearly shows the Mishnah at the center of the page with the various comments by the Rabbis surrounding it. However, the software version of the Talmud allows the reader to search the entire collection in a matter of seconds. It is also available online at:
http://www.come-and-hear.com/talmud/

Tyndale, William, "A Pathway in the Holy Scripture" in G.E. Duffield (ed.), *The Work of William Tyndale* (Appleford, Berkshire: Sutton Courtenay Press, 1964). 2–24
Tyndale's apologetic and rationale for his ground-shaking translation of the Bible into the vernacular English of his day. This and other works of Tyndale are available at WilliamTyndale.com along with a page with links to other sites on the Reformation.
http://www.williamtyndale.com

IV. Church History Resources

Bingham, D. Jeffrey, *Pocket History of the Church* (Downers Grove and Leicester, England: InterVarsity Press, 2002)
A companion volume to *Pocket Dictionary of Biblical Studies* with concise, informative articles on church history.

Cross, F.L. (ed.), *The Oxford Dictionary of the Christian Church* (London and New York: Oxford University Press, 1958)
Widely recognized as the authoritative reference on the history of the Christian church and its influence on Western civilization.

McKim, Donald K. (ed.), *Historical Handbook of Major Biblical Interpreters* (Downers Grove: InterVarsity Press, 1998)
A practical and informative introduction to the various periods, methods, and actors in the history of biblical interpretation.

V. Commentary Series

The Ancient Christian Commentary. Tom Oden (ed.) (Downers Grove: InterVarsity Press, 1998—)
Primarily a collection of comments from the early church fathers on the biblical text with little explanatory material included. Excellent resource for quickly surveying how the early fathers read a particular passage.

Blackwell Bible Commentaries. John Sawyer, David M. Gunn, Christopher Rowland and Judith Kovacs (eds.) (Oxford: Blackwell Publishing, 2003—)
This series emphasizes the various ways the Bible has been read and interpreted through the ages. Particular attention is given to readings that may not be as well known or were reflected in art, music and other media.

Evangelisch-Katholischer Kommentar Zum Neuen Testament. Joachim Gnilka Norbert Brox, Ulrich Luz and Jürgen Roloff (eds.) (Zürich: Benziger Verlag, 1975—)
A joint Roman Catholic-Lutheran project that includes the history of the text's interpretation in the commentary. Several volumes have been translated into English and published by Augsburg Fortress Press. Most notable is Ulrich Luz's three-volume commentary on Matthew.

The New International Greek Testament Commentary. I. Howard Marshall and Donald Hagner (eds.) (Grand Rapids and Cambridge: Eerdmans and Paternoster, 1982—)
While the emphasis of this series is on a careful exegesis of the Greek text and its theological significance, several of the volumes incorporate the history of the various passages' interpretation and impact through history. In particular see the volume on 1 Corinthians by Anthony Thiselton.

VI. Specialized Studies

Begbie, Jeremy S., *Theology, Music and Time* (Cambridge: Cambridge University Press, 2000)
A fascinating study that examines how music theory can inform our understanding of time, and the implication of those ideas for theology.

Green, Barbara, *Jonah's Journey's*. Barbara Green (series ed.) *Interfaces* (Collegeville, Minn.: Liturgical Press, 2005)
Surveys the history of Jonah's interpretation, but really wants to show how the world behind the text, the world in the text, and the world in front of the text are all united in the search for meaning. The first half of the book devotes a fair amount of attention to how the early church fathers read Jonah.

Guyer, F.E., "The Dwarf on the Giant's Shoulders", *Modern Language Notes* 45 (1930), 398–402
Very informative discussion on the history of the metaphor of the dwarf standing on the shoulder of a giant. May be difficult to locate.

Hornik, Heidi J. and Mikeal C. Parsons, *Illuminating Luke: The Infancy Narrative in Italian Renaissance Painting* (London: T&T Clark, 2005)

——, *Illuminating Luke: The Public Ministry of Christ in Italian Renaissance and Baroque Painting* (London: T&T Clark, 2005)
These are the first two in a three-part series on how Luke's narratives have been portrayed in classical art. Not only are these fascinating books to read but the authors follow a Reception Theory approach in their work.

Kelly, J.N.D., *Early Christian Creeds* (London: Longman, 1982³)
A widely respected study on the earliest formulations of the Christian faith. The sections on the creedal statements

and oral traditions preserved in the New Testament are especially insightful.

Longenecker, Richard N., *Biblical Exegesis in the Apostolic Period* (Grand Rapids: Eerdmans, 1975)
Explores the practices and principles by which the apostolic authors interpreted the Hebrew Scriptures as they composed what would become the New Testament epistles.

Pelikan, Jaroslav. *The Illustrated Jesus through the Centuries* (New Haven and London: Yale University Press, 1997)
Pelikan investigates the impact of Jesus on cultural, political and social history. The illustrated edition contains a wealth of full-color reproductions that vividly demonstrates how visual depictions of Jesus have been transformed across the centuries.
Also see his *Mary through the Centuries: Her Place in the History of Culture* (New Haven and London: Yale University Press, 1996).

Reasoner, Mark. *Romans in Full Circle: A History of Interpretation* (Louisville: Westminster John Knox Press, 2005)
Reasoner traces the history and interpretation of twelve passages in Romans by examining (primarily) the works of Origen, Augustine, Abelard, Aquinas, Luther, Erasmus, Calvin, Karl Barth, N.T. Wright and James Dunn. While written for an academic audience it is still very readable.

Sherwood, Yvonne, *A Biblical Text and Its Afterlives: The Survival of Jonah in Western Culture* (Cambridge: Cambridge University Press, 2000)
A fascinating study on the history of how the book of Jonah has been interpreted, with special attention given to readings that lay outside mainstream of the Jewish and Christian traditions. Sherwood is also working on the volume on Jonah for the Blackwell Bible Commentary series.

Stevenson, Kenneth W., *The Lord's Prayer: A Text in Tradition* (Minneapolis: Fortress, 2004)
A wonderful read that reveals the history of how interpretation, theology and liturgy overlap and can equally inform one another in regard to Jesus' famous prayer.

Trexler, Richard C., *The Journey of the Magi: Meanings in History of a Christian Story* (Princeton: Princeton University Press, 1997)
A scholarly study on how the magi in Matthew chapter 2 have been interpreted through the centuries.

Trumble, Angus, *A Brief History of the Smile* (New York: Basic Books, 2004)
Has little to do with the Bible, but is a fascinating study on how we have perceived one of our most basic expressions of emotion, the smile. One chapter is on the Mona Lisa, but the book as a whole contains a much wider discussion of the history of the smile.